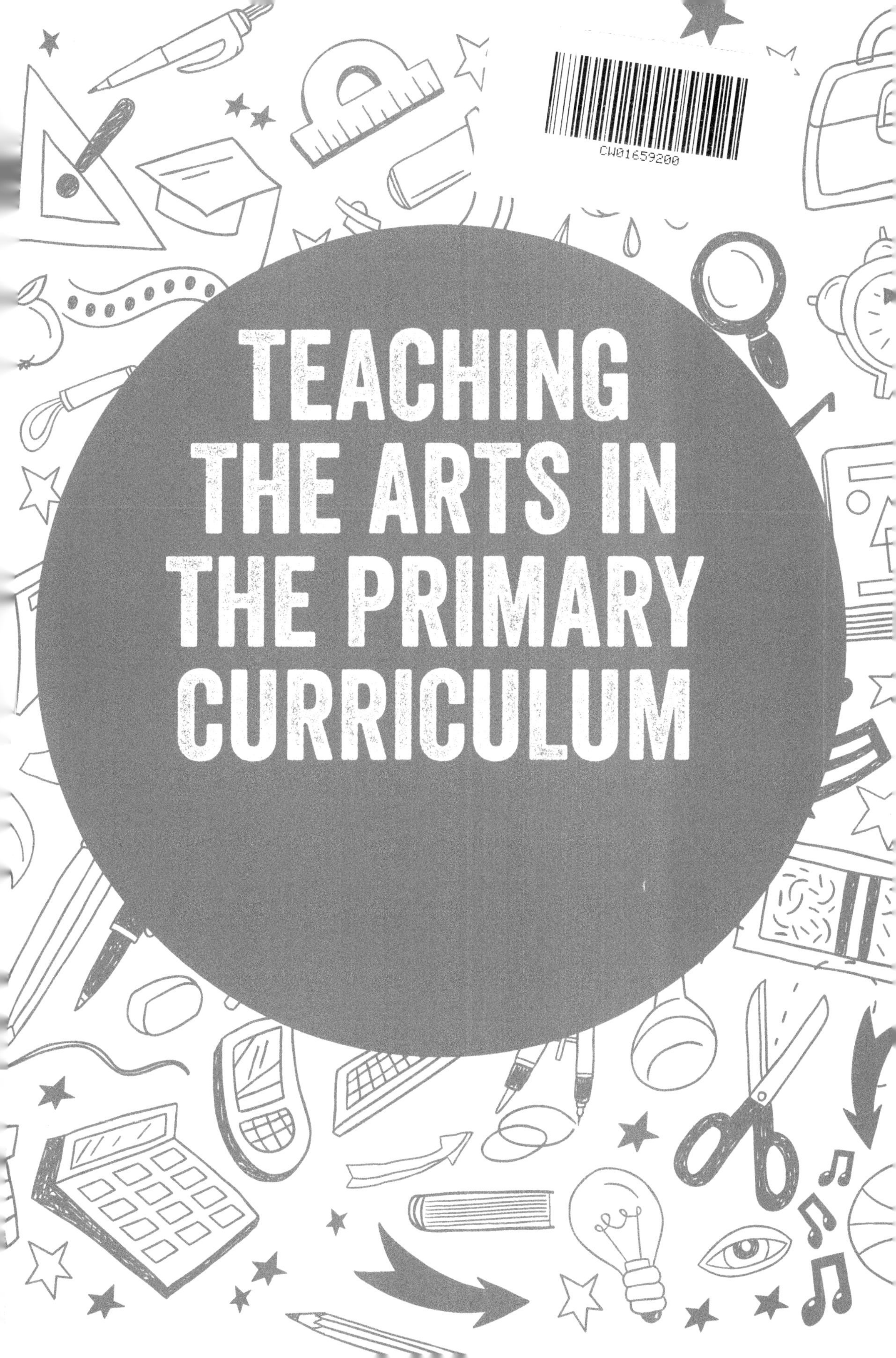

TEACHING THE ARTS IN THE PRIMARY CURRICULUM

Sara Miller McCune founded SAGE Publishing in 1965 to support the dissemination of usable knowledge and educate a global community. SAGE publishes more than 1000 journals and over 800 new books each year, spanning a wide range of subject areas. Our growing selection of library products includes archives, data, case studies and video. SAGE remains majority owned by our founder and after her lifetime will become owned by a charitable trust that secures the company's continued independence.

Los Angeles | London | New Delhi | Singapore | Washington DC | Melbourne

TEACHING THE ARTS IN THE PRIMARY CURRICULUM

EDITED BY

SUSAN OGIER &
SUZY TUTCHELL

Learning Matters

Learning Matters
A SAGE Publishing Company

Learning Matters
A SAGE Publishing Company
1 Oliver's Yard
55 City Road
London EC1Y 1SP

SAGE Publications Inc.
2455 Teller Road
Thousand Oaks,
California 91320

SAGE Publications India Pvt Ltd
B 1/I 1 Mohan Cooperative Industrial Area
Mathura Road
New Delhi 110 044

SAGE Asia-Pacific Pte Ltd
3 Church Street
#10–04 Samsung Hub
Singapore 049483

Editor: Amy Thornton
Senior project editor: Chris Marke
Project management: River Editorial
Marketing manager: Lorna Patkai
Cover design: Wendy Scott
Typeset by: C&M Digitals (P) Ltd, Chennai, India
Printed in the UK

First published in 2021

Library of Congress Control Number: 2021931916

British Library Cataloguing in Publication Data

A catalogue record for this book is available from the British Library

ISBN 978-1-5297-4248-0
ISBN 978-1-5297-4247-3 (pbk)

CONTENTS

ABOUT THE EDITORS

Susan Ogier is a senior lecturer in primary education, specialising in art and design. She works at the University of Roehampton. She is the author of *Teaching Primary Art and Design* (SAGE/Learning Matters, 2017) and a series of children's books, as well as professional and peer-reviewed journal articles and book chapters. She has been involved in several EU-funded cross-curricular education projects, developing learning materials that link art and design with citizenship and digital processes. Her most recently published book in the Learning Matters series is *A Broad and Balanced Curriculum in Primary Schools* (SAGE/Learning Matters, 2019).

Suzy Tutchell has a lifelong commitment to and involvement in art education. Having been an art subject leader for many years in a variety of London-based primary schools, she moved on to advisory work as a creativity and early years consultant, and has been working in higher education for the past ten years. As a lecturer, she currently leads the art specialism on the BA Primary Education programme at the University of Reading. She is a practising artist whenever possible and continues to develop her own knowledge and identity as an artist-teacher. She has more recently been involved in research projects relating to gender equality and art across all phases of education. Her publications include *Young Children as Artists* (Routledge, 2014) and *Mastering Primary Art and Design* (Bloomsbury, 2020, with Peter Gregory and Claire March), as well as a section entitled 'The Herstory of Art' in *Celebrating 100 Years of Women's Voices* (University of Reading, 2020).

ABOUT THE AUTHORS

Rebecca Berkley is an associate professor in music education and head of postgraduate taught programmes at the University of Reading. Having previously taught music in primary and secondary schools, she now teaches trainee and graduate music teachers. Rebecca's scholarship focuses on how children and adults learn musicianship, as well as how to empower all teachers to teach music with confidence.

Miles Berry is principal lecturer in computing education at the University of Roehampton. He teaches on the secondary computing education teacher training programme and its digital media degree. His research focus is on uptake and achievement in computing education. Prior to joining the University of Roehampton, he was a teacher, ICT coordinator and headteacher. He is a board member of England's National Centre for Computing Education (NCCE), Computing at School (CAS) and the BCS Academy of Computing. He is a fellow of the British Computer Society (BCS), the Royal Society for Arts, Manufactures and Commerce (RSA), Advance HE and the Chartered College of Teaching, as well as a member of the Raspberry Pi Foundation. He gives regular keynotes and continuing professional development (CPD) workshops on computing and education technology in the UK and abroad, and has worked on a number of international consultancy projects involving technology-enhanced learning, curriculum development and CPD.

Alastair Daniel is the principal lecturer in early years and primary English education at the University of Roehampton. Having started his teaching career as a secondary school teacher of mathematics, he quickly shifted his specialism to the performing arts (specifically drama and dance) – disciplines that he carried with him when he moved into special needs education and the primary sector. Prior to entering academia, he worked peripatetically in schools in the UK and Belgium, teaching English through storytelling and drama, and he currently researches the pedagogy of drama and storytelling.

Karin Doull is a principal lecturer in primary history at the University of Roehampton. She is an experienced teacher and teacher educator, with over 30 years in education. She is a fellow of the Historical Association and a senior fellow of Advance HE. She is also a chartered teacher of primary history. She co-authored *Mastering Primary History* (Bloomsbury, 2019, with Christopher Russell and Alison Hales). She is editor-in-chief for the *Primary History* journal and writes extensively for that publication. She has provided primary history workshops in collaboration with the Historical Association, the British Museum, Historical Royal Palaces and the British Library.

Kerenza Ghosh is a senior lecturer in English education at the University of Roehampton. She has made chapter contributions to two academic books about primary education and has co-authored an article about student teachers' use of comics in the primary classroom. She has presented research papers at conferences in the UK and Europe, and has a published chapter entitled 'Who's Afraid of the Big Bad Wolf? Children's Responses to the Portrayal of Wolves in Picturebooks' (in Janet Evans, *Challenging and Controversial Picturebooks: Children's Responses to Visual Texts*, Routledge, 2015). She recently completed a master's in critical approaches to children's literature at the University of Cambridge.

Emese Hall has worked within teacher education since 2005. Her research interests include a focus on drawing and visual literacy, as well as teachers' professional learning. She is vice president of the National Society for Education in Art and Design (NSEAD), was previously a member of the National Expert Subject Advisory Group for art and design education, and is a former South West regional network coordinator for the Cambridge Primary Review Trust (CPRT). She is also co-editor of the pedagogy volume of *The International Encyclopedia of Art and Design Education* (Wiley, 2019).

Leigh Hoath is a senior lecturer in science education at Leeds Trinity University. She is also editor of the Association for Science Education's (ASE) *Primary Science* journal. She has interests in teacher research, pedagogy and working in the outdoor setting, as well as science education as a whole. She works as a consultant for industry outreach at BBC Teach and is a hub leader for Primary Science Quality Mark (PSQM).

Nasreen Majid is an associate professor of primary mathematics education at the University of Reading. Previously, she was a primary teacher, predominantly working in urban settings across London and the South East. She has international teaching experience in Indonesia, where she led mathematics across the primary age range. She was an advanced skills teacher (AST) for mathematics, and has championed the teaching and learning of primary mathematics throughout her career. She currently leads a range of modules with trainee teachers, developing a deeper understanding of the teaching of mathematics.

Lewis Morgan studied at Leeds Beckett University before undertaking his teacher training. He is a teacher at Cookridge Primary School and the science coordinator across the school, and has taught for eight years across all Key Stages. His current role also involves teaching on undergraduate programmes at Leeds Trinity University.

Scarlett Murphy is a lecturer in primary English education for both undergraduate and postgraduate programmes at the University of Reading, having held the post of assistant director for primary PGCE. She directs the English curriculum modules and contributes towards the English specialism pathway, leading on the use of Shakespeare within the primary classroom. Before joining the University of Reading, she was assistant head in a primary school, leading on mathematics and English. Her research interests include the exploration of how impostor syndrome affects women in leadership roles, and she has recently become an associate fellow of Advance HE.

Vicky Randall is a senior fellow at the University of Winchester, where she is subject coordinator for physical education in initial teacher education. Prior to working in higher education, she was a physical education teacher, subject leader and regional subject adviser for physical education in South London. She has worked across a number of national and European professional networks to promote and develop primary physical education, including the Department for Education (DfE) formed Physical Education Expert Subject Advisory Group, the European Primary Physical Education Network (EPPEN) and the All-Party Parliamentary Group on a Fit and Healthy Childhood.

Hermione Ruck Keene began her career as a primary teacher, specialising in music, and is now a senior lecturer in creative curriculum and primary education at Oxford Brookes University, where she lectures on the BA Primary Education and PGCE courses, and an honorary lecturer at the University of Exeter. She was a postgraduate research associate on the EU Horizon 2020 project 'CREATIONS: Developing an Engaging Science Classroom', looking at fusing creative pedagogies from the arts with science teaching. Her PhD research explored musical identity, roles, participation and democracy in the context of a music summer school.

Stephanie Sharp is the programme director on the BA Primary Education (QTS) programme and the English specialism Leader. She is responsible for teacher training and is a module convenor on children's and young adult literature. She contributes to the BA Education Studies programme on creative learning and the arts, lecturing on representations of disability and promoting social justice through children's literature. She is a member of the teaching panel at the Museum of English Rural Life (MERL), supporting the development of published teaching materials related to the museum's collections and working collaboratively with teachers from a range of school settings and the Wellcome Trust.

Alison Silby is a lecturer in primary English education and is assistant director for the Primary School Direct programme at the University of Reading. She contributes to the English specialism pathway, leading on the teaching of poetry and the study of literature. She works in close partnership with a number of schools to develop and review initial teacher education training across providers. Her specific research interests include the exploration of ways in which pupils engage with reading and writing across the primary curriculum. She supervises PhD and EdD students within the Institute of Education at the University of Reading.

Robert Watts trained, worked and exhibited as a painter, and taught in Inner London schools for ten years before joining the University of Roehampton in 2000. In his role as senior lecturer in art and design education, he teaches and supervises student teachers on undergraduate and postgraduate programmes. From 2005 to 2015, he was programme convener for MA art, craft and design education, and is currently course leader for the PGCE secondary art and design programme. His research focuses on the use of visual and child-centred methodologies to understand children's perspectives. In 2016, he completed a PhD entitled *Children's Perceptions of Beauty: Exploring Aesthetic Experience Through Photography*, and in 2019 he was awarded a research grant by the British Academy/Leverhulme Trust that will enable him to develop his study on a national scale. Since 2005, he has co-edited two books on primary art education, written several articles for academic journals, and published over 200 creative projects and articles on primary education in various publications. A selection of this work can be found on his website: **www.artandeducation.co.uk**

Harriet White is a lecturer in primary education. Her teaching career began in 2002 at the Glen Helen Ecology Institute, where she studied outdoor education and natural history. Here, she found not only her vocation for teaching and learning, but a lifelong commitment to ecological and outdoor education. She has an undergraduate degree in zoology and her teaching experience is diverse. She began employment at the University of Exeter in 2012 and has led early years and primary education courses. She is particularly interested in sustainability education, and has worked with various partners to research and develop resources to support education for sustainability.

Anita Wood began her teaching career in 1994 in primary schools in Tower Hamlets, East London, where she taught all year groups from reception to Year 6 and coordinated literacy and English as an additional language (EAL) in large primary schools. In 2004, she began working in teacher education. She currently teaches at the University of Exeter, leading modules on the PGCE and undergraduate courses. She is currently involved in research on multilingual socialisation and education for sustainable development (ESD). Her core fields of interest are EAL and the teaching of English and drama in primary classrooms.

FOREWORD

I am delighted to write the foreword for this important and thoroughly engaging book. It is a tremendously welcome addition to texts on primary education written by curriculum experts that inform, educate and inspire. This book does all three and much more, written at a time of unprecedented challenge to teachers and teacher educators during a pandemic that, as I write, is far from over. Covid-19 has brought tragedy to many families and caused much turmoil. Schools have responded with innovation and commitment to continue learning for children and support parents and carers admirably, and we owe them a huge debt of gratitude for their professionalism and dedication. From adversity has risen a new spirit: one that is determined to seize this opportunity to review what is taught in schools and how it is taught, as well as offering a new vision for the primary curriculum that was urgently needed. Debates on the narrowed curriculum, high-stakes testing, increased accountability and pressures from different stakeholders are well rehearsed. These have left teachers and school leaders looking for inspiration and a new road to travel that will prepare children more appropriately for the twenty-first century, and more specifically to reclaim arts education as a vital part of the primary curriculum jigsaw. We have seen for too long now the dominance of core subjects in primary schools, and it is timely that this must change. This book offers an excellent rationale for this change by championing the place of arts education and its unique contribution not only to any curriculum design, but to children's lives.

We often talk of a book being a 'page-turner' and hear the phrase, 'I couldn't put it down.' This is one of those books! On reading it, I wanted to read the next chapter, and the next. I also wanted to pause to savour the ideas in the book, ideas that will inspire teachers and light up children's imaginations. Creativity is a dominant theme of the book. It is also highly evident, in the writers' wisdom and passion for their subjects, as to how each chapter fits together to complement the next while enabling the elusive whole curriculum that we desperately seek. As the authors in this book ably represent, arts education offers so many benefits to children's development, wellness, and ability to think and be creative, as well as rekindling what has sadly been reduced in too many schools. It enhances and unites the curriculum, as well as promoting achievement and inclusivity.

The whole curriculum – the broad and balanced curriculum – is at the very heart of the organisation I am proud to represent, the National Primary Teacher Education Council (NaPTEC). We are a group of teacher educators from a range of providers, with this very much at the core of our guiding principles. We reflect this in our conferences, regional events and lobbying of government. Susan has been a dedicated champion of this in her work with NaPTEC, and she – together with

Suzy – has assembled a writing team that strongly advocate the arts, as well as providing us with ideas and techniques for high-quality teaching, underscored by their indomitable passion for the arts. It educates and challenges, demands our reflection and critical thinking, and delights us as readers. It is therefore with the utmost pleasure that I write this foreword. This is not a book solely for the pandemic. This is a book that is part of a powerful vanguard for change in schools. It is an essential read for all those with a deep regard for the curriculum in primary schools and for those who hold dearly the importance of the arts to enrich teaching, and thus children's lives.

Dr Jonathan Doherty
Chair of NaPTEC

INTRODUCTION

SUSAN OGIER AND SUZY TUTCHELL

The arts and humanities define who we are as a people. That is their power – to remind us of what we each have to offer, and what we all have in common. To help us understand our history and imagine our future. To give us hope in the moments of struggle and to bring us together when nothing else will.

Michelle Obama

They say, 'You don't know what you've got till it's gone.' This book has been conceived by the collective concern of the authors of the chapters that follow: that arts subjects are rapidly becoming endangered species in children's education. Pre-global pandemic, evidence was gathering that the arts were squeezed almost to extinction from the primary and secondary curricula in England as schools bowed to external pressures and strived to secure places at the top of league tables which measure only English and maths (B. Cooper, 2018; Daubney et al., 2019; Spielman, 2017).

That, of course, was then, before all of our lives changed with the advent of Covid-19, and nothing has shown us more explicitly what we have lost – and are continuing to lose – as social distancing and hygiene take priority to keep us all safe in our daily lives and in our classrooms. In the spring of 2020, the world of education had an enforced reflective pause: the relentless target-setting, testing and fear of Ofsted seemed to fall away from the minds of teachers of all phases of education during this international crisis, and concerns over children's well-being came to the forefront of teachers' priorities. Children having been in isolation for weeks on end, missing the comfort, structure and rhythm of the school day, has taken its toll on the younger generation as many teachers have tried to grapple with the intellectual, physical, emotional, social and mental costs of children missing school – and life cannot just return to normal as though nothing has happened. The appropriateness of our exam system was called into question as 16+ exams were cancelled and a grades fiasco ensued. This affected a whole generation of young people and perhaps highlighted the challenges of a high-stakes testing system that measures children's capabilities and potential in a narrow way.

For many, however, the pause during the pandemic brought out our creative side. Try to recall some of the most important moments of lockdown that inspired you and gave you hope in the darkest of days. Was it the moment when the Italians were singing or playing music from their balconies? Was it the creative videos that were doing the rounds on social media that made us all laugh? Perhaps it was having access to the world's galleries, museums, theatres and cinemas, who opened their virtual doors to us, and which we visited in our thousands from our own armchairs.

In the most terrifying days of the global pandemic, the arts are what kept people interested, inspired and connected. Many people and families rediscovered their creative selves and used these pursuits to get them through the day. During this time, it was engagement with the arts that lifted spirits and inspired isolated individuals to connect in new ways with their communities. Back at school, teachers battled with how to provide a suitable curriculum for children returning to school after months of being home, and often turned to creative activities to encourage, reassure and re-engage. There now seems to be a renewal of understanding of the fundamental importance of the arts, so perhaps this is a good time to re-evaluate their place and relevance in children's lives, as well as re-establishing this firmly in the centre of every early years and primary curriculum. Importantly, schools must ensure that the creative arts and learning through the arts are not squeezed out, and that the temptation to narrow the curriculum does not win. Now, more than ever, we need classrooms that are alive and alert, where children are encouraged to be their creative selves.

This book is designed to enable you to consider the value of arts education as a meaningful learning experience for children of preschool and primary ages. It will help you to develop the subject knowledge you will need to be able to offer a high-quality arts experience for children in your school. It will help you to reflect on how the arts can have a lasting impact on children's learning and lives, through developing a deep understanding of where and how high standards in arts education can and should occur in the early years and primary curriculum. It will help you to think about an education system that responds to the skills predicted to be needed by a future generation who will be part of our cultural and creative industries, as well as for innovation and growth in the UK. It will reinforce the potential for the wide range of intellectual, physical, social, mental and emotional development through learning opportunities that engagement in arts practice facilitates across all subject areas, allowing every child to achieve and feel valued.

In these pages, we present a spectrum of insights from a team of educational experts who are not only great advocates for learning in and through the arts, but who also have a deep understanding of what children need as a holistic learning experience.

How to use this book

You might wonder what a chapter on science, or maths, or sustainable development, is doing in a book on the arts. Alongside chapters on what could be considered the traditional arts subjects, such as visual art, music, dance and drama, we want to show you that learning in any subject area can be enhanced and deepened by adding the magic ingredient which the arts bring. This book brings together expert voices from the world of primary education to help you reflect on and understand more of what children need in order to develop and flourish as well-rounded human beings, so that you can consider how to embed these factors in your own curriculum design.

You can expect to:

- develop enthusiasm and confidence to teach a wide range of arts subjects, and feel enabled to plan opportunities for promoting the arts in early years and primary education with purpose and intent;
- establish the fundamental principles of arts education and understand how these can be easily implemented within any early years and primary curriculum;
- gain a contemporary view of what learning in the arts is, and make connections between arts disciplines and the worlds that exist in schools and beyond;
- explore the impact of teaching arts subjects to children to reinforce the relevance and importance of access to high-quality, pedagogically sound arts education for all children in their formative years.

The structure of this book

The chapters have been ordered to reduce the notion of hierarchy and to promote all topics and subjects as having equal importance. Therefore, traditional arts chapters (i.e. visual art, music, dance and drama, poetry) are interspersed with chapters that cover the arts through transdisciplinary means. You might wish to read the book straight through or pick out chapters of particular interest or relevance to you in your studies, or in relation to school experience. We hope that ultimately, you will have read the whole book. We have included reflective questions and case studies in each chapter to encourage you to reflect on the ideas and consider ways to include the arts in your teaching – every day and in every way. We hope that this will encourage you to experiment with these in practice, as well as discussing the research, theories and concepts with colleagues, peers, mentors and tutors. We hope that you will find ways for children to be engaged and motivated through the arts so that their individual dispositions and talents can flourish. To this end, the initial chapter, 'What is learning in the arts?', challenges perceptions of the status and value of arts subjects within the primary curriculum. This chapter sets the scene for subsequent chapters by establishing key learning opportunities and objectives, leaving you in no doubt as to what can be achieved by engaging children in and through the arts.

The second chapter continues along this theme, to emphasise the key role that the arts play in enabling children to understand, contemplate and become activists for a sustainable future. 'The arts and education for sustainable development' is a forward-looking advocacy for how we might empower and encourage children to think about and respond to the problems that they face as they grow up and develop in a global society.

Each major arts discipline has a designated chapter, bringing together contemporary ideas as well as highlighting current research and thinking within subject areas. The chapters on visual art (Chapter 4), music (Chapter 6), poetry (Chapter 8), dance (Chapter 10) and drama (Chapter 13) all offer refreshing approaches and include ideas for the classroom. We are shown how other arts areas, such as storytelling and creative writing, which are often not utilised to their full potential, can be celebrated and reinstated in terms of their value (Chapters 5 and 12, respectively). Unusually, in a book focused on the arts, the remaining chapters look at the arts as a transdisciplinary vehicle, which allows us to understand subjects such as science (Chapter 7), the humanities (Chapter 3), maths (Chapter 11) and computing (Chapter 9) in far-reaching ways. These chapters help us to consider the interconnectivity of the arts, as well as how the arts are an essential part of how we learn and how we live, exploring the co-dependency of a wide range of subject areas.

We hope that you will use this book to bring joy and creativity to your teaching in all areas of learning across the early years and primary age ranges. We hope that you will use it to get to know the children you teach as capable, competent, curious citizens, as well as using the ideas put forward by the authors of these chapters to energise and invigorate the curriculum in your school.

1

WHAT IS LEARNING IN THE ARTS?

SUSAN OGIER AND SUZY TUTCHELL

KEYWORDS: ARTS; CREATIVE AND CRITICAL THINKING; EMBODIED LEARNING; MULTISENSORY; SELF-RESOURCEFUL

CHAPTER OBJECTIVES

This chapter will help you to:

- understand what the arts are, as well as why they are important in the early years and primary curriculum;
- understand why we need learning in the arts to provide a balanced and holistic education for children;
- consider the interdisciplinarity that arts learning facilitates;
- develop awareness of cultural diversity through the arts, as well as applying concepts around cultural capital to planning for learning;
- consider how we can create a place for the arts in daily practice.

LINKS TO THE TEACHERS' STANDARDS

This chapter maps to the following Teachers' Standards:

TS1 Set high expectations which inspire, motivate and challenge pupils

TS3 Demonstrate good subject and curriculum knowledge

TS5 Adapt teaching to respond to the strengths and needs of all pupils

See the Appendix for links to the ITT Core Content Framework.

Every child should have access to arts and culture, and to the benefits that access brings. The arts are a positive force in society: children feel more confident in their ability to create, challenge and explore, to be part of society, and to make change happen. The arts empower children. They contribute to the development of all aspects of a child's potential and personality: studying the arts fosters creativity, innovation, empathy, and resilience. The arts enrich young lives, making them happier and healthier.

(CLA, 2019)

Introduction

In this chapter, we shall define what we mean when we are talking about 'the arts'. We shall discuss the contribution that the arts make to children's lives and why they are an important component of a well-rounded education. We shall focus on the wide-ranging nature and value of arts subjects within the education system and beyond by establishing a rationale for arts learning that is common across discipline contexts. We shall offer suggestions for re-establishing a meaningful place for the arts in any early years and primary curriculum, as well as underpinning this with tested pedagogical models and examples from educational research.

Why do we need to define the arts?

You are perhaps wondering why we need to define the arts at all. Everybody knows what the arts are – right? 'It's what you do in your spare time, isn't it?' There was certainly a huge spike in all sorts of creative activity happening while everyone was in lockdown, and many of these arts-based activities were essential in keeping ourselves sane during those challenging times. However, the sad fact is that participation in arts subjects has declined dramatically in the education of young children in English schools and early years settings in recent years, and we do need to remind ourselves of why this trend should urgently be reversed (B. Cooper, 2018). In schools where the arts are not taught consistently or regularly, it is easy for teachers to lose confidence in their own subject knowledge in these areas; and before you know it, the arts have dropped right out of the curriculum, or have been relegated to extracurricular activities, which means that not all children will have access. To fully understand how arts subjects can not only be re-established as key learning experiences for every child, but can be utilised across the curriculum to motivate and inspire children, is to view these areas of learning in new and different ways.

REFLECTION

How would you define the arts? Why do you think arts subjects are part of the curriculum for young children in primary schools? Reflect for a moment on your own experiences of learning in the arts and make a list of the positive and negative memories of this.

Your personal experiences in arts engagement in your own life are likely to have impacted on how you feel about teaching these subjects, as well as where you place them on a scale of importance within the busy curriculum. This will take a key role in influencing how you design a syllabus for the children in your class; but beyond this, we must be mindful of external factors that shape the curriculum which we offer, and we need to consider the effects of that.

What do we mean by 'the arts'?

The *Encyclopædia Britannica* states that the arts form 'modes of expression that use skill or imagination in the creation of objects, environments or experiences that can be shared with others' (*Encyclopædia Britannica*, n.d.). The same source goes on to name traditional categories that we might easily recognise:

- performing arts (theatre, dance, music);
- visual arts (painting, drawing);
- plastic arts (sculpture, modelling);
- graphic arts (painting, drawing, design);
- architecture (often including interior design);
- literature (poetry, drama, story);
- decorative arts (enamelwork, mosaic, crafts).

(*Encyclopædia Britannica*, n.d.)

From this list, we can begin to realise the expansive nature of where the arts lie in the domain of learning: that the arts as modes of expression and participation stretch far beyond traditional perceptions of the main four – art, drama, music and dance. Have you ever considered that everything around us, such as furniture, mobile devices, clothing, architecture and even town planning, is fundamentally camped within the arts? It has all been imagined, visualised and designed. Even experimental chemistry and surgical procedures require attributes such as flexible and creative thinking as well as manual dexterity: skills that are learned through practising the arts. So, when we question, 'What are the arts?' it is perhaps much more pertinent to wonder, 'What is the role of the arts?' and acknowledge that what we are doing is *thinking through the arts*. We are using the language and skills that we learn through arts engagement and participation to make vital connections in every aspect of our lives.

THEORY FOCUS: THE ARTS AS A WAY OF THINKING AND KNOWING

Sullivan (2001) describes this as *transcognition*; to understand what this means, we need to recognise how artists (in the broadest sense of the word) work and think. Artists, Sullivan explains, derive imaginative thoughts and ideas not only through an initial stimulus and motivation, but also *during the process of making*, and these ideas change and evolve as a result of their own critical reflection while they are engaged in the practical activity of making. Once the work is given an audience, alternative meanings and interpretations will also inform the work as part of a dialogic process. The creative process is an active one and is always open-ended. Artists - of any discipline - are unlikely to feel as though their job is ever done, so this is a very different way of thinking about how lines of enquiry progress and develop, and very different indeed to how school curricula operate. In schools, we are much more used to celebrating the end product, ticking items off a list, working towards the achievable measures that rule our curriculum. But artists do not think in this way. They think more like scientists, with enquiry as the key driver and with questions that they are determined to answer by finding all sorts of diverse means to that end. They then find ways to interpret and reinterpret, and finally communicate this through the most appropriate modes of expression. For children, this is what Malaguzzi (1994) calls 'the hundred languages'. Artists will research via multiple channels to collect the information they need to inform their work. For example, a dancer will watch the flight of a bird or insect so that they can interpret this through their movement; an actor will research the life and times of their character in order to give a convincing performance; a composer might reference patterns found in nature to create a new piece. Watch the following TED Talk, where Cindy Foley refers to this as *transdisciplinary research* and encourages us to think like an artist: **www.youtube.com/watch?v=ZcFRfJb2ONk&vl=en**

REFLECTION

What do you understand about the relevance of *transdisciplinary research* in the primary classroom? Do you offer children the opportunity to make connections across different areas of learning?

This could be interpreted as cross-curricular learning, sometimes known as 'topic work'. But labelling work in this way can have a reductive effect if we are not careful. Hayes (2010) acknowledges that among other concerns, sceptics of this approach believe that without distinct subject-specific learning, children do not gain enough knowledge and skills to be able to synthesise their learning well enough for this method to be effective. Subject-specific learning can become so diluted that children are not sure of the learning objectives in anything. The sceptics might argue that cross-curricular learning is an inappropriate throwback to ideologies of the 1970s and notions of 'discovery learning'. However, as with all pedagogical ideologies, extreme versions of either separating subjects out entirely or combining subjects so that learning becomes haphazard and fuzzy are not satisfactory solutions. It is, however, more constructive to design a curriculum so that subject-specific learning is apparent, and creative approaches are implemented so that children understand the connections between disciplines of learning (Ogier, 2019). A balance is always best, and the arts are the areas that facilitate this best of all.

Spotlight on early years

In England, there is a worrying drive to formalise early childhood education in the proposed revision to the early years foundation stage (EYFS) framework (DfE, 2020b). There is in fact a long-standing tradition of integrated learning and arts inclusion in early years pedagogy both in the UK and in developed nations across the world (Hamilton et al., 2019). There is a lot that we can take from this integrated pedagogical paradigm to include the arts as praxis when designing curricula for both younger and older children. Early years educators understand and value the arts both as disciplines in their own right and as a vehicle for learning in other areas. As a mode of multisensory engagement, the arts can encourage what Kress (1997) relates to the concept of *synaesthesia*. This involves the transposition of sensory information, such as colour, shape and sound, into understanding in order to make sense of what is being experienced. He suggests that young children are naturally synaesthetic but that this is educated out of them in systems where the written word rules. He also reminds us that 'this fact of synaesthesia is essential for humans to understand the world' (pxviii). What is education for if not to help children discover just that?

International models that we can look to as examples of excellence, where the arts are valued and integrated, might include the Reggio schools, where the youngest citizens explore lines of enquiry through all of the expressive arts and an *atelierista* is a natural part of the teaching team. New Zealand's *Te Whāriki* has holistic core principles through which to ensure all children grow to become 'competent, confident learners and communicators, healthy in mind, body and spirit, secure in their sense of belonging and in the knowledge that they make a valued contribution to society' (Taguma et al., 2013). In this paradigm, the arts are acknowledged as being the 'first literacies' as children learn to comprehend and convey meaning through the many symbols of communication that the arts afford. You can find out more about these arts-inclusive models where the child is central by searching online.

Why teach the arts?

Michael Rosen (2014) advocates that the arts provide a home in the classroom for 'a set of humane and democratic educational practices'. This might seem like an idealistic notion when considering many classrooms across the country today. Children are placed in rows, heads down, working silently, while the teacher instructs in maths and English from the front. This seems more reminiscent of an English Victorian classroom rather than the vibrant, engaging and inclusive learning environment that we might aspire to. While this might seem like an exaggerated image, it might also help us to pause and consider the importance of why we teach the arts.

Curiosity, mystery and a lifelong love of learning

At the core of a classroom that embraces and encapsulates an arts-based pedagogy is a commitment to curiosity and mystery. It is a pedagogy that requires enquiry of the learner (and teacher), and so participants learn to express the 'mysterious' through their rapidly growing curious minds, understandings, thoughts and feelings. As Gentle (1986) stated over 25 years ago, 'All children are born curious ... they have a natural curiosity and like to touch and hold things, to manipulate them and include them in their play' (p53). There is no doubt that being curious keeps us all playful and creative. Interestingly, an elderly grandparent can revert to a very playful existence under the guide of their young grandchild, reflecting the longevity and lifelong ability to playfully learn and discover new things – right up until the day we die.

Curiosity feeds the mind to explore and find out more. It is the search engine that we all own which helps us to discover and layer our strata of understanding (Tutchell, 2014). Our brain's busy and intensive cognitive laboratory continually develops the ability to rationalise and realise. Curiosity motivates learning; a child is captured in a moment of 'wanting to know', and so they are motivated to find out and consequently learn something new. Importantly, the quenching of curiosity inevitably leads to added breadth and depth of knowledge (Peterson and Seligman, 2004).

REFLECTION

Think for a moment about the last time you were curious. What did it feel like? How did it spur you on? What did you discover in that moment which was new to you? Moments such as these are multitudinous in our daily lives. We all have this capacity to explore and investigate, especially children. It is one of the most astounding and wonderfully fruitful attributes of childhood. Children's innate and overwhelming desire to find out and become immersed in curiosity-driven quests allows them to discover, think and refine (Tutchell, 2014).

THEORY FOCUS: THE ARTS AS AN AGENT FOR LEARNING

The arts as an agent or vehicle for learning offer a useful theoretical perspective, and help us to find justification for why they are so key in children's education. Elliot Eisner was a visionary in the field of arts and education. He advocated, 'When there is no challenge, when everything is satisfactory, there may be little motivation to stretch one's thinking, to try something new, to experiment, to revise, to appraise, and to start again' (Eisner, 2002, p36). He maintained that the arts were critical to develop skills in children and young people, and advocated a ten-point strategy explaining clearly what the arts could offer (Eisner, 2002). More recently, Art in Action (2019) has contemporised Eisner's ten points to suggest the following five critical skills of an arts education, adapted here:

Creativity: Having the ability to think imaginatively, express yourself and bring fresh ideas is essential to innovation and progress.

Collaboration: Working together for a common purpose teaches children that their contribution is important, which is perfect for the collaborative nature of the arts.

Confidence: The arts create a safe space for students to explore their talents and build their confidence, and so they are more likely to take risks and step out of their comfort zones to try new things in other areas of their lives.

Cultural awareness and empathy: The arts provide a unique platform to discuss many different cultures, socio-economic levels and current events.

Critical thinking: The arts necessitate a creative process that includes conceptual and interpretational thinking which helps to build critical thinking skills, including observation, reasoning and problem-solving.

Intellectual and critical learning through the arts

To consider why we teach the arts is to emphasise the academic importance and integrity intrinsically woven into arts-based learning. Whether this is through problem-solving, engaging in rhythmic movement, or exploring sounds and words, sharing enjoyable, creative experiences will encourage social and emotional interactions and development. During these processes, children are naturally engaged in higher-order thinking, mastery and critical learning. The misconception of the arts as simply a practical, doing and making activity is prevalent in our education system. This perception misses the really crucial point that learning through the arts offers a deep and intellectual mindset. This is partly due to the behaviours of curiosity, discovery and exploration that engage the learner to go through a process which delves deep into their cognitive mindset. The deeper they go, the more they learn to reach outcomes and decisions. Increased learning in this way develops children's metacognitive skills, where they are able to plan, monitor and evaluate with a conscious awareness in any given subject. Alex Quigley and Eleanor Stringer (2018) posit that 'An effective learner will monitor their knowledge and cognitive processes, and use this understanding to make judgements about how to direct their efforts.'

Embodied learning – active and participative

Learning in an active and participative way ensures a level of enquiry-based learning, where children look, find and decide with inquisitive minds. Enquiry has no boundaries and can invite all of us in – it is fully inclusive and requires deeply rich levels of participation and interaction. The key thing about learning through the arts is that it is active and often irresistible: we participate, we engage, we move, culminating in what we call embodied learning (Gregory et al., 2020; Kosmas, 2018). According to the embodied approach, both body and mind are able to synthesise knowledge significantly by integrating physicality within learning. In that way, as Atkinson (2010) states, 'we experience, understand, and act on the world through our bodies' (p599).

Why do the arts matter now?

For decades, teachers have proclaimed that arts education is important. However, in recent years, barriers – such as the focus on science, technology, engineering and mathematics (STEM) education, the silo culture of subjects in schools, and a reduction in budgets for arts resources and opportunities – have taken their toll on this approach to teaching and learning. So, it really is time to remind everyone that the arts encourage the development of powerful cognitive capacities which have wide relevance in many areas of life, such as the capacity to think critically, to be creative, to be reflective, to solve problems, to explore alternative points of view and to make connections.

Social engagement

Learning through the arts promotes life skills such as collaboration and positive self-expression. The impact that the arts have on children's emotional and social development make them an imperative in the classroom. Responding and working with one another through expressive, creative and embodied learning lays strong foundations for a sense of community, respect and well-being. The interactions of learning, as we have already commented on, can be moments in time, but importantly they offer essential moments of understanding when the heart, body and mind operate simultaneously.

Stimulating heads and hearts

As humans, we are a combination of emotional mind and rational mind. These two minds work in tight harmony to create our experience of life. Activities in the arts invite children to play with the balance of 'head and heart'. There are no wrong answers in creative activities, and risk-taking is definitely encouraged. Through improvisation and experimentation with the arts in a non-judgemental environment, children learn more about themselves and their world. Mindful and emotional engagement in learning is personal and individually owned, but it can be a part of something bigger. Children learning together creates a shared experience, and that can become a powerful motivating factor. Socially interactive, exciting and vibrant learning opportunities, in which children are encouraged to retain a sense of agency, ensure that each individual feels part of that bigger picture (Carden, 2019).

Cultural capital, diversity and social mobility

Cultural capital, founded by Bourdieu in the late twentieth century, is the accumulation of knowledge, behaviours and skills taken from our backgrounds, family influences and society around us. The disparity attached to this is the wide and varied backgrounds that children come from. The relevance of cultural capital in school, however, can easily be embedded by promoting a range of arts and cultural learning opportunities to widen children's understanding of each other. The arts can provide a base for social equilibrium for children in this way. Perhaps your class has children in it who have never stepped foot in a gallery or have never watched a play unfold in an auditorium. That is where the classroom as an arena for arts learning is so very important. It is in this space that their worlds can transform and expand. Too often we think about our classrooms as walls, floors, ceilings and desks, rather than considering the transformative qualities that they can possess in order to enable a living, breathing generation of children to be a part of what cultural capital actually means. If children are exposed to a wide range of different cultures and art forms regularly, as well as being encouraged to interact, discuss and debate, and create, we shall enable social mobility to take place in our classrooms, thus empowering younger generations to continually aspire to own their culture.

Now, more than ever, learning and teaching through the arts is crucial as we arm our children with the skills and aptitudes that they need to move further through their educational lives and into employment. Adaptation, self-learning and resilience are characteristics that they have all had to adopt and manage due to the closure of schools and a home/school life becoming the norm. This transference of locational learning naturally requires a creative approach. Children around the world have had to be highly creative and innovative in order to learn, problematise and understand new subjects, topics and questions without the physical and face-to-face scaffolding of the school environment. We can take some really important positives from this and use what we have learned in the future. We should maintain the creative strength that we have rediscovered during this unprecedented time and use this to great effect in our classrooms. Use Table 1.1 as a planning guide for learning in the arts. This quick reference table will give you a range of learning objectives to choose from in all of the key arts subject areas, as well as providing an overview of key skills and concepts and cross-curricular links.

Table 1.1 What is learning in the arts?

Art form	**Art form specific**	**Learning that occurs across all disciplines**			**Curriculum links**
		Intellectual/ cognitive	**Emotional/ social**	**Physical**	
Art and design	• Visual communication • Hand-eye coordination • Understanding a range of materials • Understanding of how to use tools • Understanding and confidence in engaging in visual art processes (e.g. drawing, painting, printmaking) • Sculpture and crafts	• Curiosity • Decision-making • Critical thinking • Playfulness • Research skills • Embracing ambiguity and dealing with the unknown • Imagination • Idea generation • Improvisation • Developing memory and making connections • Reasoning	• Enjoyment • Motivation • Self-esteem • Expressive • Relief from stress • Developing an understanding of the need for balance in life • Self-confidence • Empathy • Social skills and the ability to collaborate • Contemplation of the human condition	• Developing fine motor control and refining movement • Manipulation (e.g. using tools correctly and safely) • Gross motor strength and control • Healthy bodies • Healthy minds • Stamina	• Science • Literature and language • Humanities • Mathematics • Digital media and computing

(Continued)

Table 1.1 (Continued)

Art form	Art form specific	Learning that occurs across all disciplines			Curriculum links
		Intellectual/ cognitive	Emotional/ social	Physical	
	• Recognise and use formal elements of art and subject-specific vocabulary (e.g. texture, line, form, shape, colour, colour mixing, pattern, tonal values, foreground, background, support, brushstrokes, pour, splash) • Spatial awareness • Visual literacy • Sense of place	• Evaluating • Ability to reflect • Initiative • Understanding historical and social contexts • Learning about other cultures • Developing aesthetic sensibility • Creativity • Ability to work within timescales • Concentration • Listening • Ability to take on new learning quickly • Entering dialogic debate and being able to justify choices • Ability to organise • Negotiation • Sense of audience • Seeing and understanding connections • Processing thoughts and actions • Communicating ideas • Interpret • Timing	• Playfulness • Risk-taking • Self-discipline and the ability to work independently • Resilience - learning to accept disappointment and keep going • Perseverance • Sense of freedom to express thoughts and ideas • Adaptability • Flexibility • Accepting constructive criticism • Ability to lead and follow • Participation • Feeling part of a community • Sense of achievement • Mindfulness • Being calm • Managing emotions - self-regulation	• Sensory development and awareness • Self-image • Multisensory • Muscle development • Being active • Being still	
Music	• Sensory awareness (e.g. sound, touch) • Memory • Ability to lead and follow				• Mathematics • Science • English/ Literature • Humanities

Art form	Art form specific	Learning that occurs across all disciplines			Curriculum links
		Intellectual/ cognitive	Emotional/ social	Physical	
	• Patience • Developing and refining auditory skills • Understanding beat, rhythm and scales • Sounds in the environment • Understanding echoes • Listening for patterns • Short- and long-term memory • Harmony and sympathetic vibrations • Timbre • Teamwork/ collaboration				
Dance/ movement	As well as the items listed in the 'Physical' column: • Gross motor • Fine motor • Healthy self-image • Balance • Control • Dexterity • Agility • Vocabulary in practice (e.g. gesture, leap, stretch, hold) • Rhythm • Spatial awareness • Working with others • Understanding of anatomy and physiology				• Music • Science • Art

(Continued)

Table 1.1 (Continued)

Art form	Art form specific	Learning that occurs across all disciplines			Curriculum links
		Intellectual/ cognitive	Emotional/ social	Physical	
Drama/ performance	• Oral communication • Teamwork and cooperation • Dialogue • Respect for colleagues and authority • Learning to work to deadlines and under pressure • Healthy self-image • Short- and long-term memory development • Ability to lead and follow • Balance • Control				• Art and design • Literature and language • Physical education (PE)
Literature and language arts	• Developing language and learning new vocabulary • Understanding forms of expressive language • Creative writing • Scriptwriting • Poetry • Storytelling • Learning about structure and sequencing • Reading • Writing • Speaking • Listening • Composition (e.g. spelling, grammar, dialogue) • Playing with language • Using humour and puns				• Art • Design • Drama • Humanities • Technology • Computing

Art form	Art form specific	Learning that occurs across all disciplines			Curriculum links
		Intellectual/ cognitive	Emotional/ social	Physical	
Photography/ film/digital media	• Visual literacy • Communication of vision and intent • Composition • Light • Colour • Tone • Texture • Understanding of technology • Understanding and care of equipment • Vocabulary and language development (e.g. viewpoint depth, value, frame) • Digital literacy and programming • Editing • Design • Presentation • Self-analysis • Sense of place				• Art • Mathematics • Science and technology • Computing

CASE STUDY

Maria Vinney is a teacher-educator at the University of Winchester, having previously been an early years and primary teacher, an art coordinator and a headteacher. She uses the arts to show how powerful they can be to help children believe in themselves - to tackle life's challenges in an increasingly complex world.

Year 5 children Jade and Nigel are putting on a performance in just one week - a performance that will change their lives. It is a demanding process. From start to finish, the children are challenged by taking risks, becoming resilient and doing things that they did not believe they could. Jade and Nigel have personal challenges that make school not easy as they both find learning and playing difficult to navigate. Jade has a troubled home life and Nigel has poor concentration skills and a physical difference that makes life hard. The arts performance, however, is a transformative experience for these children, who are able to achieve and succeed.

(Continued)

(Continued)

Everything about the performance is generated by the children from scratch in an open-ended way, from script to scenery. The journey the children take, from the first steps into the unknown at the beginning to an all-singing, all-dancing spectacular on Friday night, is a magical demonstration of the power of the arts. Every single child has their chance to shine - there is no one star of the show, because they all are.

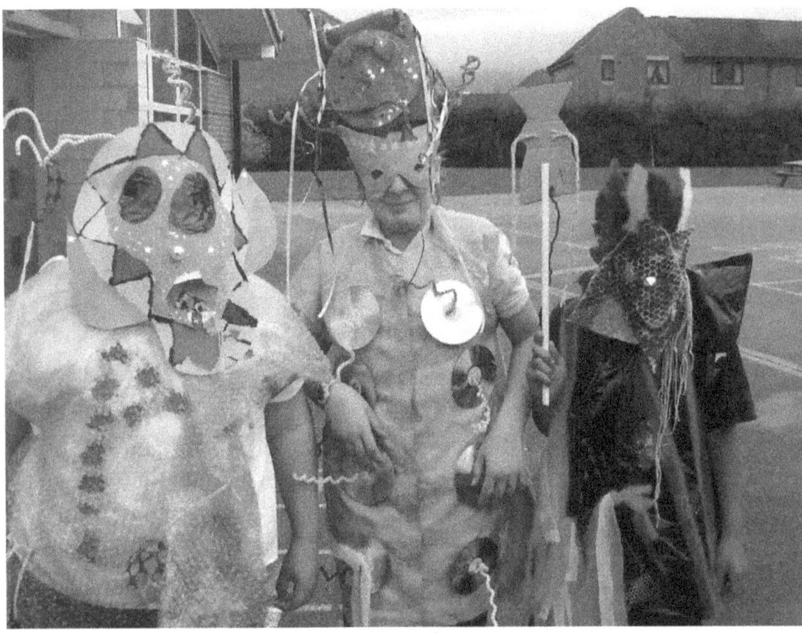

To begin, teachers use a range of motivating and inspiring strategies. For example, words cut from newspaper headlines and reordered will become the title of a song or story that children cannot wait to write down. Crossword puzzle answers, read across the page, can generate ideas and lead to wonderful starting points. All ideas are accepted and valued, collaboration is encouraged, and perseverance is praised.

Nigel and Jade join in enthusiastically with 'Zip Zap Boing!', a frantic daily warm-up game to build confidence, boost self-esteem and help children to see that it is OK to make mistakes. On the night, Nigel and Jade sing their hearts out - happy and confident and enjoying their moment, a chance to show how brilliant they are. At the end, I spring up from my seat and give an impassioned speech. I talk about how this experience sums up, for me, what education is all about, and I can feel the energy in the room. Each year, I sit in the audience and watch many Nigels and Jades, and I always end up with a lump in my throat. Each time, I think, 'How can we give them that same feeling of empowerment, that positivity, that zest for life and all things learning in our daily practice?' Here is where we are building memories. For me, education is much more than the curriculum content which we and the government of the time decide that children need to know. Good education is about how you make people feel, and the arts are at the heart of that.

REFLECTION

How has this case study affected your thinking about the value of the arts in education? When teaching arts through immersive and enquiry-led approaches, have you ever been surprised by the engagement and motivation of children who often find school and learning hard? For some children, these activities can be a great leveller, and help to raise their self-esteem and sense of self-worth.

How can we include arts in our daily practice?

When you consider designing your curriculum, whether for the whole school or within your class or year group, go back to the theory focus box entitled 'the arts as a way of thinking and knowing' and try to look at planning through this lens. Rather than starting with the facts and figures and then wondering how you are going to embed these in children's minds, start with the stories, images, movements and sounds that exist within the content. How will you inspire children to feel that this matters to them, and how will you bring that to life? How will you use the arts as a compelling learning experience that challenges children, involves them holistically, and drives them to be excited and curious in their research of the world around them? For example, in science, teach the concept of forces through dance; in maths, teach geometry through art; and in English, teach punctuation through music. In the chapters throughout this book, you will gain more ideas of exactly how to do this – and more.

DEEP DIVE

Intent

- Does your school have a vision for where the arts fit in?
- Do you have clear and consistent planning for arts education across the school to ensure that a broad and balanced curriculum is on offer? Long-term planning should be ambitious, coherent and progressive in all areas of the arts, as well as easily adaptive for all children.

Implementation

- What evidence do you have to show that your long- and medium-term plans are being used, developed and reflected upon?
- How is leadership in arts subjects managed and respected, and how are those leaders gaining subject-specific skills and knowledge through continuing professional development (CPD)?

Impact

- What is the impact of this work having on the children?
- Are the pupils able to discuss and articulate their learning clearly and cohesively?

CHAPTER SUMMARY

In this chapter, we have considered what we mean by the arts in education and why the arts are an essential part of children's learning. We have discussed how the arts impact on our daily lives and the implications for children growing up in an increasingly complex world where the arts have been marginalised, while at the same time they are needed more than ever before. We have helped you to consider how early years pedagogy can offer inspiration for including the arts across the curriculum, as well as helping you to think like an artist when planning. We have provided a quick reference table to help you assign learning intentions to your planning and integrate arts learning while also challenging and motivating pupils in all aspects of the curriculum. The case study offers an insight into how this can be made a reality in your school.

Further reading

Arts Council (2018) *Early Years Arts and Culture: Current Practice and Options for Future Development.* Available at: www.artscouncil.org.uk/sites/default/files/download-file/Early_years_arts_culture_310119_0.pdf

Cultural Learning Alliance (CLA) (2019) *The Arts for Every Child.* Available at: https://culturallearningalliance.org.uk/wp-content/uploads/2019/10/Arts-for-every-child-CLA-Social-justice-briefing.pdf

2

THE ARTS AND EDUCATION FOR SUSTAINABLE DEVELOPMENT

EMESE HALL, ANITA WOOD, HERMIONE RUCK KEENE AND HARRIET WHITE

KEYWORDS: CURRICULAR INTENTIONS; EDUCATION FOR SUSTAINABLE DEVELOPMENT; LEARNING IN AND THROUGH THE ARTS; TRANSDISCIPLINARY; VALUES

CHAPTER OBJECTIVES

This chapter will help you to:

- define and exemplify education for sustainable development (ESD) and its relevance to children's learning in and through the arts;
- share practical ideas for curriculum planning and learning activities, both inside and outside the classroom.
- provide suggestions for supporting teachers' professional learning and enquiry.

LINKS TO THE TEACHERS' STANDARDS

This chapter maps to the following Teachers' Standard:

TS1 Set high expectations which inspire, motivate and challenge pupils

TS3 Demonstrate good subject and curriculum knowledge

See the Appendix for links to the ITT Core Content Framework.

Introduction

This chapter will explain what is meant by education for sustainable development (ESD), starting with UNESCO's (2019) definition. In terms of illustration, we will consider how ESD can be delivered through the arts as a vehicle for authentic and creative learning in the early years and primary phases. We argue that the arts and ESD make perfect learning partners. Particular attention will be given to links between theory, research and practice in the areas of storytelling, visual arts and music. Readers will learn how each discipline offers unique educational opportunities, and suggested resources and case studies give further insights. The chapter will present some practical ideas for curriculum planning and learning activities, both inside and outside the classroom, as well as providing suggestions for supporting teachers' professional learning and enquiry.

What is education for sustainable development?

Considering the discourse and critique around a definition of ESD, we will draw upon the UNESCO (2019) definition:

> *ESD empowers learners to take informed decisions and responsible actions for environmental integrity, economic viability and a just society, for present and future generations, while respecting cultural diversity. It is about lifelong learning, and is an integral part of quality education.*

Importantly, there is an argument that we are now in a post-sustainability context, in that we need to 'start asking an everyday question: "What should we do next?"; there is a need to radically rethink education in terms of its culture, purpose, content and direction' (Jickling and Sterling, 2017, p5). In looking at ESD through a post-sustainability lens, we must take a holistic view of both environmental and social justice, through transdisciplinary, transgressive education with urgency, agency, imagination and hope.

There is a need to address the elephant in the room, which is that we have a triple crisis: dehumanisation, economic inequality and ecological catastrophe (*The Guardian*, 2009). The Paris Agreement demonstrates a global acknowledgement that the climate crisis is 'an urgent and potentially irreversible threat to human societies and the planet' (UN, 2015a). The climate crisis presents considerable and intensifying risks for food security, water availability, health, housing, infrastructure, agriculture and natural ecosystems (IPCC, 2014). These multiple threats disproportionately affect children right now, and future generations of children will also suffer the consequences (Sanson and Burke, 2020). Children in poverty will be at significantly higher risk (Dzvimbo et al., 2017), and worryingly these trends are already evident globally (Behrens, 2020).

Children are not ignorant of this crisis or the impact it will have on them. Since the first school strike for climate in 2018 by Greta Thunberg, hundreds of thousands of children and young people have participated in climate strikes. This movement is passionate, imaginative and meaningful, showing enormous amounts of agency and courage. However, resistance has been strong from schools and some professional teachers' associations (Barrance, 2020). With a rise in eco-anxiety, it is perhaps no wonder that 'many young people have a rather pessimistic view of climate change and the future on a global scale. Consequently, many lack a sense of empowerment and agency regarding this threat' (Ojala, 2018, p11). Not only are we not actively empowering our students to act, but we are actively disempowering children from acting by devaluing their heartfelt protests. Article 12 of the UN Convention on the Rights of the Child (UNCRC) 'establishes the right of every child to freely express her or his views, in all matters affecting her or him, and the subsequent right for those views to be given due weight, according to the child's age and maturity', and in article 15 to 'take part in peaceful protest' (UNICEF, 1990). Some schools and organisations heed this and work towards nurturing authentic pupil voice, such as through UNICEF's Rights Respecting Schools (**www.unicef.org.uk/rights-respecting-schools/**), but this practice needs to be more widespread. We must recognise that children's protests are motivated by hopes of a better world, and their passion and imagination are invaluable to creating this better world.

One of the steps that we, as educators, must take is to encourage ourselves and our children to *imagine* a world that is just – environmentally, socially and economically. Imagining new futures is critical to deal with the complex problems that we face. Despite alarming research in the decline of childhood creativity (Kim, 2011) and curiosity (Engel, 2011), we know that children and young people are gifted with a desire to learn, be curious, explore and play, which Piaget (1930) identified as vital in knowledge construction. If we consider imagination, creativity and curiosity as different but similar attributes, we can form a meaningful pedagogical narrative of what we wish to achieve. This is what should inform our curricular intentions.

To create the right conditions to support the development of children's imaginations, education should consider this as a 'cognitive and affective endeavour' (Eckhoff and Urbach, 2008). Imagination involves the head, hands and heart; it is transdisciplinary and open-ended, as well as requiring time, space and resources. Imagination is required for us to tell new stories, make new songs, create new things, have divergent ideas, and evoke empathy and compassion. Imagination is also required to shape a values-based curriculum that fosters all of the above.

Debra Kidd's (2020) excellent book *A Curriculum of Hope* uses transdisciplinary learning enquiries based on children's interests and their set curriculum to create learning experiences that use the imagination to cultivate trust and meaningful learning experiences. Deep, meaningful questions about the world drive children's interest, imagination and agency in their learning, as well as driving hope. Being encouraged to imagine an impossible future, with support from teachers and communities, will empower children to be courageous, radical and hopeful, which is exactly what the world urgently needs.

Storytelling and education for sustainable development

> *Tell me the facts and I'll learn, tell me the truth and I'll believe, but tell me a story and it will live in my heart forever.*
>
> First Nation saying

Narrative is a powerful way of understanding the world (Bruner, 2004). Children can be both receivers and creators of stories – decoders and encoders. The stories with which they engage might be oral, written, digital or multimodal. We can experience a story from a safe emotional distance or become part of a story through oral retelling, drama and role play. When paired with ESD, stories can help children to understand the world and all of its possibilities. Importantly, Style (1988) views the curriculum and stories as both a 'window' and a 'mirror':

> *It is limiting and inaccurate to only educate our children provincially when they must live their lives in a global context, facing vast differences and awesome similarities. They must learn early and often about the valid framing of both windows and mirrors for a balanced, ecological sense of their place(s) in the world.*

Story-making and story-receiving can lead to hopefulness rather than hopelessness in the face of global challenges. Stories can provide children with a sense of agency and the confidence to initiate change in an uncertain world.

Oral storytelling has a different quality to the reading aloud of a book. Tilkin and Paulus (2012) suggest that it allows us 'to dream awake, side by side, to imagine a possible world' (p27). When combined with ESD, Holland (2021) describes it as an act of 'earth care'. Storytelling is sometimes seen as the preserve of gifted 'tellers', but in reality it is something we all do. We all tell stories in conversations with our families, friends and children. Teachers who use oral storytelling find that learning is richer for it, perhaps because the telling of a story creates a genuine relationship between the teller and the listener and is a memorable form of learning (Bruner, 2004). When teaching about challenging issues such as sustainable development, we can take a moderated approach. For example, children can internalise a story in a way that is appropriate for their stage of development.

In recent years, the publication of children's books with the principles of ESD at their heart has proliferated. Books such as Nicola Davies' (2013) *The Promise* have a clear message about individual agency in the face of the climate emergency. Her work has a wealth of resources to support teachers in the classroom, and she has created a global community of readers and followers: **www.thepromise.earth**

For older children, the work of Gill Lewis provides a 'window' (Style, 1988) into other worlds. In *Sky Dancer*, she encourages us to consider the challenges of rewilding landscapes in the UK (Lewis, 2017). In *Gorilla Dawn*, we discover the impact of mining for metals in the Democratic Republic of the Congo on the local community, miners and mountain gorillas (Lewis, 2015). Lewis' books consider the challenges of sustainable and equitable development, as well as the environment and our place within it. They raise as many questions as they answer and open up valuable dialogue with pupils. Populating our classroom bookshelves with books such as these, books that offer 'windows' into other worlds, is vital in building children's sense of global citizenship.

Children are often the receivers of stories but they can also be the creators. The 17 UN Sustainable Development Goals (UN, 2015b) are underpinned by an approach that encourages 'envisioning' – what Hicks (2012) would describe as 'possible futures'. The environmental story of which we are all part has a 'present', but we do not yet know the 'ending' of our current climate and environmental emergency. Hicks (2012) suggests that there are 'probable futures', 'possible futures' and 'desirable futures'. Digital storytelling, where children film their own experiences of sustainable development, is an approach used by UNESCO (2014). *The Story of an Unknown Island*, a powerful film by children from Sagar Island, is an excellent example (**https://vimeo.com/58776012**). It allows us to see one small island through the eyes of its young inhabitants and promotes discussion about possible futures.

Only our children will know the ending of our current story, but they do not need to be passive recipients. When children are given the space to create and represent their own stories, we begin to see the huge opportunities for a brighter possible future. Teaching with and through narrative can empower children to be agents of change – global citizens who shape their own narratives.

The visual arts and education for sustainable development

Education in the visual arts involves three components: the productive, the critical and the cultural (Eisner, 1972). In addition to making art, we want children to develop aesthetic sensitivities and take a genuine interest in visual and material culture – not just the work of famous artists, but everyday experiences. The National Society for Education in Art and Design's 2019 manifesto recognises that 'art, craft and design education is a building block of social cohesion' and 'vital for personal development, health and wellbeing' (NSEAD, 2019). Now more than ever, children can benefit emotionally as well as educationally from engaging in high-quality visual arts education that promotes urgency, agency, imagination and hope.

ESD has strong links to an approach known as issues-based art education (IBAE), which foregrounds learning *through* the subject. Although IBAE is more commonly used with older students, it has huge potential within early years and primary contexts. Some of the opportunities of IBAE include: engaging in creative risk-taking (Halsey-Dutton, 2016); promoting critical consumption of contemporary arts and culture (Chang et al., 2012); enhancing students' understanding in terms of who they are, where they are, and their relationships to others (Smith, 2011); and the potential for deep inquiry and action (Li, 2018). By examining real-world problems through the lens of the visual arts, teaching can holistically address the productive, critical and cultural components highlighted by Eisner (1972).

To do justice to Eisner's three components of visual arts education and to maximise the potential benefits of IBAE identified above, we can usefully move beyond the notion of learning *in* and *through* the subject to include learning *about* and *with* the subject (Lindström, 2012). Figure 2.1 illustrates how the goals (either convergent or divergent) and means (either intrinsic or extrinsic) of visual arts education differ according to whether the focus is on learning *about*, *in*, *with* or *through* the subject. There is no hierarchy; all have their distinct roles and values (Lindström, 2012).

Perhaps because it is deemed to be an accessible ESD theme and easy (and cheap) to resource, 'recycling' is a popular topic explored in primary schools. However, we must avoid superficially addressing this issue and underestimating children's learning capacities – a one-off activity decorating plastic milk bottles does not stretch or challenge learners. Figure 2.2 takes Lindström's (2012) four ways of learning to create a 'Plastic Pollution' project plan with transdisciplinary aims. This starting point provides a springboard for detailed planning that is as applicable to teaching in

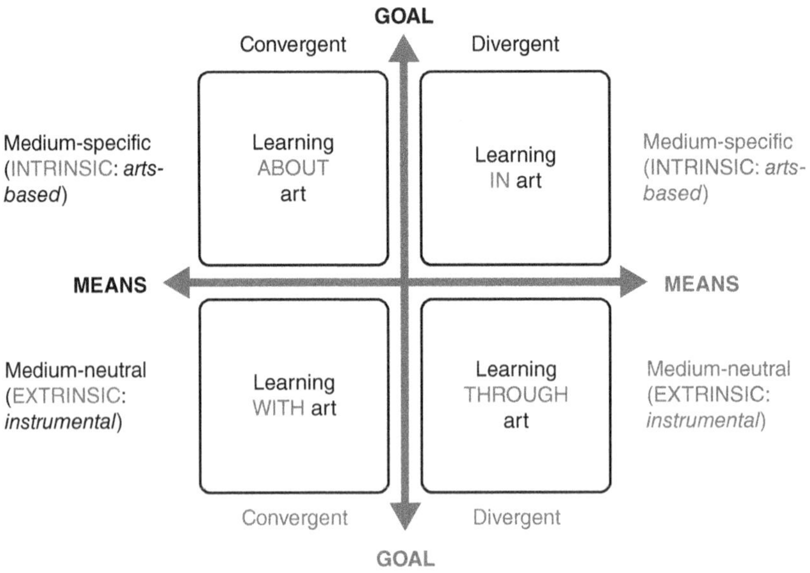

Figure 2.1 Four ways of learning in art (adapted from Lindström, 2012)

the early years as it is for working with older learners, depending on the level of teacher input and scaffolding needed to build on pupils' 'funds of knowledge' (Moll et al., 2013, p172).

We want children to see themselves as part of a wider visual arts community (Hetland et al., 2007). The artwork pictured in Figure 2.3 shows an outcome from a collaborative project between children and professional artists which was aimed at raising awareness that bottle caps are not always recycled. Created as part of a series of out-of-school learning workshops during a craft festival, it is likely that during the process of physically making the artwork children were engaged in learning conversations *about*, *with* and *through* the subject. The artwork itself provides an excellent stimulus for an in-school project drawing on the objectives of the 'Plastic Pollution' project shown above, with great scope for fostering pupil imagination and agency in addressing a real-life issue.

Learning **ABOUT** art	Learning **IN** art
➢ Be aware of artists who use plastic waste in their work	➢ Explore how to combine/join different plastic items
Learning **WITH** art	Learning **THROUGH** art
➢ Understand the science of plastic as a material (e.g. its manufacture)	➢ Reflections upon personal use of single-use plastics

Figure 2.2 Example project: 'Plastic Pollution'

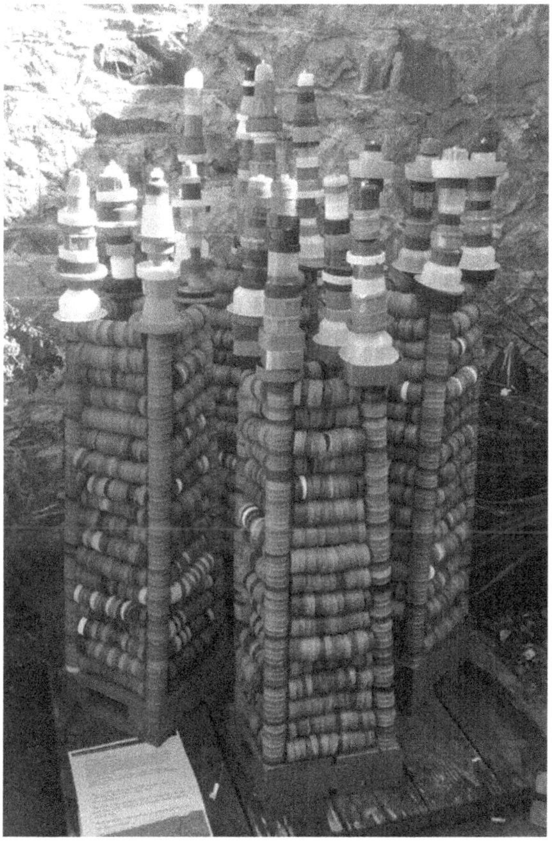

Figure 2.3 Towers of Hope, *displayed at Devon Guild of Craftsmen (photo: E. Hall)*

CASE STUDY

The Erasmus+ research project *Visual Art Education in New Times: Connecting Art with Real Life Issues (CARE)* aims to connect ESD with visual arts education in primary schools. The research focuses on the professional learning of pre-service and in-service teachers in each of the four partner countries (Cyprus, England, Greece and Malta), which will be complemented by investigations into pupils' learning in visual arts education and ESD. Contemporary art will have a central focus; it is known that drawing on contemporary art can be an effective way to 'develop reflective practice and an understanding of pedagogical issues' (Jové and Farerro, 2018, p333). Likewise, various creative strategies exist for this integration (Marshall, 2010), which opens the scope for many possibilities both inside and outside the classroom. Local training programmes will help teacher participants to develop professional learning communities, assisting them in designing relevant lessons and activities in their schools. The research findings will be shared on the project website: **http://care.frederick.ac.cy/**

Music and education for sustainable development

Music is a powerful social force that binds us together. It offers endless opportunities to enable education for a '"good life" of well-being, flourishing, virtue, and happiness for the benefit of oneself and others' (Elliott et al., 2019, p7). Music supports social justice (Jorgensen, 2015; Woodford, 2005) and prompts teachers and learners to focus on the 'big questions' and values that guide our lives. However, inequality of access to appropriate music education on the basis of race, social class and geographical and socio-economic context is a prevalent problem in the UK and beyond (Bates, 2019; Bull, 2019; Daubney et al., 2019). We cannot address all of these issues, so we have chosen to focus on the decolonisation of the curriculum.

Social and racial divides underpin many music curricula (Hess, 2014), and the call to decolonise the music curriculum has grown in urgency since the Black Lives Matter protests of 2020. What does 'decolonise' mean? This definition comes from the non-profit organisation Decolonizing the Music Room:

> *Our decolonizing work means centering BBIA (Black, Brown, Indigenous, and Asian) voices, knowledge, and experiences to challenge the historical dominance of white Western European and American music, narratives, and practices that has resulted in minimization and erasure throughout our field. There is no end point of being 'decolonized', only constant learning, reflecting and growing.*
>
> (Decolonizing the Music Room, n.d.)

This definition invites us, as educators, to keep learning, reflecting and growing – attitudes that underscore the values of ESD.

What does decolonisation look like in practice? Music teachers use a familiar repertoire: songs learned during training, online and published resources, and songs from their own personal childhood learning. We need, though, to reflect on our 'music classroom canon' (Kelly-McHale, 2018, p61) and consider our repertoire choices. We need to question our world views, shaped by a lifetime of musical engagement and received wisdom. This can be an uncomfortable process. When Nate Holder shared his poem 'If I Were a Racist ...' to a social media group for music teachers, it was removed as it was believed to be provoking unnecessary anxiety. Holder's poem is challenging and thought-provoking. Here is one verse:

> *If I were a racist,*
>
> *I'd call all non-white music*
>
> *'World Music'*
>
> *After all, it's them and us.*
>
> (Holder, 2020)

Holder asks difficult questions: Why do we teach 'African drumming'? Africa is a continent, not a country. Why do we teach 'African songs' if we do not know their exact origins or meanings? The poem demands that we interrogate our practice, question what we take for granted, consider the 'whiteness' of the spaces in which much music education happens, and confront that anxiety which might cause us to shy away from reading it.

A growing list of 'songs with a questionable past' is being compiled by Lauren McDougle (2020). Reading this list can be disquieting; but as McDougle urges us, we do not need to feel guilty about previous repertoire decisions, but to educate ourselves on our future choices. This might mean excluding certain repertoires, or informing ourselves and our pupils in far greater depth about the context, history and meaning of a piece of music.

CASE STUDY

The Voices Foundation, which promotes singing in primary schools, recently reconsidered their practices in the light of the Black Lives Matter protests (Voices Foundation, 2020). With the support of experts, they reviewed their song bank to interrogate the contents for racist or anti-Semitic associations. The result was that one song ('Jump Jim Joe') was excluded from the online song bank. For a more detailed consideration of this song, see Kelly-McHale (2018).

CASE STUDY

Teachers must also create a community-based, locally appropriate and flexible curriculum (Alexander, 2010). Feversham Primary Academy, located in a part of Bradford that is 98 per cent Pakistani Muslim, received widespread media coverage following a marked improvement in SAT results, partly attributed to up to six hours of music per week with their teacher, Jimmy Rotheram (Halliday, 2017). Rotheram describes his first school concert as a 'disaster' that failed to engage or connect with the community; so, for the next performance, he invited Islamic nasheed singers to participate.

Feversham's music curriculum is informed by the Kodály method, which focuses on children's musical vernacular (cultural and linguistic context). Rotheram integrates traditional Arabic Na'ats and contemporary nasheeds into the Kodály-inspired curriculum. Polish and Hungarian songs also feature in the classroom repertoire, ensuring that the whole of the school community is represented.

DEEP DIVE

Intent

How will you show your intention to engage children with ESD in engaging and imaginative ways? Consider creating a policy document to begin the process.

Implementation

What action will you take, such as planning in continuing professional development (CPD) sessions or inviting speakers, to encourage a wide uptake of teaching ESD through a broad and balanced curriculum? Think about implementing a whole-school arts project based on ESD themes, which can be celebrated with exhibitions, music and drama events.

Impact

How will you measure the impact? What concepts are children, teachers and families taking on board, and what changes do you expect/see happening?

CHAPTER SUMMARY

Our intentions for this chapter were threefold: to define and exemplify ESD and its relevance to children's learning in and through the arts; to share practical ideas for curriculum planning and learning activities, both inside and outside the classroom; and to provide suggestions for supporting teachers' professional learning and enquiry. We trust that we have given readers some insights into the exciting potential offered by the arts to enhance children's knowledge, skills, attitudes and values in the area of sustainable development. Encouragingly, Ofsted's new focus on a broad and balanced curriculum presents a golden opportunity to foreground the role and value of children's learning in and through the arts. During an Ofsted 'deep dive' into one or more arts subjects in your school, it is vital to emphasise how learning *in* the subject is complemented by learning *through* the subject - the arts and ESD make perfect learning partners. In making meaningful links to ESD through the arts, we shall empower children and help them to become more creative and compassionate human beings - both now and in the future.

Further reading

Cambridge Primary Review Trust (CPRT) (2016) *Sustainability*. Available at: https://cprtrust.org.uk/about_cprt/cprt-priorities-in-action/sustainability/

UNESCO (2019) *What Is Education for Sustainable Development?* Available at: https://en.unesco.org/themes/education-sustainable-development/what-is-esd

3

AN EYE ON THE PAST: CURIOUS EXPLORATIONS INTO 'THE OTHER'

KARIN DOULL

KEYWORDS: AUTHENTIC; HISTORY; INTERWOVEN; PLACE; STORIES; TIME; VOICE

CHAPTER OBJECTIVES

This chapter will help you to:

- consider how the arts allow us to understand more completely the authentic voice of people from other times and places, especially those who left no written records;
- recognise the interwoven relationship between the arts and the humanities both as sources for and expressions of learning;
- provide examples of projects that generate stimulating learning for both the arts and the humanities.

LINKS TO THE TEACHERS' STANDARDS

This chapter maps to the following Teachers' Standards:

TS3 Demonstrate good subject and curriculum knowledge

TS4 Plan and teach well structured lessons

TS6 Make accurate and effective use of assessment

See the Appendix for links to the ITT Core Content Framework.

> *Curiosity about what appears 'other' remains intense and can be mobilised by many factors, including time, place, culture or religion.*
>
> (Jordanova, 2006, p191)

Introduction

The humanities subjects explore the human experience through time and place. All aspects of civilisations and societies in different environments and across the past are investigated to help us understand our own connectivity and identity. In this, the point of study must be more than factual gobbets of information about past events or distant places. To engage in a meaningful way with these subjects, we should, as educators, present the richest view we can of that human experience (H. Cooper, 2018; Kidd, 2020). To do this, we need to reflect on the emotive responses that are encapsulated within the realm of the arts.

This chapter will consider how the arts reflect aspects of human experience from different periods and in relation to particular environments, suggesting how our understanding of time and place can be communicated through creative outcomes. It will consider how aspects of substantive and pedagogical knowledge can be developed through investigating the visual arts, music and dance of a particular group. It will also explore how this understanding may be communicated through responses that go beyond factual descriptive writing. It will show a coherence between the arts and humanities that allows us to interweave experiences in such a way as to add colour, sound and movement to place and time.

Considerations in relation to humanities learning

> *History is eclectic, hence the range of its debts to and the complexity of its relations with other disciplines.*
>
> (Jordanova, 2006, p80)

Cooper (1992) describes history as an 'umbrella subject', while Owens (2018) talks about the 'chameleon' nature of geography, suggesting here that these subjects explore the entirety of human dimension in place and time in concert with other aspects. We can investigate the geographical features that contribute to the development of a civilisation just as we can use historical context to add depth to a geographical enquiry. In a similar approach, we can consider what specific forms of art or music tell us about the past or a specific location or consider how individual artists are representative of their time or place. These linkages and connections enhance the depth and breadth of our investigations to better represent the world as children see it – holistic and interrelated.

Interdisciplinary or cross-curricular teaching has long been a staple of the primary curriculum (Barnes and Scoffham, 2017; Eaude, 2017), not least because children's experiences are not compartmentalised. It engenders increased enjoyment and involvement (Kelly, 2009; Percival, 2020). It can also promote efficiency of coverage (H. Cooper, 2018; Harnett, 2000). It is, however, important to recognise the confusion that this type of teaching can engender within children's learning. Children consider that they are studying a 'topic' without recognising particular subject disciplines (Ofsted, 2011a). Time allocation for explicit subjects may be unclear within the framework of the study (Ofsted, 2011a), leading to gaps in knowledge and poor subject-specific understanding (Ofsted 2011a, 2011b). It is clear, therefore, that the integrity of individual subjects needs to be safeguarded when planning interdisciplinary teaching. This is achieved through understanding the essence and boundaries of each subject, enabling them to be combined with confidence and without distortion (Turner-Bisset, 2005).

REFLECTION

Think back to your own experiences of studying or planning for a topic. How easy was it to identify the following?

- How did the different elements feed into each other?
- What progress was being made in understanding concepts or using processes?
- What was significant about the knowledge acquired?
- How were the different subjects used to enhance each other's understanding?

You might have reflected on the level of depth of knowledge and understanding that planning a topic can facilitate. Sometimes it is easy for us, as adults, to clearly see the links across subject areas, and this helps us to be excited to plan a topic. Can we, however, be equally as sure that children are aware of these links? Are we explicit enough about the learning in discrete subject areas so that depth of understanding is forefronted?

Reading the clues

How do the arts allow us to understand people from different times and places? Our first consideration here is to return to the idea of the essence of a subject. What makes an activity history- or geography-specific?

Historical understanding is created from a complex interplay of substantive subject knowledge (facts), conceptual understanding and the effective application of processes. We need to be aware of how this contributes to what Dawson (2004) describes as a sense of period. Key to this is a recognition of how historical learning is developed, including concepts of chronology, significance, interpretation, causality and characteristic features.

The evidence that we select and the sources that we use to investigate history may well be in forms related to the arts. To support historical learning, we need to consider what we want children to understand when we use the arts as a vehicle in this way. The questions that we select will shape how children approach the resource.

Learning through song

On 16 August 1819, a crowd of 60,000 gathered to hear the radical politician Henry Hunt speak on electoral reform. They were attacked by the Manchester and Salford Yeomanry; 18 were killed and 600 were injured. Using a contemporary ballad about the Peterloo Massacre will allow us to consider:

- how relevant a source this is in relation to bias (*historical interpretation*);
- what factual information it provides and how accurate it is (*substantive subject knowledge*);
- why the ballad was created (*causality*);
- how effective the ballad might have been at the time (*significance*).

The use of a contemporary ballad allows us to access popular feelings about the event through the use of vernacular language in a dramatic form. Ideally, we also want children to hear what the song would have sounded like, so learning and singing the song will bring an extra dimension to the experience. The questions relate to developing history while the singing of the ballad employs musical skills. Without the questions, the activity may promote musicality without identifying historical significance. More information can be found here: **www.historyworkshop.org.uk/s2-e3-the-ballads-of-peterloo/**

Geo-graphicacy

Geography also requires an amalgam of different elements. While enquiry is central to any geographical learning, it is based securely on substantive knowledge and accessed through certain skills, such as graphicacy and map use (Barlow and Whitehouse, 2019). Enquiry provides the focus for the development of conceptual understanding:

- shape and space;
- scale and connection;
- proximity and difference;
- relational thinking.

Once again, it is the focus of our questions and the intention to promote historical thinking that shape geographical enquiry, rather than the source that we select. The following example demonstrates how a piece of contemporary art can expand children's understanding of a specific place, as well as helping us to consider what difference might have been evident by using a photograph, rather than a painting of the same place.

Look at *Market* by Juan Sisay here: https://i.pinimg.com/originals/30/ab/00/30ab003e2e4ea62ef6c3cacee4188116.jpg

More information about Sisay can be found here: **www.artemaya.org/bio-sisay.html**

Santiago Atitlán is a town in Guatemala on Lake Atitlán between two volcanoes. It is a centre of indigenous Mayan culture. Juan Sisay lived there all of his life until he was murdered, at the age of 99, during civil unrest.

The following are some questions that will generate geographical discussion:

- What activity is happening here, and how do you know this? (*space and place*)
- What is this place like (e.g. geographical features, climate)? (*substantive subject knowledge*)
- What is being sold in the market? Does this relate to markets that you know? (*proximity and distance*)
- How do you think the artist feels about this place? (*relational thinking*)

One of the important facets of this source is that it is made by someone for whom this is 'their own place', so the impressions are more authentic than those of a tourist or outsider. This tells us how they see their world.

More than a Roman shield or model volcano: art as a vehicle for learning

It is a fallacy to assume that historical and geographical understanding is best demonstrated through extended writing. This has its place, and it is certainly a feature that Ofsted will look for, but it is not always the most appropriate or powerful demonstration of understanding.

Returning to Peterloo, students read testimony from the event, listened to ballads, and looked at maps and contemporary images, including George Cruikshank's well-known cartoon *Massacre at St Peter's* (**https://ageofrevolution.org/200-object/george-cruikshanks-massacre-st-peters/**). After exploring the images, students were asked to work in pairs. One person re-enacted one of the roles by creating a tableau in dance, while the other sketched their position. A collage of the event was created using a limited but dramatic palette. This was then allied with a 'found poetry' haiku created from witness accounts (see Figure 3.1).

Liberty and death

Dealt out blood and destruction

Hear the dreadful cries

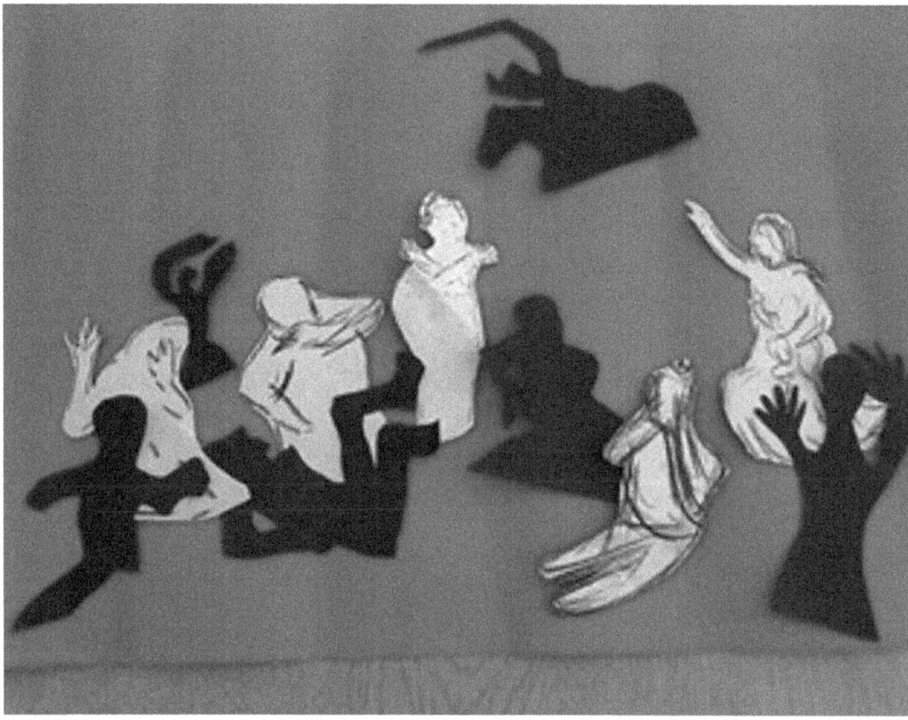

Figure 3.1 Children's artwork in respsonse to Massacre at St Peter's

The investigation used historical skills to evaluate sources of evidence and gather information to understand why the event happened (*causality*) and how it was represented (*interpretation*). The outcome, however, was in the form of dance, art and poetry. Not only was the activity memorable, but it demonstrated valid understanding (Dixon and Hayes, 2014).

Similarly, a local geography study created maps and trails, took photographs, and carried out interviews with residents, including the local vicar. He then featured in a song that was written about the area to the tune of The Beatles' 'Penny Lane':

> *In Dagnall Street there is a vicar praying very hard ...*
>
> *200 couples he has married there with their golden rings and everything*

Here, music was used to create something relevant to the area that could be shared as a group (*relational thinking*) because this resonated so closely with their sense of identity within this specific place (Kelly, 2009). Both of these activities engaged the affective and cognitive domains – the heart as well as the head (Goodhart, 2020).

REFLECTION

Think about how you might explain to a visitor why you have selected a piece of artwork or a song as a relevant source to engender learning.

Think about how you might explain to a parent what evidence of learning the *Massacre at St Peter's* painting demonstrates and why it is appropriate to use this.

Why is it valid to enhance the curriculum in this way?

History and geography connect children to themselves as inhabitants of a place or as part of a chain of remembrance. This identity is a powerful motivator that can be enhanced through allowing children's voices to be heard. The arts create personal and collective responses to stimuli, recognising the different perceptions that children bring to activities (Ogier, 2019). A local area project can allow children to take and selectively present photographs of their own place. Here, we might find that the view which children have of where they live is not the same as our own perceptions (Barlow and Whitehouse, 2019; Kent and MacIntosh, 2015). Likewise, we could create soundscapes of place, telling the story through the human and natural sounds that make a particular environment (Lee et al., 2015). Perhaps we could consider 'inheritance tracks': What music have children inherited from their families? Can we create a compilation linking to particular places and sounds? How has music been transformed as it travels either through time or place? One of the aspects that we can develop through activities such as these is to link the local to the global, to focus here on *proximity* and *difference*.

Dance is also a powerful tool to develop children's agency, allowing them to use embodied learning to demonstrate understanding. In studying the Great Fire of London, the evocative language of Samuel Pepys and John Evelyn could be used as a basis for telling the story through creative movement. Evelyn vividly evokes the destruction – 'the stones of St Paules flew like granados, the Lead mealting down the streetes in a streame' (Gyford, 2009a) – while Pepys talks of running, clambering and flinging as 'the poor pigeons ... were loth to leave ... but hovered ... til they were, some of them burned, their wings and fell down' (Gyford, 2009b). Using eyewitness accounts adds veracity and immediacy. Dance allows children to explore the event emotionally and from different perspectives (*historical interpretation*).

Creativity, through problem solving and recognising correspondence within disparate foci, is a feature of the humanities (H. Cooper, 2018; Cooper et al., 2006; Turner-Bisset, 2005). When visiting a museum or site, children might be asked to collect a series of images that display a theme without directly disclosing the theme itself. They might be asked to sketch significant artefacts that could be used to create a museum logo or a product for the gift shop. The focus is on the selection that the children make, as well as their ability to justify their choices.

REFLECTION

Can you guess the theme in this series of images from Butser Ancient Farm?

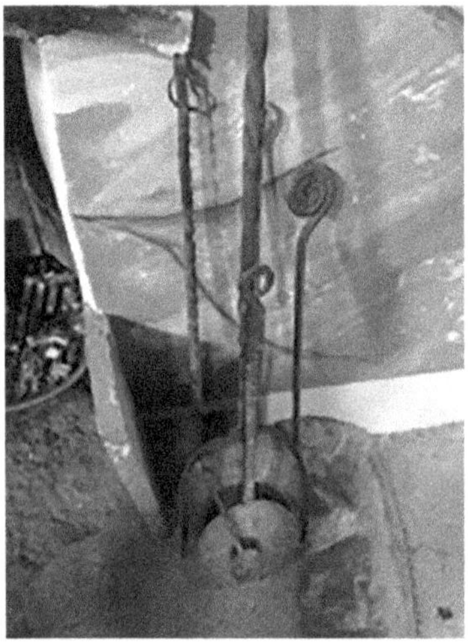

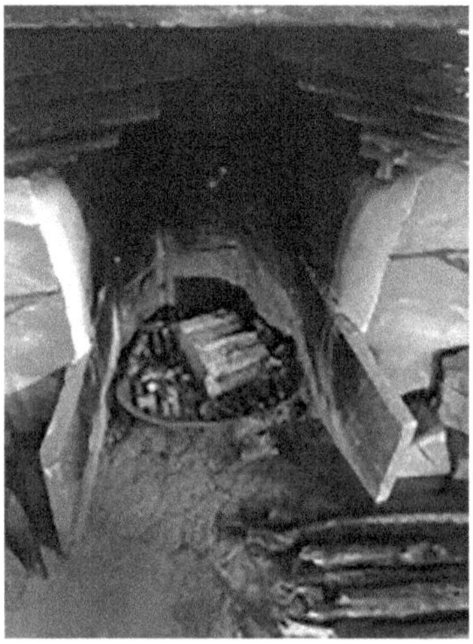

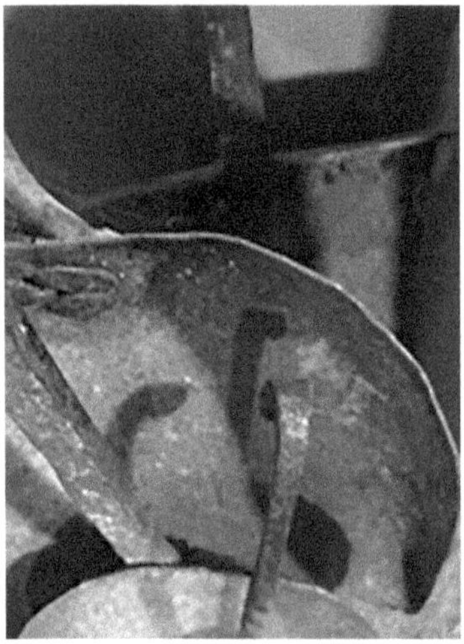

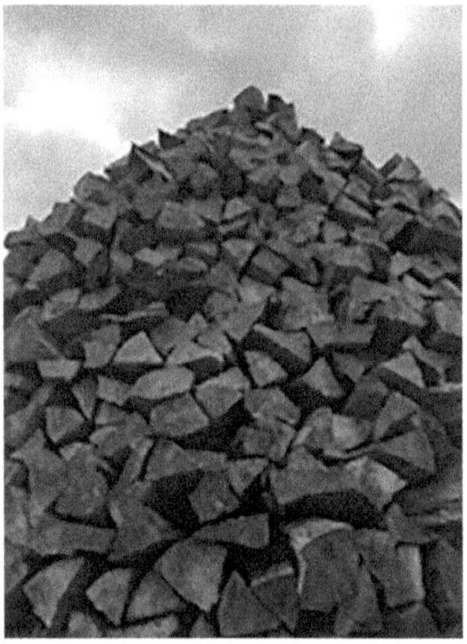

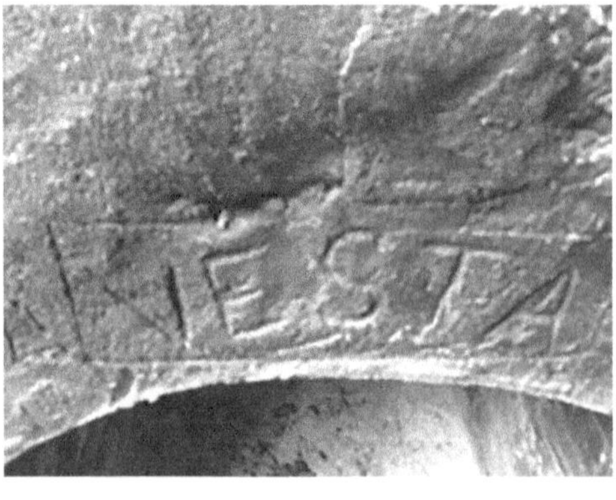

Central to both history and geography is enquiry; ideally, this also involves fieldwork and experiential learning (Barlow and Whitehouse, 2019; Doull et al., 2019). Through a first-hand investigation of place, children create impressions that shape their understanding. These can be recreated visually through pictorial or photographic trails or journey sticks. (A journey stick is where objects collected along a route are linked together on a stick or a piece of string. An urban journey stick will probably have rubbish, paper, small stones, perhaps a lost glove, and so on. A journey stick for the countryside might include feathers, flowers and plants, perhaps some sheep's wool, and so on.)

Museums allow children to engage with a range of images, audio and artefacts that they would not otherwise have access to, for example in the above Reflection activity. They help children to understand the reality of the past in a way that is not possible through the internet or books. Seeing the *real* object, one that you have previously looked at online or in a book, can generate enormous excitement and engagement. It can also help us to understand colour and size. Museum visits for history and geography can introduce children to a wide range of artistic styles and influences, creating visual references to slot into their long-term memory.

Subject knowledge and schemas

The term 'knowledge-rich curriculum' is very current at the moment. It stems from the work of E.D. Hirsch, who significantly influenced the thinking of Michael Gove and Nick Gibb as government ministers with responsibility for education. Gove (2009) saw knowledge as being at the centre of the curriculum. This thinking is reflected in the current Ofsted framework, which focuses on 'knowing more and remembering more' as the definition of learning (Ofsted, 2019c). In relation to history and geography, this has led to a focus on factual information often related to a perceived canon of knowledge. While it behoves teachers to be 'knowledge-rich' themselves in order to make valid selections of information, in itself this is a limited notion. To understand the significance of an event, place or individual, we must be able to create connections both with prior knowledge and knowledge from other disciplines. In doing so, we are able to create relevant schemas and develop children's understanding of place and past. Gove and Gibb both identified a need for 'core knowledge', a body of knowledge that all children should acquire. Selection also leads to omission, however, with the question of who should make the selection. In this, it is similar to issues raised by the term 'cultural capital'. Whose culture are we promoting? In suggesting that there is a body of knowledge about history and geography, or in relation to art or musical works that should form a 'core knowledge' for children, we create an imbalance. These ideas are rightly being challenged through the movement to decolonise the curriculum, to reflect a more diverse and inclusive syllabus.

Our task, as teachers, is to widen our own knowledge and seek out examples of diversity across the different subject disciplines. We need to show children more diverse examples of people and places.

REFLECTION

One of the first representations of black characters in Britain is that of John Blanke, the black trumpeter to Henry VIII who asked for (and received) a pay rise for the quality of his music (you can find his image at **www.nationalarchives.gov.uk/pathways/blackhistory/early_times/blanke.htm**). When looking at this portrait of trumpeters, think about how the artist has shown us the difference between Blanke and the other musicians.

What representations of black individuals can you find? What examples of historical black artists or musicians do you know?

Early years focus: extending learning and considering progression

History and geography are also represented in the early years framework under the focus of 'understanding the world'. How can we help young children to learn about their world and their past?

- We should always start with the experiences of children using terms that they can understand.
- Physical and concrete examples create a stronger reality and understanding. They allow children to explore objects using their senses and create discussion possibilities.
- Sometimes, because we know what an object is, we forget how different it might appear to children.
- Make good use of picture books to introduce ideas. These help to visualise either the past or a different place.
- For young children, we should ideally link to the near past. In the same way, any geographical investigations should start with children's knowledge of their own place. For example, when exploring the local high street, nursery children might look at old photographs and then compare them with what they saw. They could then draw either a modern or old version with their own commentary.

CASE STUDY: CRITICAL AND CREATIVE THINKING IN THE EARLY YEARS

The following are some discussion examples from when children were examining an old stone hot water bottle:

> *It's very heavy.*
>
> *It's got a lid, so it must keep something in ... maybe it's for perfume?*
>
> *I think it's for carrying something.*
>
> *No, I know, it's like what those ladies that wear clothes like Syreeta's mum wears carry on their heads. I saw it on telly.* (Indian women carrying water)

Here, we see children using what they have previously seen to make sense of what they are looking at.

Supporting all children

Visual sources are also powerful tools to use with children with English as an additional language (EAL), who may need help with specific or technical vocabulary. Pictorial vocabulary sheets also provide support.

Embodied learning is a potent strategy used to support children with special educational needs and disabilities (SEND). Telling a story through dance or role play can give voice to those who struggle with literacy. Physically investigating artefacts can allow children to make full use of their senses.

Bringing in colour and sound

Let us use the example of early Islamic civilisation to explore how we might plan an interdisciplinary theme.

Around 900 CE, Baghdad was the centre of an extensive trading network. Caravans of traders and pilgrims criss-crossed the caliphate. Caravanserais were set up to provide shelter for the night. Images such as those in the illustrated Maqamet manuscripts provide miniature scenes of daily life that can be used as a starting point for this activity.

You could also include some clips of musical instruments, such as the oud (a lute-like instrument), the zither, the flute, and small drums for percussion.

Consider using some of the following suggestions to engage all children through the use of colour and sound:

- Imagine that you have been travelling all day and have now settled for the night.
- How would you feel? What sounds would you hear? What smells would you encounter? What would you see looking up at the night sky? What is it that you would want to do most, or first of all?
- Create a multimedia group collage with drawings in the style of the aforementioned miniatures. Then add written quotes to show how the travellers are feeling.
- Create a piece of role play.
- Write a shared poem and then audio-record it, adding sound effects such as fire burning and camels grumbling.
- **www.youtube.com/watch?v=iz7wtTO7roQ** (fire sounds)
- **www.freesoundeffects.com/free-sounds/camels-10019/** (camel sounds)
- **www.youtube.com/watch?v=QGGbZRFt1NE** (archive video of a camel caravan)

CASE STUDY: CONTROVERSIAL AND EMOTIVE HISTORY – THE STORY OF THE PARTITION OF INDIA (HISTORY, MUSIC AND ART)

In 1947, India became independent. At the same time, the country of Pakistan was created. States that were predominantly Muslim became East and West Pakistan, while those that were predominantly Hindu formed India. The Punjab and Bengal provinces were split down the middle. As independence dawned on 14 and 15 August, between 10 and 14 million people were on the move. Up to 2 million were killed during the ensuing violence.

Student teachers worked with children in Years 5 and 6 to explore this event. The title of the workshop was 'Journey to Hope', with a focus on loss of the old and the hope for a new life. The journey by foot or by train was the focus for creating a storyline.

The context for this project was historical in nature, while the vehicle for understanding the learning was through art, role play and music. This was also evident in the project outcomes.

Music

- Voice and body percussion were used to create the sounds of a train.
- Spoken thoughts were chanted, either individually or in chorus (e.g. 'Where am I going?' 'I feel lost.' 'I want to go home!'). Varying timbre, speed and volume were encouraged.
- Children were taught about and investigated raga scales.

Role play

- Children created freeze-frames and dramatic scenarios from observing photographs.

Art

- Children explored their feelings, both positive and negative, and wrote associated words in decorative, colourful texts (see Figure 3.2). These words were used for vocal percussion.

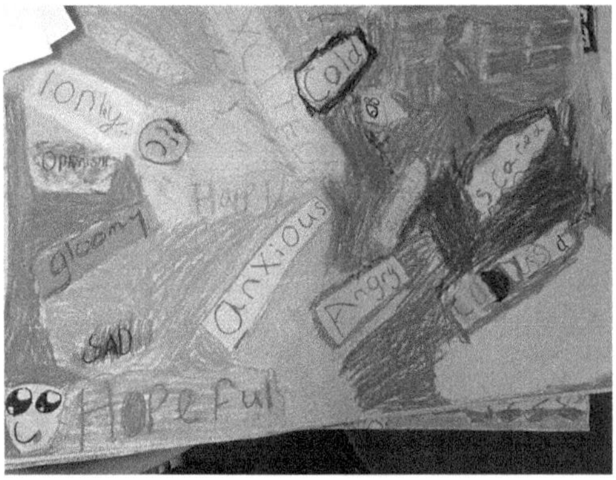

Figure 3.2 Visual representation of emotions

- Children used fragrant spices as painting materials to create a sense of confusion and violence. This was particularly fun, and the classroom smelled fabulous (see Figure 3.3).

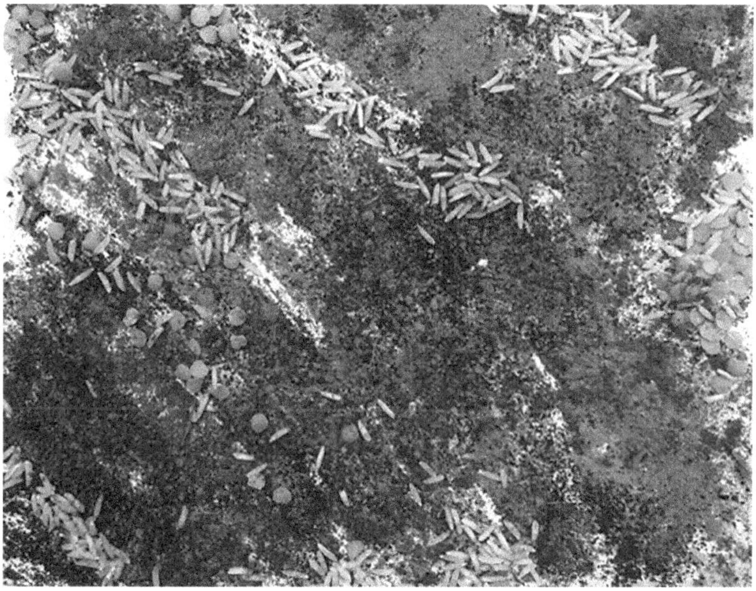

Figure 3.3 Painting with spices

- The final outcome of the *Journey to Hope* artwork (see Figure 3.4) shows that the first panel has light, joyful colours and many positive words to symbolise life before the rupture. The middle panel shows the journey itself - dark and frightening. The final panel is representative of a mixed viewpoint, with some hope for the future but also sorrow for what was lost. The children used the narrative gleaned from eyewitness accounts and images to represent an affective journey during the partition (*historical interpretation*).

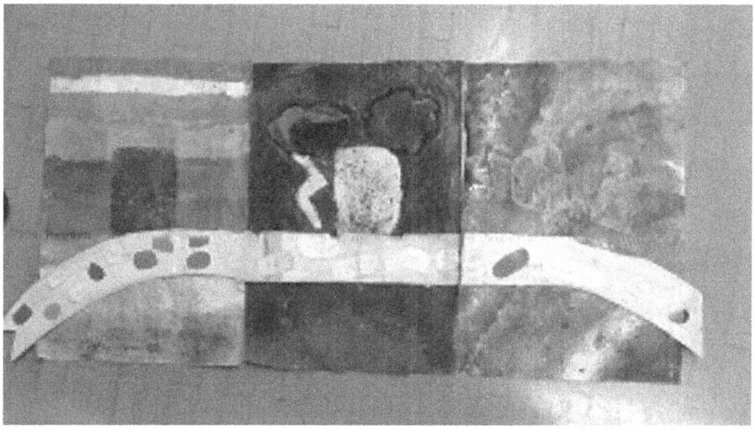

Figure 3.4 Journey to Hope

CASE STUDY: OCEAN EXPLORERS (GEOGRAPHY AND MUSIC)

Seeking to capture the relationship of island people with the water around them, as well as how this is reflected in their music, this project looked at the Pacific Islands and how they are defining themselves in the contemporary world. The focus was to help the children understand something about people whose lives and cultures are different to their own.

Geography

Maps were used to locate the place, both in terms of the wider world and in relation to the children's location (*scale and connection*). It was also important to investigate the children's understanding of the word 'island' both in relation to Rapa Nui (Easter Island) and Great Britain (*relational thinking*). Comparing images of high streets and residential areas both here and there provided more opportunities to recognise similarities and differences. Areas for further development were the role of tourism and attempts to revive agriculture after deforestation.

Music

Different examples were offered using some traditional instruments and including elements of traditional dance:

- tourist films of traditional dance;
- the work of contemporary local band Matato'a (**www.youtube.com/watch?v=mVAvhOxgx-M** - be aware of nudity);
- another example of a contemporary band, Rapanui Hinariru (**www.youtube.com/watch?v=Cpzs8QomEhs&list=RDQ3nafVG_urE&index=4**).

The children listened for traditional instruments such as sonorous stones and conch shells, as well as the use of voice. They explored timbre, rhythm and dynamics, and became aware of the differences between the authentic music of the local bands and the dance display put on for tourists. They also had a chance to experiment with sonorous stones, using them as part of their own spoken compositions.

The children were able to look at the lyrics of one song, 'Here Ma'Ohi' (https://lyricstranslate.com/en/here-maohi-beloved-brethren.html). In doing so, they were able to begin to understand not only how the music was created, but what it was trying to say. Considering this affective domain again enhanced their understanding of place and the issues of the people who lived there.

DEEP DIVE

Intent

When developing interdisciplinary projects, how have you ensured that you have created meaningful learning for each subject? What substantive subject knowledge have you identified, and how are you ensuring that key concepts linked to each subject are developed?

Implementation

How does your project help children to understand the lives of people at other times and in other places? Does your humanities project allow children to act as historians or geographers, asking and answering valid enquiry questions? Will you make use of fieldwork or museum visits?

Impact

Have you allowed children to demonstrate their understanding through a range of ways using the arts as well as extended writing? How will you share children's progress with parents and carers through the use of presentations, displays and home-school project tasks? How will you raise the status of humanities subjects within your school to lasting effect?

CHAPTER SUMMARY

> *History and Geography have much in common. Both are ancient but also contemporary. Both address seemingly limitless territory yet remain lodged in our imaginations: hard to grasp but indispensable.*
>
> (Bonnett, 2008, p8)

This chapter has considered how the humanities and the arts act in concert to enhance children's understanding of the human experience. Examples have been given that demonstrate how the arts provide vivid sources of evidence about past times and different places. Some of these provide a voice directly from those who might not otherwise be heard (e.g. those who have no written culture). Here, artefacts, images, dance and music speak for them. In addition, we have also seen how children can use the arts to create more varied responses themselves to communicate their understanding through both the cognitive and affective domains. Human lives, either those of the past or of other places, reflect a tapestry of experience enriched by the colours of the arts.

Further reading

Barlow, A. and Whitehouse, S. (2019) *Mastering Primary Geography*. London: Bloomsbury.

Cooper, H. (2018) *History 5–11*. London: Routledge.

Doull, K., Russell, C. and Hales, A. (2019) *Mastering Primary History*. London: Bloomsbury.

Kidd, D. (2020) *A Curriculum of Hope: As Rich in Humanity as in Knowledge*. Carmarthen: Independent Thinking Press.

4

ART AS A WAY OF LEARNING ACROSS THE CURRICULUM

ROBERT WATTS

KEYWORDS: AESTHETIC EXPERIENCE; CREATIVITY; EXPLORATION; IMAGINATION; VALUES IN ART EDUCATION

CHAPTER OBJECTIVES

This chapter will help you to:

- consider the role of teaching and learning in art as a skill for life;
- consider the values that underpin practice;
- reinforce the notion that learning should be enjoyable;
- explore a range of principles for teaching and learning in art;
- reflect on how these principles offer a model for teaching and learning across the primary curriculum.

LINKS TO THE TEACHERS' STANDARDS

This chapter maps to the following Teachers' Standards:

TS1 Set high expectations which inspire, motivate and challenge pupils

TS4 Plan and teach well structured lessons

See the Appendix for links to the ITT Core Content Framework.

Art is the means by which we communicate what it feels like to be alive.

Antony Gormley

Introduction

It is the early 2000s, and I am sitting in a large, dark room in a London gallery at a training event for primary teachers. I am one of 100 teachers looking up at a huge screen, at a painting of a woman, elaborately dressed in beautiful robes, a child at her side and an angel at her feet. The woman must have been dead for 300 years, but right now she is towering over us, staring straight at us – and we are mesmerised. Our heads are full of questions: Who was she? What made the artist capture this person, this moment, this place? How did they learn to paint fabric so perfectly, so beautifully, so lifelike that you feel you could reach out and touch it? The trainer's voice interrupts our thoughts: 'And in a maths lesson,' she declares, 'children could count the number of pearls in her hand.'

For decades, educators have explored ways to connect art with other areas of children's learning. In response to the marginalisation of art in the curriculum, they have sought to quietly sneak the subject in through side doors, covered in blankets labelled 'maths' or 'English', hoping to secure it a more central position on the school curriculum stage. The gallery educator was one of many whose heart was in the right place when she pointed hopefully at the pearls in the woman's hand. But most of the teachers, sat quietly in the dark, would have known that counting pearls in a painting would get them only so far with a class of 6-year-olds on a wet Friday afternoon. There are, however, genuine connections between art and other subjects, and at the heart of these connections is a collection of values.

This chapter explores the idea that the values which underpin art education can also inform approaches to teaching and learning across the primary curriculum. It argues that art offers a way of learning which can both heighten children's appreciation and deepen their understanding of other subjects. The chapter begins with a brief account of John Ruskin's principles for teaching art in the mid-nineteenth century. It goes on to identify five key values in art education before exploring ways in which these values can inform teaching and learning beyond the art lesson and across the primary curriculum.

THEORY FOCUS: LEARNING TO SEE WITH JOHN RUSKIN

One day last spring, I was looking at what I thought was a dead damson tree in my garden. The previous autumn, a bonfire had scorched its branches, which were now lifeless. It had never looked wonderful before this happened, but now it looked awful. I decided to cut it down. But as I went to make the first incision, I noticed a tiny green shoot in the bark. Somehow the tree had survived the scorching and was ready to carry on doing what it was meant to do: being alive.

To celebrate the resurrection of the damson tree, I decided to draw it. I found a sketchbook and set to work. I imagined my children admiring the finished piece, how they would insist we remove it from the book, frame it and display it. The drawing, unfortunately, was awful. It looked nothing like the tree. In fact, I would show it to no one. But as I went to rip the page from the book, I heard a voice: 'It doesn't matter what the drawing looks like,' it whispered, 'what matters is the experience of *drawing*, and the experience of *looking*, and the process of *learning to see*.'

The voice, I realised, belonged to John Ruskin. Ruskin is remembered as a nineteenth-century philosopher, philanthropist and social reformer, but he was also an art critic, artist and teacher who was particularly passionate about the process of drawing. In the 1850s, Ruskin embarked on a crusade to persuade people of the value of drawing, initially by publishing two books on the subject and subsequently through a series of lectures. These lectures were not, however, delivered to a gathering of privileged academics. Instead, Ruskin rose to his feet in the humble surroundings of London's Working Men's College and addressed an audience of impoverished East Enders. His message was clear:

> *The art of drawing, which is of more real importance to the human race than that of writing and should be taught to every child just as writing is, has been so neglected and abused, that there is not one man in a thousand ... who knows its first principles.*
>
> (de Botton 2002, pp220-1)

Anyone, Ruskin argued, could learn to draw. Yet Ruskin's belief in the importance of drawing arose not from a sense that everyone should explore their creative potential, but instead from a conviction that drawing could help people to take greater pleasure in their daily work: 'My efforts are directed not to making a carpenter an artist,' he explained, 'but to making him happier as a carpenter' (Atwood, 2011, p53). Had Ruskin lived a century later, his vision of equality of opportunity would doubtless have stretched beyond the confines of an all-male environment. But regardless of the gendered language, his message is clear. Ruskin teaches us that the process of observational drawing makes us look more closely at the natural world, the built and natural environment, and each other. Though we are engaged in the activity of drawing, we are not necessarily seeking to create works of art that others might want to see. Instead, we are learning to pay attention to the details, to the essence, to the beauty of what is before us. As Ruskin said: 'Now remember, gentlemen, that I have not been trying to teach you to draw, only to *see*' (Cook and Wedderburn 1903-1912: xx, my emphasis).

THEORY FOCUS: VALUES IN ART EDUCATION

Some 150 years after Ruskin taught his drawing lessons in the East End of London, I found myself on the other side of the city teaching my own class of primary school pupils. I sought to squeeze art into a crowded timetable and began to wonder what children thought of the subject. One afternoon, the class finished work early; with nothing else planned, I chalked a few questions on the board: Why do children make art? Why do adults make art? Will you make art when you grow up? Why is art important?

(Continued)

(Continued)

The range of responses that children offered persuaded me that these were questions which I should explore in more depth. Within a year, and with the help of a number of student teachers, I gathered responses to the questions from over 300 children, which led me to write my first journal article (Watts, 2005). While researching related literature, I came across Downing et al.'s (2003) study that examined teachers' perceptions of the value of art in schools. If we look at the combined responses from teachers and children, five broad themes emerge:

- the value of developing knowledge and skills;
- the value of experimentation;
- the value of decision-making and diverse responses;
- the value of aesthetic experience;
- the value of the enjoyment of making art.

We will explore each of these themes in turn. As we do, you might start to visualise how each value could underpin children's learning beyond art lessons.

REFLECTION

Think of lessons you have planned, children you have taught, and the work they have produced, as well as how the following values in art education might influence children's learning across the curriculum. How do your values affect what happens in your art classroom?

Analysis

Our personal values can affect how we come across in the classroom. For example, if we are nervous or unconfident about teaching art, that will quickly rub off on children and affect their attitudes towards learning in this subject area. It is important, therefore, that you start to develop an understanding of what the key principles and pedagogy are in art, craft and design so that children always have a positive experience.

Knowledge and skills

Many primary teachers underestimate their artistic knowledge and skills. I often hear them claim that they do not know one end of a paintbrush from another, let alone how to use it to mix colours or tones. Yet most have far more knowledge and skills than they realise, and a few hours spent going back to the basics of colour-mixing or observational drawing can help them to re-engage with art. Children love to see teachers demonstrating a process to them. Whether you are showing them how to blend colours or tones of paint on the page, print a repeat pattern, or mould a piece of clay into something resembling the Gruffalo, your class will almost always watch and listen. You might not think that you are an expert, but the children in your class will disagree. It is easy to forget how impressed children are when teachers *show* them what to do rather than *tell* them what to do.

A good demonstration can inspire even the most hesitant of children to engage with an activity. But being 'good' at demonstrating need not mean weeks of rehearsals before taking centre stage. Enthusiasm goes a long way. When you introduce a new technique to children, try to immerse yourself in the experience. Ask children to describe what you are doing, invite questions about the techniques you are demonstrating, and ask about their perceptions of the process. Explain what you are doing by 'thinking aloud', drawing children's attention to the challenges and rewards of the process. Above all, show children that you are *engaged* with the process, applying skills that you have practised and curious about what will happen next.

Experimentation

We sometimes assume that if children are making things, then they are being creative. But what do we mean by this? Open almost any book on art education and you will find a discussion of definitions. Sir Ken Robinson, for example, in his 1999 report *All Our Futures*, suggests that creativity involves 'Imaginative activity fashioned so as to produce outcomes that are both original and of value' (Robinson et al., 1999, p30). Csikszentmihalyi (1990) focuses on the importance of innovation within a particular field, while Vygotsky's (2004) notion emphasises how a creative approach, through rejecting a dependence on established methods, plays a key role in human development:

> *If human activity were limited to reproduction of the old, then the human being would be a creature oriented only to the past and would only be able to adapt to the future to the extent that it reproduced the past.*
> (Vygotsky, 2004, p9)

Creativity essentially involves experimentation, and it is essential to provide children with time to experiment. At the start of an art lesson, encourage children to play with materials without seeking specific outcomes. Remind them that ideas do not always work at the first attempt, and show them that they may need to return to ideas to rethink and refine them. When planning a sequence of lessons for older children, allow them time to experiment for the first one or two lessons. Perhaps they do not need to produce anything that they will keep; perhaps the paper or clay will be recycled. The important thing is that they are experimenting and finding out what they can do with materials. The language you use to support children is important. While older children may like to reflect on how experiments in art relate to those in other subjects, younger children will be more drawn to the notion that they are *playing*. What they see as play, we recognise as investigation, exploration and experimentation.

Decision-making and diverse responses

Alongside experimentation, another key feature of creative learning is decision-making. So often in art lessons, children miss opportunities to make decisions about their work, and their outcomes can lack individuality. For example, having followed instructions or copied examples, by the end of the lesson one child's work is indistinguishable from the next. If we offer children choices, we encourage them to make decisions – and when they make decisions, their work is more distinctive, more personal and more original. American art educator Elliot Eisner summarises this principle beautifully: 'While the teacher of spelling seeks uniformity of response, the arts teacher seeks diversity of response' (Eisner, 2002, p44). As primary teachers, we might find Eisner's words a little troubling. During an art lesson, we might reassure a child, 'There's no right or wrong', and they might well reply, 'Well, there was this morning when you told me I'd got all my spellings wrong.' The aims, methods and outcomes of a spelling lesson will always contrast with those of an art lesson – few teachers would encourage children to adopt a creative approach to their spellings.

The solution to this problem is to communicate to children how much you value diverse responses in art lessons. You can share this both implicitly and explicitly. Before an art lesson, prepare a range of resources. At the start of the lesson, offer children choices (e.g. A3 or A4 paper, thick or thin brush, working alone or in pairs). During the lesson, look for the unexpected. Seek out children whose responses surprise you rather than those whose work matches your original expectations. At the end of the lesson, choose examples that illustrate diverse responses to the task. Emphasise to children that you had not anticipated work such as theirs, and that you are pleased to see it. In a lesson I observed recently, a class of children were drawing cityscapes with silhouetted views of skyscrapers. One boy decided to adopt a bird's-eye view of the same scene, and his teacher was delighted. She seized on the drawing to share it with the class, showing the children how she valued their unique perspectives – how she was seeking, in Eisner's words, *diversity of response*.

Aesthetic experience

The marginalisation of art in the curriculum is sometimes justified by the argument that few children grow up to be artists. This argument is increasingly easy to dismantle – partly because increasing numbers of children grow up to pursue careers related to craft and design, and partly because visual images have assumed an increasingly important place in their world. We need not teach art only because we want children to grow up to be artists. We can teach art in order to raise children's levels of engagement with the visual world – in other words, to develop their aesthetic experience.

The notion of aesthetic experience may sound remote from the concerns of primary teachers, a theme more suited to philosophical debate than a Year 3 classroom. The meaning of the word 'aesthetic' is perhaps most easily understood if we think for a moment about its opposite: 'anaesthetic'. We know what anaesthetics do: they make us less sensitive. Aesthetics, it could be argued, do the opposite: they make us more sensitive. An aesthetic experience, we might tell children, is about the way something looks and how it makes you feel, and it is interesting to reflect on why it makes you feel that way and what you want to say about it. An aesthetic experience, we could say, is like the first line in a conversation – one that you might rehearse in your head when you first see something and then are compelled to tell someone about it.

REFLECTION

Think about a time when you saw something that you considered beautiful. Can you remember how that sight affected your senses and feelings? That is what we mean by having an aesthetic experience.

Much of my own research has centred on understanding children's aesthetic experiences (see Watts, 2018). What do children notice about the world? What do they find attractive, engaging or beautiful? How do they articulate their responses to beauty? What I have found is that most children have something to say on the subject – and some have plenty to say. Questioning children about their aesthetic experiences – what they love to look at, and why – is a wonderful way to develop our knowledge and understanding of their way of thinking about the world.

Enjoyment

Ask young children why they make art – they will tell you, 'Because it's fun.' If you prompt them, they might offer many other responses (see Watts, 2005), but the main reason that children make art – and like, even love, art – is because they enjoy it. It may be that children's enjoyment of creative work is instinctive. Denis Dutton (2010) argues that humans have a deeply rooted impulse for making art, one that has changed relatively little in the 10,000 years since our ancestors painted animals on their cave walls. Children do not make art because adults tell them to. They make art because it is something that comes naturally to them, such as playing or laughing. They make art because it is fun.

Children make art long before they are even aware such a thing exists. Babies and toddlers are driven to find out how they can impact on their environment, and their early attempts at mark-making are an extension of their playful investigations. Yes, they are experimenting; yes, they are investigating. But if they could articulate their motivation for scribbling crayons across the page, they would say, 'Because it's fun.' This impulse does not disappear when they start school. Younger children look forward to art lessons, aware that the rules are relaxed, that this is something which they can enjoy. If children were allowed to redesign their teachers' lesson plans, we would find a section stating, 'Children will have fun in this lesson when ...'

Art as a way of learning across the curriculum

In this final section of the chapter, we will draw out the key messages from the previous section and reflect on their relevance to children's experiences across the curriculum. The examples below illustrate how art offers a way of approaching teaching, learning and thinking about other subjects. You will doubtless be able to build upon these examples by adding your own.

Knowledge and skills

Art educators often celebrate the freedom of expression we find in young children's paintings and drawings. In art, we say, there is no right or wrong. Some children, however, are uncomfortable with this message. They like it when something is either right or wrong – and they want to get it right. In art and design, these children may be drawn towards making precise images, shapes and patterns, and the perfect way of developing this line of enquiry is through exploring geometry.

Children begin to learn about geometry as soon as they recognise and reproduce regular shapes, however haphazardly. As they grow older, children become more capable of creating complex shapes and patterns that draw on both their mathematical knowledge and artistic skills. It is important for teachers to develop and demonstrate these skills. Begin by learning to construct a 'flower of life', a simple design consisting of seven overlapping circles (see Figure 4.1). This is an ideal opportunity to model how we can become immersed in an activity, patiently assembling shapes into a composition. For further inspiration, explore the resources recently produced by the Harmony Project (see the further reading section at the end of this chapter).

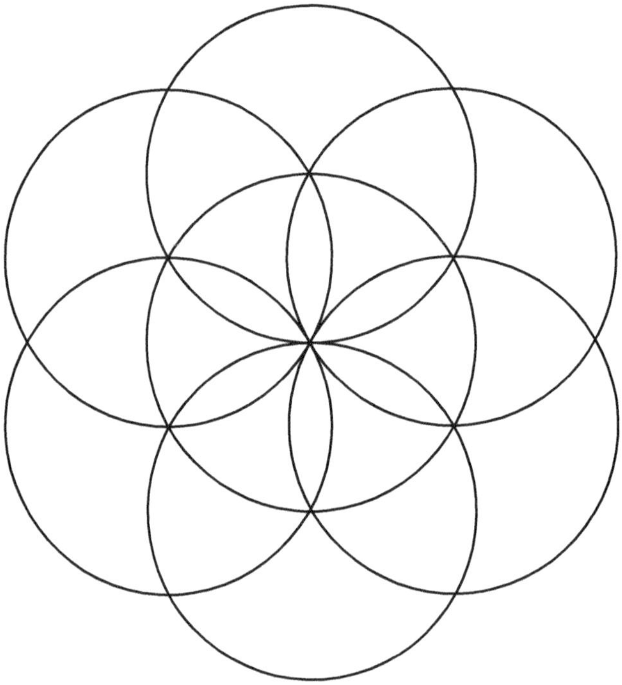

Figure 4.1 Flower of life

Experimentation

Demonstrating an art process to children is an opportunity for you to share the rich language of art. Art educator Lesley Butterworth illustrates the value of this language with her list of 100 words that describe techniques which artists, craftspeople and designers carry out. The list, which ranges from 'spin, weave, stitch' to 'sketch, throw, smear' (Butterworth, 2020), is valuable not only for the diversity of techniques that it represents, but also because it highlights the wonderful richness of art-specific language. Emphasise these words to children and they will be tempted to try them out for themselves. Encourage them to draw on this language when they describe their own work in progress and respond to others' work at the end of a lesson.

Diverse responses

Earlier, we reflected on how teachers should value unexpected responses from children. One sign of a successful art lesson is that it concludes with a celebration of diverse images or objects, none of which look quite like any other. This principle is easily applied to other curriculum areas. Try to provide children with opportunities to develop and demonstrate their individuality – look for children who offer innovative responses to questions, responses you may not have anticipated. Try to create a learning environment that encourages reflective thinking, for example by drawing on the principles and practices of philosophy for children (P4C). Teachers who use P4C in their practice aim to create *communities of enquiry* that challenge children to articulate their ideas and ensure that individual voices are heard. The process of questioning children, suggests P4C expert Robert Fisher, is at the heart of this process: 'Questioning is the primary form of education, drawing out true knowledge from within rather than imposing knowledge from outside' (Fisher, 1998, p140).

Aesthetic experience

One of the magical qualities of art is that it can inspire us to look afresh at aspects of the world which we thought we knew. While subjects such as science and geography might develop children's knowledge and understanding of the world, art can guide them towards appreciating its aesthetic qualities. Art offers a way of re-engaging children with nature. These days, few of us are able to take the time to pause, look, notice, or be absorbed by what we see. It need not be a view of rolling hills or a spectacular sunset; it might be a flower, a feather, or weeds pulled from cracks in concrete. If children feel frustrated that their drawing is not 'right', that it does not do justice to the beauty of their subject, then remind them that they are not learning how to draw; they are learning to *see*.

Enjoyment

Finally, while we might value art for the opportunities that it offers children to develop knowledge and skills, to experiment, to respond in diverse ways, and to encourage them to engage with the natural world, they are more likely to value it because it is fun. Teachers can be forgiven for forgetting that art was once enjoyable. It may be many years since they last enjoyed experimenting with materials in the carefree way they did as children. When we watch young children making art, absorbed in the process, exploring, experimenting, making mistakes and making a mess, we are reminded that this is how they learn best. At a time of increasing concerns about children learning remotely, alone and through screens, art offers a reminder of the physicality of learning. Children learn best by doing, by making, by experiencing, by playing.

Conclusion

Much has been written about the value of art in education. Art offers opportunities for children to be creative, to explore, to experiment, to be imaginative, and to learn a range of practical skills along the way. But it also has the potential to inspire and enrich children's learning across the curriculum in meaningful ways. And while primary teachers are often encouraged to 'bring art in' to other subjects by providing children with opportunities to draw maps, illustrate stories or colour-in pictures, these activities do little to reinforce its real value in the curriculum. One of the most important values of art is that it offers a unique model for a way of learning that has the potential to not only enrich children's experiences of the broader curriculum, but also raise their levels of engagement with education.

DEEP DIVE

Intent

How will you communicate the values and principles that underpin good practice in art education to staff, and hence to pupils in your school? Check your school's policy for the subject area of art and design, and make sure it reflects sound principles.

Implementation

What will you put in place to ensure that staff training is rigorous and consistent in the messages which are transmitted through continuing professional development (CPD) sessions for art and design education, and how will this transmute to subsequent action in the classroom?

Impact

How will you capture the results of this work? What is evident in displays around the school, portfolios or sketchbooks? Are children able to articulate their learning in the subject area of art and design? What do the wider school community, parents and carers understand and feel about the status of this subject in your school or class?

CHAPTER SUMMARY

In this chapter, we have reflected upon values and principles that underpin best practice in art, craft and design learning. We have considered the importance of allowing time for children to experiment with materials, to play, to enjoy learning in ways that are completely natural to them. We have reminded ourselves that learning in art and design is primarily a tool to help them see and understand the world in new ways, as well as a vehicle to engage them in their learning in practical and meaningful ways.

Further reading

Eisner, E.W. (2002) What the arts teach and how it shows. In *The Arts and the Creation of Mind*. New Haven, CT: Yale University Press, pp70–92.

The Harmony Project (2021) *HRH Prince of Wales – The Harmony Project*. Available at: www.theharmonyproject.org.uk/tag/hrh-prince-of-wales/

5

STORYTELLING: THE SOCIAL ART OF LANGUAGE

ALASTAIR DANIEL

KEYWORDS: MEANING-MAKING; NARRATIVE COMPETENCE; STORYTELLING

CHAPTER OBJECTIVES

This chapter will help you to:

- understand the nature of storytelling as an art form;
- recognise the developmental nature of narrative competence;
- see storytelling within a social context;
- understand how to provide a classroom environment that fosters children as narrators of their own lives;
- begin to consider the application of storytelling to support learning across the curriculum.

LINKS TO THE TEACHERS' STANDARDS

This chapter maps to the following Teachers' Standards:

TS1 Set high expectations which inspire, motivate and challenge pupils

TS3 Demonstrate good subject and curriculum knowledge

TS4 Plan and teach well structured lessons

See the Appendix for links to the ITT Core Content Framework.

The process of learning how to tell a story is a process of empowerment. We all want to narrate our lives, but very few of us have been given the techniques and insights that can help to form plots to reach our goals.

(Zipes, 1995, p4)

Introduction

In this chapter, we shall explore the role that storytelling can play in fostering a creative classroom culture for spoken language. The familiar 'performance mode' of classroom storytelling will be presented alongside a more process-oriented model, and they will both be considered in relation to creativity. We will identify some key competencies that children need in order to create and shape their own narratives. We will also consider how we can support children in their development of these competencies, as well as exploring opportunities for storytelling across the early years foundation stage (EYFS) and the national curriculum.

Becoming 'our own narrators'

The word 'storytelling' is a rather slippery term because of its use in multiple contexts to refer to a range of practices. Just as novelists, choreographers and artists are all praised as storytellers, in the school context 'storytelling' often refers to story-reading, story-writing and story-acting. By contrast, we will be very specific in this chapter; the word 'storytelling' will be used to refer to the oral recounting of a narrative (or part of a narrative) that is reliant on the linguistic resources of the speaker (and is performed in the absence of a written text).

Defining storytelling as a process of oral recounting, with the speaker relying on their own linguistic resources, could make it seem like a more challenging practice than it actually is. After all, storytelling is how we communicate with each other, sharing the narratives that we have shaped from our memories as well as common experiences. This is true whether we are recounting a recent disaster with the staffroom photocopier or recalling shared moments from a residential visit. In fact, I suggest that telling stories is so embedded in our communication that we often do not realise this is what we are doing, and we respond to stories without recognising these are what we are hearing.

For the purposes of this chapter, then, storytelling includes activities such as children telling each other traditional tales, recounting historical events, relating what has happened during the day while walking home, or narrating an adventure enacted with small-world figures. Apart from the oral nature of the telling, the principal characteristic here is that the teller steps outside of events to narrate them as a sequence. In doing so, they make connections between characters, their motivations and their actions; as a side note, this is true whether or not the 'story' that is being told has an identifiable beginning, middle and end, or is rather a 'fragmentary' story.

Storytelling, then, will happen inside the classroom (and outside of it) as a natural part of children's talk, even if it has not been planned as such. In current policy documentation, the expectations of the national curriculum (DfE, 2013b) are less explicit than those in the EYFS, where storytelling is embedded (as we shall see below), but this does not alter the fact that storytelling is an essential life skill which we cannot ignore. Story is both the means by which we make sense of the world around us and through which we represent ourselves to the world. To explain their experiences, needs and fears, children tell stories; to understand the experiences, needs and fears of others, they listen to stories. Developing the skills of oral storytelling, then, is to develop one of the fundamental skills of oracy, so that, as Zipes (1995) suggests, 'learning how to tell a story is a process of empowerment' (p4).

Storytelling as an art form

Having established above the ever-present nature of storytelling, we perhaps need to question the notion that storytelling can be considered an art. However, as children tell stories, they make choices between a range of narrative elements, shaping both the language they use and the expression of that language – choices which draw on elements of their expressive repertoires and their funds of life experiences. As such, storytelling aligns both with Brian Boyd's (2009) definition of art as 'cognitive play with pattern' (p15) and Anna Craft's (2002) recognition of choice as a core element of creativity (p44). The teacher's role, then, is to foster children's expressive repertoires and enable them to make imaginative and storied connections with their experiences of the world. Of course, the modelling of storytelling is an essential part of such a fostering, which means that adults in the classroom also need to develop their own narrative and storytelling competencies in a range of contexts. Without doing this, it is hard to see how they will be able to model expressive and coherent storytelling themselves, recognise children's stories as they arise (including fragmentary stories), and explicitly support children's developing storytelling competencies.

As highlighted above, storytelling is embedded both within the EYFS (as part of communication and language in both the 2017 document (DfE, 2017) and the proposed reforms of 2020 (DfE, 2020b)) and the national curriculum (DfE, 2013b), where it sits within the subject area of English. But as we have already seen, children encounter story – and tell stories – throughout the day, so we need to avoid confining explicit references to storytelling to, say, the use of traditional tales in the primary English curriculum or communication and language in the early years. Rather, narrative approaches (and storytelling in particular) can be exploited in every area of learning (Daniel, 2012), helping children to make connections between character, intention, action and result: from mathematical problems in narrative form, to tales of scientific discovery; from recounting historical events, to telling the stories of those people who did not make it into the history books; from telling stories that are inspired by works of art, to creating pictures that contain a story to be told.

Meaning-making and story-shaping

We have already established that children need to share their stories with those around them. However, while in the context of the classroom we may think of a story as being a complete unit with a beginning, middle and end, the narratives that children and adults share during the day are often fragmentary rather than complete. In narrative research, such fragmentary or 'small' stories are recognised as vital to people's communication (Georgakopoulou, 2015; Ochs and Capps, 2001). To make pedagogic use of the full range of classroom storytelling practices, therefore, we need tools that can be applied to both complete narratives and these small stories. Drawing on the work of Alexandra Georgakopoulou (2015) and Elinor Ochs and Lisa Capps (2001), I have chosen four aspects of storytelling that will help us to consider how we can best support children as developing tellers. These are: tellership (*who* is telling?); ways of telling (*how* are they telling?); sites (*where* and *when* is the telling taking place?); and tellability (*what* is the point of the story?). To these I will also add a fifth aspect: cohesion (*why* do things happen in the story?) (see Figure 5.1).

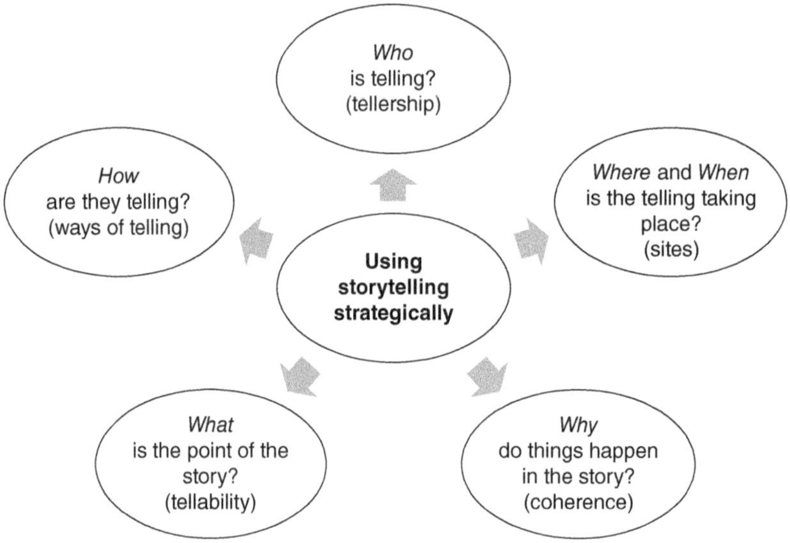

Figure 5.1 Aspects of classroom storytelling

Tellership (who is telling?)

In everyday encounters, tellership is the 'involvement of conversational partners in the actual recounting of a narrative' (Ochs and Capps, 2001, p24). A single individual may control a story during a conversation, but group members may also take turns to fill in details and comment on the tale's believability (and truth). In such cases, we can think of tellership as being distributed rather than individual. However, such distributed tellership is not limited to verbal contributions to the telling, but can also be seen in the back and forth between the teller's narrative and the non-verbal responses of their audience, which becomes part of the performance.

Distributed tellership, I suggest, is vital in understanding how storytelling happens in the classroom, enabling it to be seen as a co-construction or dialogue between the teller(s) and those listening, rather than simply as a monologue. It also recognises that the role of the storyteller can be shared with pairs or groups, depending on the intended learning of the activity, shaping narrative together and giving it expression.

Ways of telling (how are they telling?)

Although Georgakopoulou's (2015) definition of 'ways of telling' emphasises the linguistic content of storytelling (vocabulary and grammatical structures, as well as the way that the plot is organised and makes reference to the world), I will extend this meaning to include the ways in which that language is expressed. When the teller narrates a series of events, they take an evaluative stance towards those events, not only through what they say, but also the way in which they say it.

Teachers, then, need to attend to what is being said through both the words that are chosen in a telling and how those words are expressed – something which applies whether the teller is a child or an adult. Practically, this means that children need the direct teaching of oral language use – direct teaching of both words and expression. At the same time, they need to see the purposeful and explicit modelling of effective communication skills by the adults in the classroom. These elements are both *linguistic* (e.g. vocabulary, rhetorical devices, figurative language, other narrative conventions) and *non-verbal* (e.g. gestural movements, spatial awareness, physical tension).

Sites (where and when is the telling taking place?)

Children tell and listen to stories throughout the day and in different situations, each of which will place demands on the child as a storyteller. These contexts are referred to by Georgakopoulou (2015) as 'sites'.

Teachers therefore need to be strategic in creating supportive contexts and activities in which children can explore the notion of story, as well as making creative and meaningful choices as they develop their 'ways of telling'. Stories can be told around a classroom table, on the floor of the hall, sitting in a 'pirate ship' climbing frame, or walking through the woods. Each place and time will help to shape the choice of story, the ways of telling and the tellership.

Tellability (what is the point of the story?)

We tell a story because we think that it is worth hearing, and the tellability (or reportability) of a story is what makes us want to share it. Commonly, this tellability is related to the inclusion of unexpected events (Labov, 2013; Ochs and Capps, 2001), or the story's particular relevance to a specific group of people (Georgakopoulou, 2015).

The feedback that children receive in relation to tellability is formative in helping them to both recognise this quality in their own stories and shape their narratives to exploit it. Specific feedback (from adults and peers) can be framed to explicitly identify tellable elements: 'I liked the way that ...' 'I was surprised by ...' 'It was unexpected when ...'

Coherence (why do things happen in the story?)

A range of research (Applebee, 1978; Engel, 1995; Sutton-Smith, 1981) suggests that narrative competence is marked by a developing ability to manipulate the content of a story and create coherent connections across it so that it makes sense to the listener. In order to support developing storytellers, then, teachers need sufficient understanding of how stories work so that they, in turn, can identify specific aspects of coherence or incoherence in children's narratives.

Kendall Haven's (2007) definition of story as 'a detailed, character-based narration of a character's struggles to overcome obstacles and reach an important goal' (p79) can help us to establish a baseline for this understanding in which we constantly return to a character's intention, as well as the problems that are preventing them from achieving it. This is the case even in fragmentary stories (see the first case study below), and supporting children to shape their narratives so that they make sense to the listener is a fundamental part of the process of learning 'strategies of narration' (Zipes, 1995, p4).

REFLECTION

As you go through the day, make a mental note of how many times you engage in storytelling, particularly those points when the story is fragmentary:

- Where did you tell them? (*sites*)
- To whom did you tell? Did they assist you with the telling? (*tellership*)
- Why did you share particular stories with specific people? (*tellability*)
- How did you bring the stories to life? (*ways of telling*)
- To what extent were the stories linear and the ideas organised? (*coherence*)

You may be surprised by how often you engage in storytelling.

In the classroom, ask yourself the same questions about the stories that children tell, but in addition consider whether they are spontaneous narratives or whether they have arisen out of planned and learning-oriented activities.

CASE STUDY: EARLY YEARS

During a storytelling workshop, multigenerational groups retold a traditional version of *Little Red Riding Hood* using Kawamura's (2015) wordless picture book as a visual prompt. The groups then retold the story, but this time adapting it so that the girl saves herself (reflecting an earlier tradition than is most widely known).

After a while, a 4-year-old child left his group, so I sat on the floor with him and we shared the wordless text together. The conversation went something like this:

Me: I wonder how Little Red Riding Hood could escape from the wolf?

Child: [pointing to the scissors the hunter uses to open the wolf] She used the scissors to get out.

Me: Oh, I wonder where she found them ...

Child: They were in the wolf's stomach.

Me: How did they get there?

Child: He swallowed them earlier.

Me: But it must have been very dark in the wolf's stomach; I wonder how Little Red Riding Hood found the scissors?

Child: [pointing to the picture of Little Red Riding Hood's basket] Her mummy gave her a torch in case it was dark in the woods.

This simple exchange highlights how my understanding of the way narrative works enabled me to scaffold this child's *fragmentary telling* of the story to create a whole sequence of events that fitted together. Each turn of the conversation focused on key elements of narrative to build the story. Throughout the exchange, he is being supported with making cause-and-effect (problem/solution) connections, and every suggestion he makes is 'goal-oriented'.

Strategies

The most significant strategy used to develop a storytelling classroom is, naturally, the telling of stories. But here are some simple strategies that can be used as opportunities to discuss how the choices that we make as we tell can enhance story language and expression.

Warming up to storytelling

The Lion Hunt (early years/Key Stage 1)

For younger children, tell a version of The Lion Hunt with the children – a version of the game that predates the popular *We're Going on a Bear Hunt* by Michael Rosen and Helen Oxenbury (1989) – where the children help to choose obstacles (and accompanying noises and actions) as they make their way to the lion's cave. This provides plenty of opportunities to model expression in voice and gesture, as well as rhythm and repetition.

Say It How We Mean It (Key Stage 2)

- Create a set of cards with phrases that might appear in folk and fairy tales, such as 'once upon a time', 'she looked into the mirror', 'he turned the key slowly', and so on.
- Standing around the cards, a group of five or six children take one card each.
- Taking it in turns, they read their own card aloud with expression.
- After the last card has been read, the cards are passed to the left. The last child in the group to read returns their own card to the bottom of the pack and takes a new card from the top. This child will be the one to start the next round.
- The cards are read again, but each card has to be read in a different way to the previous reader, changing the expression and its meaning.

This game provides opportunities to discuss the relationship between expression and meaning, as well as the importance of non-verbal communication, including physical posture and tension.

Teacher-directed storytelling

Teacher-directed storytelling is sometimes referred to as 'story whoosh' (Winston and Tandy, 2009, 2012). This is where the children sit around a space (e.g. in a horseshoe shape) and the teacher tells the story (either memorised or using a text as a prompt). At key points in the narrative, the teacher invites the children to step into the empty central space and bring parts of the tale to life. The children are then directed by the teacher, who either gives them lines to deliver or encourages them to explore aspects of the narrative through drama activities such as still image (sometimes called tableau). Because children do not use scripts but repeat the words that the storyteller gives them, they can be introduced to complex language (such as that of classic texts), with the dramatic activity providing contextual meaning and supporting understanding.

Group storytelling

Group storytelling is process-oriented, with the telling directed inwards to the group rather than outwards to an audience.

Resources for group storytelling might include some or all of the following:

- An object per group that can be used as a 'talking stick' (indicating whose turn it is to speak). These should not be so large that they make gestures difficult (something such as a whiteboard pen works well).
- Visual resources to help structure the story. These could be items such as storyboards, story-maps or story-dice, or other images or objects.

The children sit in groups of five or six and create a story. Whoever holds the 'talking stick' can add the next part. The talking stick should be passed from person to person *across* rather than around the group.

Once the children are used to the procedure, the rule is introduced that turns have to be passed mid-sentence rather than at the end of a sentence. This introduces unpredictability and helps to maintain the energy of the telling.

Some children may lack the confidence initially to speak for more than a few words, but there is no set length of time for which children have to speak. It is also important to note that the aim is for the story to be told; so, if someone gets stuck while telling, the others can help out.

The teacher's role is to emphasise the coherence of the story created through the connections made, as well as the meaning given to language through expression.

CASE STUDY: UPPER KEY STAGE 2

In 2019, two colleagues and I worked with children in a South London school developing their own audio version of *A Midsummer Night's Dream*. Although the project was primarily drama-based, with children given multiple opportunities to engage in 'as if' behaviour, two storytelling strategies mentioned above were central to the overall approach: teacher-directed storytelling and group storytelling. In this case study, I will outline the latter.

For the writing task of *A Midsummer Night's Dream*, groups of children were allocated one of eight scenes from the play. It was clearly important that the children were able to make sense of the scene with which they were working, and that they were not expected to understand the characters in their scene or the events surrounding them without context. While we could have taken a more didactic approach, in which the children read a synopsis and answered questions to test their understanding, we preferred to exploit the way that storytelling makes the teller recognise and create connections between characters, events, problems and solutions. The children worked with a set of A6 images that traced the plot of *A Midsummer Night's Dream*, with each image representing a scene which one group was responsible for. These images not only provided prompts for the children to remember the plot of the play, but also placed each group's scene in relation to the others. Although the start of the activity began slowly, soon the talking stick was being passed quickly across the groups and children were being expressive in their voices and actions - not only recalling the story, but also conveying their personal evaluations of the characters and events.

DEEP DIVE

Intent

How are you being strategic in creating times and spaces in which children can story curriculum content?

Implementation

Tour the school and identify spaces that might encourage different kinds of storytelling (e.g. soft seating in the reading area/library where children may recast story books, an outdoor natural environment where children could connect the landscape to stories of either its inhabitants or those who use it). Map places across the curriculum where narrative is employed in teaching and learning, and consider how oral storytelling could be used to introduce or consolidate content, as well as creating connections within it.

Impact

Consider to what extent children and teachers are incorporating oral narratives (including fragmentary narratives) into teaching and learning activities.

CHAPTER SUMMARY

The title of this chapter, 'Storytelling: the social art of language', is a phrase that I have taken from the work of the influential early childhood practitioner and researcher Vivian Gussin Paley (1990), and my argument has been that we should move beyond seeing storytelling simply as a monologic performative process, but rather as a co-construction. Within this social practice, then, children are encouraged to make choices about the stories that they tell, how they tell them, and with whom. Finally, we can recognise that storytelling, as a strategy, can be used to shape understanding, not just reflect it, and that we can support and celebrate a breadth of oral storytelling (including fragmentary narratives) inside and outside the classroom, through attention to:

- tellership (*who* is telling?);
- ways of telling (*how* are they telling?);
- sites (*where* and *when* is the telling taking place?);
- tellability (*what* is the point of the story?);
- coherence (*why* do things happen in the story?).

(Daniel, 2012; Georgakopoulou, 2015; Ochs and Capps, 2001)

Further reading

Cremin, T., Flewitt, R., Mardell, B. and Swann, J. (eds) (2017) *Storytelling in Early Childhood: Enriching Language, Literacy and Classroom Culture*. London: Routledge, pp58–78.

Daniel, A. (2017) Teachers and children: a classroom community of storytellers. In P. Hodson and D. Jones (eds), *Unlocking Speaking and Listening*, 3rd edition. London: Routledge.

Gussin Paley, V. (1990) *The Boy Who Would Be a Helicopter: The Uses of Storytelling in the Classroom*. Cambridge, MA: Harvard University Press.

6

MUSIC EVERYWHERE AND EVERY DAY

REBECCA BERKLEY

KEYWORDS: ANALYTICAL LISTENING; INTERDISCIPLINARY LEARNING; MUSICAL PLAY AND MUSICAL GAMES; NON-VERBAL COMMUNICATION; PROBLEM-SOLVING IN MUSIC

CHAPTER OBJECTIVES

This chapter will help you to:

- encourage schools to include music everywhere and every day for every child, as well as suggesting ways that this may be resourced;
- encourage all teachers to be musicians with their classes, as well as feeling confident that they can set high expectations for musical activity which inspire, motivate and challenge pupils;
- explore ways that children learn through creative music-making which emphasise musical play and non-verbal communication;
- appraise how music can support learning in focused analytical and critical listening across the primary curriculum;
- give examples of current good practice of music teaching that link to learning in other subjects.

LINKS TO THE TEACHERS' STANDARDS

This chapter maps to the following Teachers' Standards:

TS1 Set high expectations which inspire, motivate and challenge pupils

TS2 Promote good progress and outcomes by pupils

TS4 Plan and teach well structured lessons

See the Appendix for links to the ITT Core Content Framework.

We all – teachers and pupils – have the potential to bring a huge amount to inspiring music education and to get a huge amount from it; we need to find the confidence to believe in ourselves and try things.
(Daubney, 2017, p159)

Introduction

This chapter encourages teachers to include music everywhere around the primary school and every day in their teaching. The benefits of music are significant in the primary curriculum. Music provides children with essential opportunities to express their thoughts and feelings through creative musical play and non-verbal forms of communication that are not offered in other subjects. Music relies on children and adults working cooperatively to apply informed strategic thinking to solve problems and achieve a common aesthetic goal. All children may learn how to become skilled and successful as musicians. Music facilitates self-expression by enabling pupils to perform with love and care for the detail of the music. Music raises self-esteem by giving children public recognition for their artistic efforts. Children remember the delight of the sparkle and razzmatazz of a public performance for a very long time, and the public appreciation of an admiring audience tells them that they are important and valued.

The value of music in the primary school

Children love music, and it is a hugely enriching subject for them. By singing and playing and making music together, children learn a common store of melody that remains with them for life. Music helps children to belong. Children arrive in school with a great deal of musical knowledge from home and the wider community, meaning that 'a music teacher never meets a musically ignorant, untutored or uneducated pupil' (Folkestad, 2006, p136).

A musical classroom is an enabling environment for children to learn how to socialise through music play and shared creative expression (DfE, 2014a). Research suggests that musical and linguistic abilities are developed holistically in young children, with the development of one benefiting the other (McPherson and Welch, 2018). Musically rich environments where children hear, sing, play and engage in music benefit linguistic development because children develop more sophisticated skills of pitch and rhythm, discrimination and recognition of melodic contours, and speech by hearing and understanding pitch variation. Children who learn instruments experience a positive impact on their intellectual development, especially in their spatial reasoning. There is a consistently positive relationship between increased educational attainment and sustained, active engagement in musical learning. The sense of attainment through sustained work to achieve something musically challenging by using self-discipline increases a child's motivation to learn, and this in turn raises their self-esteem and willingness to try new and harder work in other subjects (Hallam, 2010).

Music is a practical subject first and foremost – it is something that you do. Primary music is built from creative music-making, which children can experience through singing, playing instruments, improvising and creating their own music. A games-based approach to teaching music works well, placing practical music-making at the centre of all learning. This can aid the retrieval of theoretical concepts of music on a solid foundation of mind–body knowledge, where cognitive and theoretical concepts are built from the physical experience of sound in the human body (Thurman and Welch, 2000). As Ofsted (2012) notes, musical sound should be the 'dominant language of musical teaching and learning' (p7) so that the children can learn in music rather than by talking about music.

CASE STUDY: MUSICAL GAMES

The children in Hedgehogs Class (aged 7-8) are sitting in a circle playing the Plasticine Man game, where they improvise vocal sounds and body percussion to tell the story of an imaginary man made of plasticine who can go anywhere and do anything (**www.singup.org**). Today Plasticine Man is at the zoo. Miss Leach, the class teacher, has a series of flash cards with pictures of animals that she shows to the children, and they vocalise animal sounds along with sound effects and actions to describe the zoo (e.g. the ticket machine, the train that drives around the site) and other scene-setting sounds (e.g. the noise of the crowd, the sun shining) to illustrate the story. She conducts the children by using hand gestures to indicate the volume and duration of the sounds.

Musical games are an ideal way for children to learn by playing and exploring through worked examples. Children can practise positive social behaviours such as leading, following, waiting, turn-taking, sharing, copying and paired working, as well as collaborating in small and large groups. Musical games enable children to explore why social rules such as turn-taking, negotiating and sharing are needed for successful collaboration with their peers. The class work together as a team, following the rules to arrive at the successful answer. They take turns in answering questions, and there is a combination of closed and open questions to allow for targeted correct answers ('What sound does a monkey make?') as well as more free responses ('How long should the monkey music last for?'). Play-based learning in music actively engages children through inclusive musical games and activities on their own, with their friends, and with adults in the classroom. The games are sensorimotor activities where children experience, make and explore musical sounds in order to understand them better.

This is a form of active learning with whole body-mind engagement to establish an understanding of core musical concepts. These include pulse and rhythm, pitch and harmony, musical structure, texture, and timbre. In addition, concepts such as integrating movement and action, body percussion, singing and vocalising, sound-making, and playing with instruments are part of this learning dynamic. Actions can emphasise fluency and dexterity of gross and fine motor skills to aid other physical maturation. Musical games always start with the teacher modelling a musical activity, so the children learn unconsciously by listening, watching and concentrating. This is the foundation of core knowledge that children can then show in the way that they create music by thinking critically. Children find and develop their own musical ideas by singing and playing instruments, as well as making sounds to create musical soundscapes, narratives and compositions.

Multisensory learning

The physical activity of classroom music is multisensory learning. Integrating sound, vision, movement and visual modes of activity such as singing and chanting, moving to the beat, and playing body percussion and instruments is very beneficial for hand, eye and body coordination. Using body percussion and props such as scarves, beanbags and balls is excellent preparation for children to learn to manipulate other tools for drawing, writing and playing musical instruments. Building lessons from musical games and activities promotes the procedural learning of musical, language and number patterns, building from practical experience towards more abstract knowledge of musical concepts and ideas. Games encourage repetition and consolidation of core concepts relating to the interrelated dimensions of music and give children real-world examples of why musical concepts work as they do. For example, playing a coordination game at different speeds allows children to explore and experience how the rhythmic feel of the music is created by a combination of the speed of the pulse (the tempo), the feel of the beat, and the particular word and movement rhythms in the music.

Learning in music supports strategic, computational thinking in other subjects and aids the development of aural memory. In music, children have to listen and remember visual and verbal instructions and translate those into a series of physical moves in order to create a specific sound. They then appraise the quality of the sound they are creating. For example, in maths, Maple Class (Year 4) are preparing to work on multiplication and division word problems, using the 6 and 7 times tables. Mr Grey starts the maths lesson with a revision of times tables and counting in multiples of 6 and 7 using the 'Concentration Navigation' game. The children have a number line displayed on the whiteboard to help them. First, the children recite in a pattern of four beats in the bar, and then repeat using a count of three and then two, which reduces the recall time and challenges them to remember this key information more quickly.

CONCENTRATION NAVIGATION

This is a playground game often accompanied by ball-catching or body percussion. It adapts well to the classroom. The chant opens with:

Concentration, concentration, concentration, navigation - let's begin!

Children recite a list while keeping a pulse pattern. In this example, the list is the 6 and 7 times tables.

The opening chant goes:

♥	♥	♥	♥	♥	♥	♥	♥
Patsch	Tap	Tap	Tap	Patsch	Tap	Tap	Tap
|	|	|	|	|	|	|	|

♥	♥	♥	♥	♥	♥	♥	♥
Con-	cen-	tra-	tion,	con-	cen-	tra-	tion,
⊓	⊓	⊓	⊓	│	│	│	Z
con-cen-	tra-tion,	na-vi-	ga-tion,	Let's	be-	gin!	

The hearts show the pulse or beat of the music, the stick notation indicates the pattern of the rhythm of the syllables in the chant, and 'Z' indicates a one-beat rest. Use a body percussion pattern to mark out the pulse. A good one to start with is to patsch (tap hands on knees) on the first beat of the four-beat pattern and then tap the other beats. You can develop the body percussion pattern to include other actions to make it more challenging.

The 6 and 7 times tables can be recited as a four-beat pattern:

♥	♥	♥	♥	♥	♥	♥	♥
Patsch	Tap	Tap	Tap	Patsch	Tap	Tap	Tap
One	times	six	is	six			
Two	times	six	is	twelve			
Three	times	six	is	eight-	teen, etc.		

And then as a three-beat pattern, which also reduces the waiting time between each repetition, and so challenges children to recall the numbers faster:

♥	♥	♥	♥	♥	♥
Patsch	Tap	Tap	Patsch	Tap	Tap
One	times	six is	six		
Two	times	six is	twelve		
Three	times	six is	eight-	teen, etc.	

(Continued)

(Continued)

And a two-beat pattern with no waiting time:

♥	♥	♥	♥
Patsch	Tap	Patsch	Tap
One times	six is	six	
Two times	six is	twelve	
Three times	six is	eight-	teen, etc.

The times tables can also be recited as a list of products to a two-, three- or four-beat pattern, either counting backwards or forwards, as here:

♥	♥	♥	♥	♥	♥
Patsch	Tap	Tap	Patsch	Tap	Tap
Six,	twelve	eighteen	twenty-four	thirty	thirty-six, etc.

Thinking aloud

Children make constant use of think-aloud protocols (Vandevelde et al., 2015) to articulate their procedural thinking as they create music in groups. Working together to perform, compose and analyse music requires children to listen with mutual respect to each other's thoughts and feelings. Group conversations in music-making meet a number of the aims for promoting spoken language in the national curriculum, as children need to make 'their thinking clear to themselves as well as others' so that they can:

- articulate and justify answers, arguments and opinions;
- use spoken language to develop understanding through speculating, hypothesising, imagining and exploring ideas;
- consider and evaluate different viewpoints, attending to and building on the contributions of others.

(DfE, 2014b)

Wyvern Class (Year 5) are investigating stringed instruments from different cultures, focusing on the guitar, ukulele, pipa (Chinese lute), kora (West African harp) and violin. Miss Bordon, the class teacher, has created a resource of texts, pictures, recordings, video, and online material from suitable websites for the children to work independently in groups to investigate the origins of instruments and the musicians who play them. One group of children are listening on headphones to an extract of *The Butterfly Lovers* by He Zhanhao and Chen Gang, in the version for pipa and orchestra. Miss Bordon tells them to listen to the extract twice without discussion, and then work together with their study partners to answer the questions, which ask them to explain how the music is constructed to tell the story. Miss Bordon leads a discussion with the group where the children share their answers; she prompts them to explain why they think the composers chose to make the music sound like this, always asking the children to use musical vocabulary to justify their answers.

These children are using literacy skills to 'retrieve, record and present information from non-fiction' and 'explain and discuss their understanding of what they have read', providing 'reasoned justifications for their views' (DfE, 2014b). Using analytical talk to promote a deeper understanding of a work of art, Miss Bordon can also challenge the children to think about cultural stereotypes in music, as well as encouraging an interest in diversity of sound and a willingness to listen to music that might be new to them.

REFLECTION

How can we challenge stereotypes in music?

White, male classical musicians are massively over-represented in the lists of 'great composers that primary children should know'. To search for a more diverse representation of musical recordings, try some of these websites as a starting point for your own research into contemporary and historical music:

- *BBC Ten Pieces*: Opening up the world of classical music to 7-14-year-olds with resources and teaching materials for developing practical, creative work in music, art and dance (**www.bbc.co.uk/teach/ten-pieces**).
- *Minute of Listening*: A curated collection of 60-second clips from folk and traditional music, jazz, rock and pop music, and classical music, with resources to make links to other curriculum areas such as black musical histories (**www.minuteoflistening.org**).
- *Institute for Composer Diversity*: Databases of recordings and printed music of work by composers from under-represented groups (**www.composerdiversity.com**).
- *A Modern Reveal*: A database of resources relating to research, printed music and recordings of the work of women composers throughout history (**www.amodernreveal.com/links**).

You are the music teacher

When adults say, 'I'm not musical', normally what they mean is that they are not trained in musical skills such as playing an instrument, and so they equate that with a fundamental lack of musicality in themselves. This is wrong – all adults are musical, just as all children are musical. As an adult, there is an enormous amount of music that you already know – all you need is to take a risk and try some music with the children.

Focused, engaged listening based on aural memory is the core musical skill, and you already have a working musical ear or thinking voice. If you do not think that you have a musical ear, let us try an experiment to find it. Pick a tune that you know very well, such as 'Happy Birthday', and imagine the sound of 100 people playing and singing it in full glorious surround sound. Visualise and watch them as they play the instruments; join in – silently – as they sing the words. Being able to hear this music in your internal thinking voice is your musical ear operating. The fact that you can remember the detail of how the music sounds, as well as how it makes you feel, is your aural memory working.

When 'listening to, reviewing and evaluating music across a range of historical periods, genres, styles and traditions' (DfE, 2013a), we ask ourselves a series of reflective questions to identify, discriminate, analyse and appraise the sounds that we are hearing, whether it is music we have created ourselves or music other artists have created. The teacher asks questions to focus the children's analytical listening in order to 'check pupils' prior knowledge, access understanding and break down problems' (TS4/CCF). For music, effective targeted questioning uses key musical vocabulary, both in the questions the teacher asks and the kinds of responses the children give back, as Glover (2000) lists here:

- *Naming musical features: introducing vocabulary relating to musical elements such as rhythm pattern, steady beat, getting louder, melody shape; or musical techniques, for example two tunes keeping together; or singing or playing techniques such as scraping and tapping the drum, sliding up with your voice.*
- *Describing what happens in the music, in musical terms: for example, 'first we heard ...', 'just before the end the jumpy rhythm got louder'.*
- *Describing the form of the music: 'the music gradually built up', 'It stopped and started again twice', 'It was in two sections'.*
- *Picking out noticeable characteristics: 'the two ways of playing the tambourine were mixed in all the way through', 'marks the music went suddenly high, became lower slowly'.*
- *Analysing some aspect of the music: 'the second pattern started the same but went different', 'the first pattern kept coming back'.*

(p62)

Music is a practical subject, and you can facilitate learning best by making music with the children. Play instruments with them, sing together, and compose with them. This pedagogy is fun, collaborative, informal and active, and will make your classroom 'a positive environment where making mistakes and learning from them and the need for effort and perseverance are part of the daily routine' (TS1/CCF). By being a musical role model, you will influence their attitudes towards music very profoundly. This is how you enact your school's *intention* for its music curriculum. You will be communicating your 'shared values that improve classroom and school culture' (TS1/CCF), of an open and inclusive musical environment for the children, which is a safe space for risk-taking in the musical problem-solving you give them to do. Working as a team with the children will make them feel supported by you as a teacher, and so they will be much more likely to strive towards the goals 'that challenge and stretch' (TS1/CCF) them, and it will be a joyful experience making music with the children.

Music teaching doughnut

To plan and prepare a music lesson, use the 'doughnut' model to determine what skills, knowledge and understanding both the children and the teacher will need for the lesson to be successful.

Consider this lesson:

*Hedgehogs class (age 5–6) play Musical Feet. Miss Leach plays 60-second extracts of different types of music from Minute of Listening (**www.minuteoflistening.org**). Today, the examples are all from orchestral music. The children respond to the music by moving around the room. They show the mood of the music by the way they move their feet: stomping, tiptoeing, skipping and sliding. When the music stops, the children freeze. Mr Purvis, the teaching assistant, moves between the motionless children and chooses someone to tell the class how they were moving their feet to the music. 'I am stamping like a giant,' says Tyra.*

Figure 6.1 shows what the musical doughnut might look like for Miss Leach as she prepares to teach this lesson.

Investing in your teaching skills

To develop your practical know-how in music-making, invest in training. In addition to the training that should be offered by your local music education hub, the following organisations offer informal training, certification courses and teaching resources.

Classroom musicianship for early years, Key Stage 1 and Key Stage 2	British Kodály Academy	**https://kodaly.org.uk**
	Orff Society UK	**www.orff.org.uk**
	National Youth Choir of Scotland	**www.nycos.co.uk/learn**
	Voices Foundation	**www.voices.org.uk**
Leading classroom singing and conducting choirs	Association of British Choral Directors	**www.abcd.org.uk/training**
	Sing for Pleasure	**https://singforpleasure.org.uk**
	Sing Up	**www.singup.org**
Playing and teaching the recorder	Society of Recorder Players	**www.srp.org.uk**
	Learn Recorder	**https://learnrecorder.com**
Playing and teaching the ukelele	Ukelele in the Classroom	**https://ukuleleintheclassroom.com**
	Uke'an Be Happy	**www.ukeanbehappy.org**
Body percussion and world music and dance	The Beat Goes On	**www.beatgoeson.co.uk**
	Inspire-Works	**www.inspire-works.co.uk**
Whole-class ensemble performing	Musical Futures	**www.musicalfutures.org**

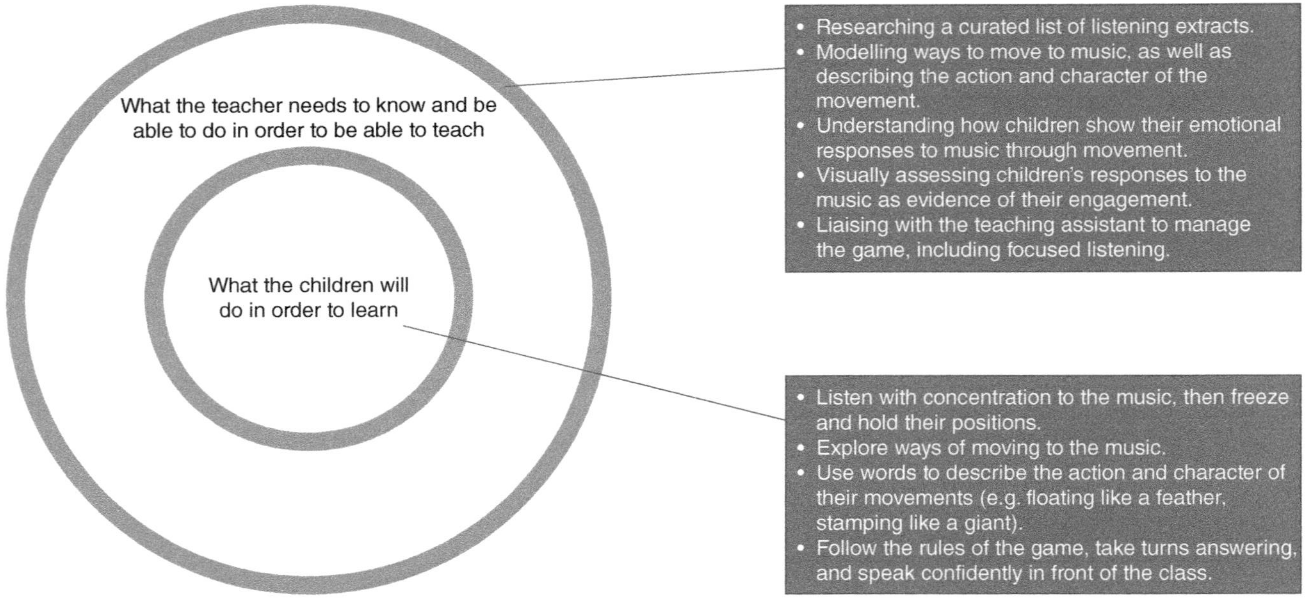

Figure 6.1 Music teaching doughnut

DEEP DIVE

Reflect on how to review the music curriculum in your school and prepare for an Ofsted inspection using the new inspection framework.

Intent

What is the school trying to achieve through its music curriculum?

Implementation

How is the school's curriculum being delivered?

Impact

How is the school engaging and inspiring pupils 'to develop a love of music and their talents as musicians' (DfE, 2013a, p7)?

Your local music education hub will be able to support you in reviewing your school curriculum, as well as offering training to support colleagues preparing for an inspection.

See also *Ofsted Music Deep Dive Resources and Information (Music Mark, n.d.).*

CHAPTER SUMMARY

Music is a tremendous cultural force in primary schools, as well as a subject that children love. Integrating creative musical learning into your teaching will enrich daily life in your classroom and give children opportunities to learn that facilitate their non-verbal communication, imagination and creative thinking. Learning in music is multisensory and supports learning in many other subjects, especially in literacy, procedural and strategic thinking, problem-solving, and spatial reasoning. Musical learning is fun and active and raises children's self-esteem. Because primary school children work best by making music together in groups, music is a great social activity, encouraging children to work as a supportive team with each other. You can include music every day in your primary school classroom - and you will never regret it.

Further reading

Early years foundation stage

Burke, N. (2018) *Musical Development Matters*. Available at: www.early-education.org.uk/musical-development-matters-download

Greenhalgh, Z. (2018) *Music and Singing in the Early Years: A Guide to Singing with Young Children*. London: Routledge.

Young, S. (2009) *Music 3–5*. London: Routledge.

Key Stage 1 and Key Stage 2

Beach, N., Evans, J. and Spruce, G. (eds) (2011) *Making Music in the Primary School: Whole Class Instrumental and Vocal Teaching*. London: Routledge.

Daubney, A. (2017) *Teaching Primary Music*. London: SAGE.

Daubney, A. (2019) *Primary Music Toolkit*. Available at: https://ismtrust.org/resources/primary-toolkit

Glover, J. (2000) *Children Composing, 4–14*. London: Routledge.

Hennessey, S. (1998) *Coordinating Music Across the Primary School*. London: Routledge.

Jones, P. and Robson, C. (2008) *Teaching Music in Primary Schools*. London: SAGE/Learning Matters.

7

SCIENCE AND THE ARTS – CLOSER THAN YOU THINK

LEIGH HOATH AND LEWIS MORGAN

KEYWORDS: ART; SCIENCE; SCIENCE CAPITAL; TEACHER CONFIDENCE

CHAPTER OBJECTIVES

This chapter will help you to:

- explore what science is and how this relates to the arts;
- consider the research and existing literature around education in science and the arts;
- consider how feelings and emotions play a role in learning in both science and the arts;
- provide a practical guide to how science and the arts can be taught meaningfully in your setting;
- link with learning in the home and community outside the classroom;
- give examples of practice and children's views on science and the arts.

LINKS TO THE TEACHERS' STANDARDS

This chapter maps to the following Teachers' Standards:

TS2 Promote good progress and outcomes by pupils

TS3 Demonstrate good subject and curriculum knowledge

TS4 Plan and teach well structured lessons

See the Appendix for links to the ITT Core Content Framework.

Science and art tend to coalesce in aesthetics, plasticity, and form. The greatest scientists are artists as well. The most beautiful thing we can experience is the mysterious. It's the source of all true art and science.

Albert Einstein

Introduction

In this chapter, we will be exploring what science is, its status in the education system, and how this is mirrored with the arts. Science capital, a theory and teaching approach explored later in the chapter, is a growing concept, and how this relates to arts learning will be discussed. We will go on to look at and consider existing literature in this area, drawing upon educational and learning theories as appropriate. We will explore how science and the arts can support each other in terms of the skills and subject knowledge to be developed. This will be supported by examples from classroom practice.

Albert Einstein, arguably one of the most famous scientists, appreciated the interconnected nature of subject disciplines; and despite being an empirical data-gathering physicist, he did not create a dichotomy between science and the arts.

Yet this is often seen in society and schools today, where children are labelled as either 'sciency' or 'arty'. We will consider some of the tensions around science itself initially, which mirror some of the issues faced by arts subjects in school, before we show how science and the arts can work to support each other in relation to learning and teaching.

The purpose and reach of science

Ofsted (2019b) reported concerns about the teaching of science nationally, suggesting that it has been deprioritised, which is not a surprise when the accountability through SAT testing at Key Stage 2 was abolished in 2009. They describe this as most worrying because it is a core subject, but they also suggest that it is a concern found in other non-core subjects – the first parallel between science and the arts. Over the years, accountability has shifted in relation to formal inspections and the 'in' subjects on which to focus. There is often an emphasis and move towards a 'topical' subject area – in addition to maths and English, of course. In May 2019, Ofsted outlined their methodology for approaching curriculum inspections (Ofsted, 2019a) and introduced the notion of a 'deep dive', which:

involves gathering evidence on the curriculum intent, implementation and impact over a sample of subjects, topics or aspects. This is done in collaboration with leaders, teachers and pupils. The intent of the deep dive is to seek to interrogate and establish a coherent evidence base on quality of education.

(p4)

Since the implementation of this framework in September 2019, there has been a flurry of activity on social media and support networks, such as Twitter, Facebook groups and online communities, about the science provision in school. While there are always going to be concerns about assessment regimes driving teaching, there is some argument that anything which brings the priority of other subjects further up the list is a good thing – again, we apply this equally to the arts and science. The debates around the need for science education are loud and clear – and have been for many years.

What appears to be in little debate is the need for science education throughout school to create a more consistent path for learners to their futures. The science, technology, engineering and mathematics (STEM) gap is often talked about in relation to careers in schools, and yet at the same time society is taking more and more for granted, as Abrahams et al. (2019) state:

> *The reality of the complex society in which we live is such that we depend on experts and professionals. Most of us are not scientists or designers of technology and yet irrespective of our academic achievements are all able to use mobile phones, send e-mails and fly around the world without needing to know, or in many cases having any desire to know, anything about the underlying science that enables such technology to function.*
>
> (p3)

Solutions are neither simple nor straightforward, but it is clear that interventions and initiatives up to this point are not having a significant effect. The conclusion from Ofsted (2019b) declares that:

> *Science has clearly been downgraded in some primary schools ... this is likely to have a serious impact on the depth and breadth of science understanding and knowledge that pupils take with them into secondary school, which may in turn stifle pupils' later curiosity and interest in the sciences.*
>
> (p5)

Science is lucky – it at least has some weight behind it as a core subject in terms of the arguments relating to education in this area. Ofsted has highlighted that it is not given sufficient attention in teaching time, bodies such as the Royal Society of Chemistry (RSC), the Institute of Physics (IOP), the Primary Science Teaching Trust (PSTT) and the Association for Science Education (ASE) all campaign for more and better science in primary schools, but there is not the same ongoing campaign in the media for the arts. In the same way that well-taught science fosters curiosity and interest, well-taught arts do the same. Science is used to offer certainty and answers to society. During the Covid-19 pandemic, politicians have used the phrase 'the science' to justify much of the decision-making behind their actions. Science is more a part of our public consciousness than it has previously been. There is a lot to be learned from this pandemic – not only about epidemiology, but also about the processes behind science and how important creative thinking is in supporting that.

Ben Shneiderman (2019) writes of how Leonardo da Vinci joined science and the arts, and that his artistic skills improved his understanding of science. His drawings of scientific phenomena were more accurate representations than they would have been without his artistic ability. There is also a bank of literature which suggests that medical professionals find that training in the visual arts improves their work (Katz and Khoshbin, 2014). For example, musically trained doctors are better at hearing nuances in heartbeats and similarly trained nurses are more accurately able to identify heart, stomach and lung sounds (Collins et al., 2014). Nobel Prize-winning scientists are three times more likely to have arts and crafts avocations than 'average' scientists, according to a study by Robert Root-Bernstein (2008) – and this is not a new observation. He states that 'In 1878, J.J. van't Hoff, who would become the first Nobel Prize winner in Chemistry (1901), proposed that scientific imagination is correlated with creative activities outside of science' (Root-Bernstein, 2008, p52).

Overall, both of these areas suffer at the hands of the focus on maths and English – and we are not downplaying their importance. But there is something about a broad and balanced curriculum that will always be a great ambition rather than the reality in classrooms. The following section will look at what children bring with them in terms of 'science capital'; again, we feel that this has parallels with children's engagement with the arts in school.

What is science capital?

Science capital is described by those who are most involved in researching it as:

> *a concept that can help us to understand why some young people participate in post-16 science and others do not. In particular, it helps shed light on why particular social groups remain underrepresented and why many young people do not see science careers as being 'for me'.*
>
> *The concept of science capital can be imagined like a 'holdall', or bag, containing all the science-related knowledge, attitudes, experiences and resources that you acquire through life. It includes what science you know, how you think about science (your attitudes and dispositions), who you know (e.g. if your parents are very interested in science) and what sort of everyday engagement you have with science.*
>
> (King's College London, 2019)

The idea of science capital builds on the notion of Bourdieu's concepts of 'capital' (see the further reading section at the end of this chapter), and our question focuses around how this can be applied to the arts. For science to be valued and seen by children as 'for them', they need to be exposed to a number of what King's College London (2019) refers to as 'science capital dimensions':

- scientific literacy;
- science-related attitudes, values and dispositions;
- knowledge about the transferability of science;
- science media consumption;
- participation in out-of-school science learning contexts;
- families, science skills, knowledge and qualifications;
- knowing people in science-related roles;
- talking about science in everyday life.

REFLECTION

- Can you apply a similar list to learning the arts?
- What would a set of 'arts capital dimensions' look like?
- Are there ways that you are already addressing this in the arts (or science) but have not been aware of them?

The researchers also outline that the approach to teaching should 're-orientate science lessons in a way that can better connect with the reality of students' lives and experiences' (Godec et al., 2017, p5). If learners and families of learners feel a disconnect from science, in the way that Abrahams et al. (2019) stated, and the teaching of the relevance to real life needs to be more explicit, as Godec et al. (2017) suggest, then we believe that the same should be true for the arts.

The British Science Association (BSA) encourage interdisciplinary approaches, stating that this provides 'a rich ground for collaborative working, questioning paradigms and engaging new audiences' (BSA, 2019). By teachers working to bring these two areas of learning together in meaningful ways, we believe that children will learn that there is not just a simple choice to be made in terms of choosing a science route or an arts route, but rather that they can be mutually supportive.

There are issues around science teachers' confidence in teaching science. They will often talk of being uncertain around the knowledge to be taught, as well as being unsure of what to do if asked questions that they do not know the answers to. Science is about uncertainty more than it is knowledge. It is OK to say to a class, 'We need to find that out.' The skills that teachers use to develop their teaching of the arts can be applied to the teaching of science. By making these subjects more learner-focused through the development of 'capital' in both disciplines, children are more likely to see the value of them both and understand that the learning of one can support the learning and skills in another. The medic who has developed communication skills through drama, the artist who has a better understanding of their materials through chemistry, and the dancer who understands muscles and forces to support their movement are better for having a more rounded approach to their knowledge.

Enabling children to see these links, as well as being able to extend them to their own lives and to the others around them, will make learning more meaningful and allow the learners to engage in a deeper way with both science and the arts.

Science and the arts: links made meaningful

When you look around, science and the arts are everywhere. The links between the two areas can be seen easily in almost all aspects of life. Zoom in on primary education, and the reciprocal nature of the subjects and their pedagogical approaches are even clearer to see.

Think back to your first years of primary school. Do you remember the lesson where you completed a worksheet, or do you remember the lesson where you created a volcano and tested which substances would react and make the biggest eruption? It is no coincidence that science and the arts feature heavily in the latter. These are the subjects where the opportunities to teach in this engaging and creative style are most bountiful. All aspects of the arts provide these memorable and valued opportunities. The day that you learned how to play a musical instrument for the first time or performed in a drama performance alongside your friend will be firmly entrenched in your memory as engaged and creative moments in your life. It is those moments of experiential learning that remind us why hands-on lessons are fundamental in our classrooms. However, many teachers approach both subjects with a waning confidence: 'I wasn't very good at art.' 'I can't play musical instruments.' 'I can't sing or dance.' 'I'm not clever enough to be a scientist.' As a result, many excellent teachers miss the point to these fantastic vehicles of learning. They do not need to be expert artists or be preparing papers to win a Nobel Prize, they just need to be able to harness and provoke feeling. The opportunities to do this across both subjects are in abundance.

To understand anything or help someone to understand, first they must feel. Art begins with a feeling or an emotion that ebbs and flows throughout a piece. We may listen to a piece of music in class and then create a piece of work that shows how it made us feel, or the children 'feel' what medium or material is best to represent their art work. Science begins and ends with a feeling. 'I wonder ...' questions are a perfect example of this: 'I wonder what tissue paper is best for mopping up a spill?' 'I wonder what the best material would be to build a boat from?' 'I wonder why a tree changes colour?' It is the feeling of wanting to know, and then subsequently knowing, that features heavily within the two subjects. Both of these feelings help to inspire, drive and motivate people – and mean that when teachers pair the subjects together, the possibilities of learning are endless. How do we, as practitioners, create these feelings inside of our students?

> *Tell me and I forget, teach me and I may remember, involve me and I learn.*
>
> Benjamin Franklin

It might be pertinent to ask, 'What is the correct pedagogical approach to take in my classroom?' The answer is vast and not straightforward; but from experience and academic research, we can piece together an approach that should have an impact in the classroom. The joy is that these successful approaches are the foundations that teaching in science and the arts are built upon. For a huge amount of the science and the arts curricula, the approaches discussed below can be implemented with ease.

Hackathorn et al. (2011) state that deeper levels of thinking and understanding can be reached when children are engaged in active learning through active teaching, and this – we feel – is the most important factor:

> *Active learning is learning which engages and challenges children's thinking using real-life and imaginary situations. It takes full advantage of the opportunities presented by spontaneous and planned, purposeful play; investigating and exploring; events and life experiences; focused learning and teaching.*
>
> (Scottish Executive, 2007, p5)

Active teaching, according to Bonwell and Eison (1991), is a process that is centred around the student and which holds the student responsible for their own learning. It has been found that excellent active teachers have used a huge variety of techniques – such as elaborate demonstrations, interactive quizzes, physical experiences, videos, dramatic performances, role play, games, and taking trips – to ensure that active learning is taking place (Hackathorn et al., 2011).

To provoke an initial 'feeling' from the students, a real, experience-rich environment must be created. The students must feel the texture of the paint and watch the colours combine to understand what is going on. Although much can be gained from just engaging demonstrations, the children need to do rather than watch. Take the example of this learning question found in almost all primary school settings: 'What minibeasts live in our school grounds?'

The teacher could provide the children with the data and images of the insects and then get them to fill in a bar model and tally chart. If we are trying to create an active learning experience, one approach could be to present the same question again, and then allow the children – through discussion, debate, opinion alleys, and so on – to decide on the best way to collect the data. Hopefully, the children will decide that they need to explore and 'get out there', so will take an active role in exploring all of the different habitats in the school grounds. Children could sketch and draw the different insects they find while tallying up how many lived in certain areas. From here, it is important that the children then take ownership in how they will convey their findings to their audience. Some may choose graphs and tables, some may choose to create a presentation, and some may choose to create mind maps; but there is no doubt that by taking control of their own learning, there will be understanding and some very happy and engaged students.

The curricula that underpin science and the arts can be aligned in a huge variety of ways, and there are many opportunities for them to support each other. Some of the strongest links can be found within the 'working scientifically' strands of the science curriculum. One of the elements of 'working scientifically' is scientific enquiry. According to the ASE, scientific enquiry is the processes and skills that we teach children to help them find out more about the world and how it works. Turner et al. (2011) define it as 'what children do in order to answer scientific questions about the world around them' (p11). What working scientifically does is promote independent thoughts and attitudes towards a range of subjects and ideas, and then allows pupils the chance to explore these. The pupils have to ask and answer questions, experiment and adapt throughout a process, showing a plethora of life skills, and then effectively communicate what they discover to other pupils and often a variety of audiences.

All of the above skills resonate deeply across the whole spectrum of the arts. The ability to present their work so that it appeals on different levels to different people is the real skill of an artist. Often they must begin with a feeling towards a subject, much like a prediction or a question, and then work – often independently – towards creating their end goal. Like many scientists, their initial thoughts may be different from others; thus, they must be confident in their own thoughts and show resilience and determination. With both subject areas, there is emphasis on practice, which allows for failure in order for skills to develop and knowledge to grow. Once a piece is finished, whether a painting, a dance, a song or theatre, it is an artist's role to present it to an audience with conviction and confidence, like a scientist presenting their findings.

This complementary style can be seen beautifully within the early years foundation stage (EYFS) environment because of how child-led and play-based it is. Set out in the Statutory Framework for the Early Years Foundation Stage (Early Education, 2012), children in this age phase have areas of learning and development. The science and arts areas are categorised as 'understanding the world' and 'expressive arts', respectively. The former involves 'guiding children to make sense of their physical world and their community through opportunities to explore, observe and find out about people, places, technology and the environment' (Early Education, 2012, p40). The latter involves 'enabling children to explore and play with a wide range of media and materials, as well as providing opportunities and encouragement for sharing their thoughts, ideas and feelings through a variety of activities' (Early Education, 2012, p46). The joy, wonder and nature of both subjects lend themselves excellently to a predominantly active learning, play-based and child-led pedagogical style of teaching. They both work hand in hand to essentially enable children to play, explore their feelings, and try to understand the world around them.

Science across the curriculum and home

This section of the chapter will outline some generic links between the science and the arts curricula before offering specific examples against national curriculum statements. I will then briefly outline three broad activities that marry together these subject areas.

Role play

Role play and dramatic performance are excellent ways to assess the understanding of anything that requires a process. Getting children to act out processes and different elements really allows them to show understanding without having to write it all down. Drama can also be used to show a huge amount of subject knowledge. The Year 5 earth and space objectives can be greatly enhanced by news shows, TV adverts and stories that develop their understanding of planets' movements around the sun.

Dance

Very much like role play, this is an excellent vehicle for showing all of the subject knowledge around different areas of scientific processes. Creating a dance performance that shows the changes of state is an excellent way of identifying the different qualities of the individual states. It is also a great way of showing the life cycles of a variety of animals – think of the chick breaking free from its shell.

Sketchbooks

A significant aspect of science is being able to observe closely and then accurately record these observations. There is no better way to teach about the finer details of the features of a flowering plant than to get children using magnifying glasses and creating detailed scientific sketches. It is an excellent way to tie in learning about great artists, architects and designers in history as many of them used these detailed sketches in their designs. Use Table 7.1 to consider the close links between arts and science subjects in a range of activities designed for Early Years.

Table 7.1 The early years foundation stage (EYFS)

The Early Years Foundation Stage (EYFS)		
The Understanding the world factor...	**The Expressive Arts factor...**	**The Task...**
Early Learning Goal • Children know about similarities and differences in relation to places, objects, materials and living things. They make observations of animals and plants and explain why some things occur, and talk about changes.	**Early Learning Goal** • They safely use and explore a variety of materials, tools and techniques, experimenting with colour, design, texture, form and function	**Collecting leaves** Getting all children out and about is the best way to combine "The Arts" and Science. You can discuss the different colours and textures of fallen leaves and then have a go at sorting them, an excellent working scientifically skill. You could sort them into different colours, crunchy and not crunchy etc. Collecting the fallen leaves creates a chance to discuss why the changes occur in the trees and plants, the seasons and then pieces of art can be created from the variety of things collected. Creating pieces of transient art is a firm favourite with EYFS children. Children can also begin to sketch and make observational drawings of the leaves and trees. Similarities and differences can not only be drawn from the trees, leaves and plants but also the different artistic styles of the individuals in an art gallery style viewing of the children's work. 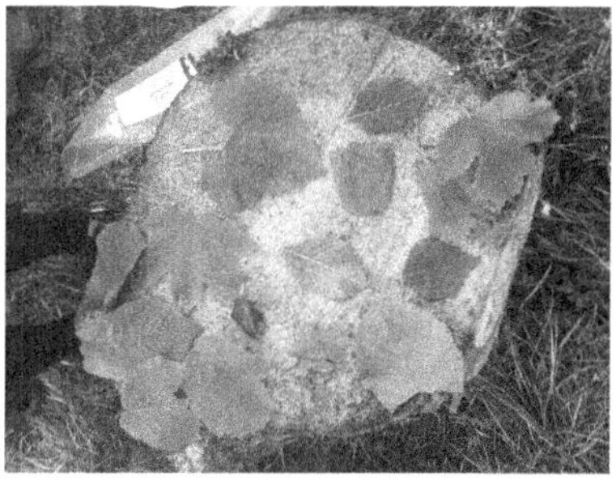
Early Learning Goal • Children know about similarities and differences in relation to places, objects, materials and living things. They talk about the features of their own immediate environment and how environments might vary from one another. They make observations of animals and plants and explain why some things occur, and talk about changes.	**Early Learning Goal** • Children sing songs, make music and dance, and experiment with ways of changing them. • Children use what they have learnt about media and materials in original ways, thinking about uses and purposes. They represent their own ideas, thoughts and feelings through design and technology, art, music, dance, role play and stories.	**Sounds of the weather** The weather is a brilliant tool to begin discussing changes in the natural world, relating to their place, and is a great place to start laying the building blocks of their understanding of sound. You could get children to build and create instruments that represent the "sounds" of different weather. They can use weather they have experienced and also different media to show them videos of extreme weather. The most extreme tends to make some wonderful instruments. You begin to point out the instruments vibrating and then they play around with different pitches. Creating dances and movements to represent the different types of weather is also a great task to begin exploring weather and their wider world.

(Continued)

Table 7.1 (Continued)

The Early Years Foundation Stage (EYFS)		
The Understanding the world factor...	**The Expressive Arts factor...**	**The Task...**
Early Learning Goal • Children know about similarities and differences in relation to places, objects, materials and living things. They talk about the features of their own immediate environment and how environments might vary from one another. They make observations of animals and plants and explain why some things occur, and talk about changes.	**Early Learning Goal** • Children use what they have learnt about media and materials in original ways, thinking about uses and purposes. They represent their own ideas, thoughts and feelings through design and technology, art, music, dance, role play and stories.	**Animals and their habitats** Any activity around animals and their homes offers a plethora of amazing opportunities for EYFS. Building habitats from different materials and acting as an animal and then having people guess which animal you are, are some of the children's best tasks. Following the instrument theme, creating or using recognised instruments to create different animal noises is a good way to begin to recognise, name and classify animals and birds.
Key Stages 1 and 2		
The Science factor...	**The Arts factor...**	**The Task...**
KS1 Plants • identify and describe the basic structure of a variety of common flowering plants, including trees *(This can be replicated in LKS2 Plants topic as well)*	Use drawing, painting and sculpture to develop and share their ideas, experiences and imagination Develop a wide range of art and design techniques by using colour, pattern, texture, line, shape, form and space	**Building models and structures to represent leaves, flowers and plants** - Children can use natural materials and a variety of art materials to create models of flowers. Children can then label the models and structures with features and roles the different parts have. 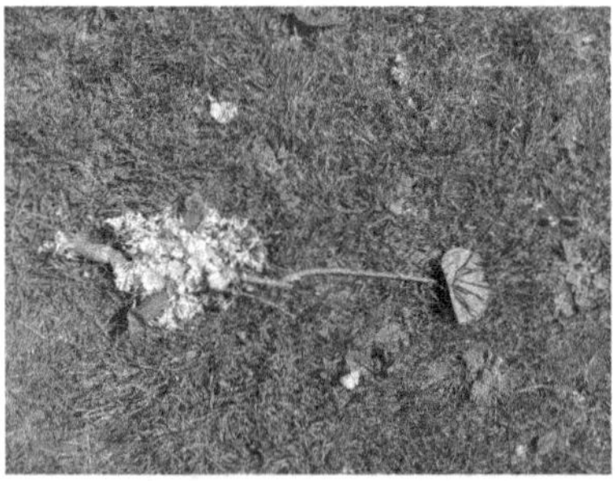 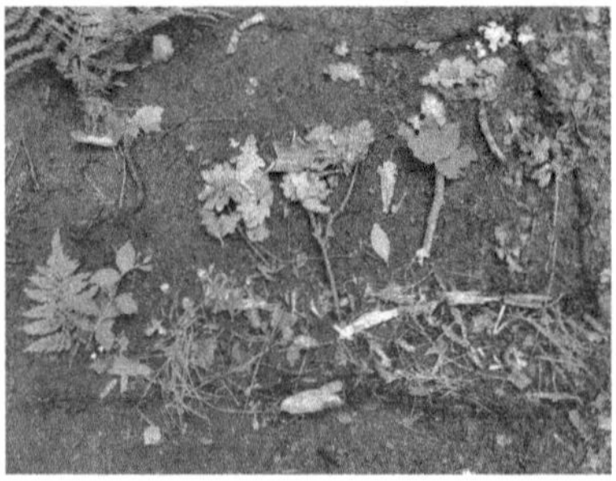

Key Stages 1 and 2		
The Science factor...	**The Arts factor...**	**The Task...**
KS1 Plants • identify and name a variety of common wild and garden plants, including deciduous and evergreen trees	Use drawing, painting and sculpture to develop and share their ideas, experiences and imagination Develop a wide range of art and design techniques by using colour, pattern, texture, line, shape, form and space	**Leaf rubbings** - Children can use a variety of crayons and pastels to take rubbings of different species of leaves. The rubbings can help identify different trees and leaves and also help to name them. Children could then use the images created to label the different parts of the leaf.
KS1 Animals Including Humans • identify, name, draw and label the basic parts of the human body and say which part of the body is associated with each sense	Use drawing, painting and sculpture to develop and share their ideas, experiences and imagination	**Building models of the body** - Getting children to create life size and miniature sculptures of the body and then labelling them is a great activity. The interactive physical nature is a lot more appealing than labelling worksheets.
LKS2 Plants • explore the part that flowers play in the life cycle of flowering plants, including pollination, seed formation and seed dispersal	Dramatic performance and role play Oracy	**Life cycle of a plant dramatic performance** - Children can each take the role of part of the life cycle and act out the life of the flower. Children can start as seeds and use physical movements to show them growing. Children can act as bees and insects to show different elements of pollination and then how the seeds are dispersed. At each stage in the cycle, children can use presentative language to describe the processes the seed is undergoing.
LKS2 Light • recognise that shadows are formed when the light from a light source is blocked by an opaque object • find patterns in the way that the size of shadows change	Dramatic performance and role play Oracy Improve their mastery of art and design techniques, including drawing, painting and sculpture with a range of materials	**Puppet show** - Children can design and create their own shadow puppets using a variety of art materials and techniques. They can then put on a shadow puppet show. This works with their writing as well as they can act out a story first before they write about it. Acting out the story, the children can explore the different sizes of shadows they can create and what materials are opaque
LKS2 Light • recognise that light from the sun can be dangerous and that there are ways to protect their eyes	Dramatic performance and role play Oracy	**TV advert** - Children can produce their own dramatic performance for selling a pair of sunglasses to you. They could be selling it to you or a "visitor" who has never seen sunglasses before.

(Continued)

Table 7.1 (Continued)

Key Stages 1 and 2		
The Science factor...	**The Arts factor...**	**The Task...**
UKS2 Space • describe the movement of the Earth, and other planets, relative to the Sun in the solar system • describe the movement of the Moon relative to the Earth • describe the Sun, Earth and Moon as approximately spherical bodies • use the idea of the Earth's rotation to explain day and night and the apparent movement of the sun across the sky	Create sketch books to record their observations and use them to review and revisit ideas Improve their mastery of art and design techniques, including drawing, painting and sculpture with a range of materials Learn about great artists, architects and designers in history.	**Exploring Artwork** - Showing the children some famous pieces of art work based on Space (Think Van Gough's "Starry Night") is a great way to start lots of discussion, using their subject knowledge, about whether or not it is an accurate depiction of Space. From this point, children can analyse it with a scientist's hat on but also from an artist's point of view as well. This technique works across the whole science curriculum as long as you can find artwork that features that aspect of the curriculum.
UKS2 Space • describe the Sun, Earth and Moon as approximately spherical bodies	Improve their mastery of art and design techniques, including drawing, painting and sculpture with a range of materials	**Solar System models** - All Space topics have to start with creating models of the planets, Sun, Earth and Moon from a whole range of art mediums! This really allows the children to explore shape and relative size. Once the models are formed you can use them in your classroom displays hanging from the ceiling.
UKS2 Animals including humans • identify and name the main parts of the human circulatory system, and describe the functions of the heart, blood vessels and blood	Dramatic performance and role play Oracy	**Circulatory system drama** - Giving the children a role in the circulatory system and getting them to act it out is a great way of getting them to remember how it all works. The children can present how each section works as the blood gets to them.

REFLECTION

Year 2 teacher, Richard, offers some insights of planning for science and arts using examples from his practice. When I reflected, I never set out to link my science lessons to art, or vice versa. It was only when I took a step back that I realised the beauty of combining the two. The ideas I had seemed to combine the best elements of both to produce engaging, thoughtful and impactful lessons. Here are a few memories from the classroom where sciences and the arts have worked together.

Case study 1

Meet Jayden. 'Oh no ... science!' he moaned as he entered the classroom and looked at the visual timetable at the side of my board. It was my first proper week with the class after a week of getting to know the teacher tasks.

'What do you mean, "Oh no"?' I asked.

'It's science ... it's boring!'

'You just wait!'

What Jayden was referring to was a science lesson where he finished labelling a worksheet of different habitats and then coloured the pictures of animals that could live in there.

We began the block of work on food chains with the theoretical knowledge needed. I checked that the children understood the terms 'herbivore', 'carnivore' and 'omnivore', and could name some animals that fit into the categories. 'Right, drama time!' I announced.

'Drama time? But it's science!' the class replied.

We headed straight outside. The aim of the performance was for the children to show me a food chain that they might find on an African savannah. They split into groups and off they went. I watched as discussions and debates erupted. Children put forward their arguments for what animals they wanted to be. 'I'll be a tiger!' someone shouted.

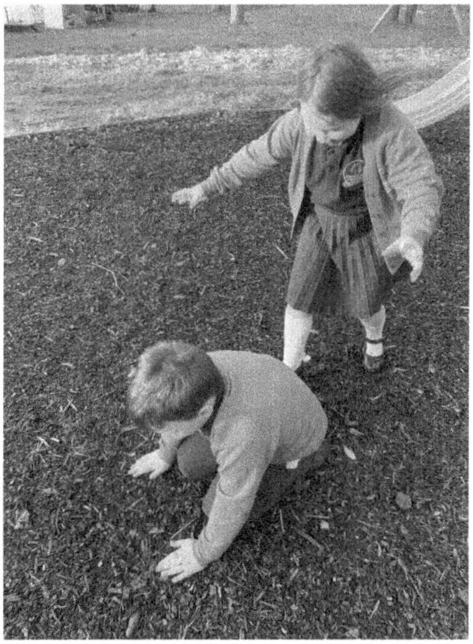

'No, you can't, they don't live in Africa!' Jayden shouted, jumping up and down with excitement at playing the part of an antelope and at the prospect of being chased by the lion.

The children all performed their 'food chain drama' and then I changed the goal: 'Now show me a food chain from a different habitat - any habitat you want.' The volume grew louder and louder as the children chattered about where in the world they would travel and what animals they would be.

(Continued)

(Continued)

As a sleek sea lion swam away in fear from a great white shark, I asked, 'Bored, Jayden?'

The grin said it all.

Case study 2

The objective was clear: identify and describe the functions of different parts of flowering plants (roots, stem/trunk, leaves and flowers), but the class I was teaching was a tricky one - a mixed-ability group with a very different set of interest levels. How could I capture them? I remembered talking to their art teacher; she had said how brilliant they had all been, when learning about great artists, at using their sketchbooks and then modelling with different materials.

The children came in from the playground and saw that their topic books had been replaced with their art sketchbooks, and a selection of art pencils were on their desks. The feeling of the room lifted as they started to murmur, 'Art! Art! We are doing art!'

They lifted their books and we headed up to the garden. The children were instructed to find a plant or flower that interested them in the school's garden. They found a quiet space and used the variety of sketching techniques that they had been shown by their art teacher to fill their pages with detailed, scientific, observational drawings of the plants and flowers. An hour passed, and still the tongues of the cheekiest boys in the class twiddled out of the sides of their mouths with concentration.

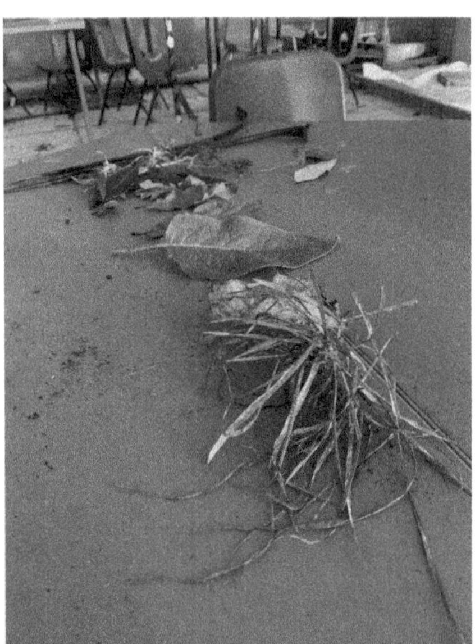

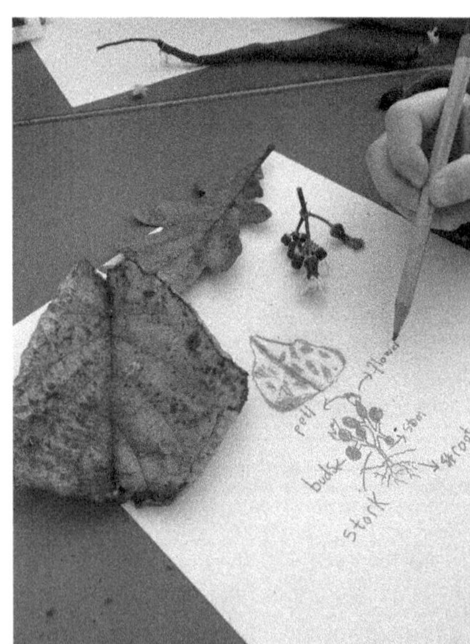

After making models of flowers inclusive of all of their features, the children returned to their careful and detailed sketches and began to label all of their parts and functions. 'I was a root! That's easy to label,' shouted Nza. I then went around and checked in on the small groups of children and looked at their detailed sketches. We had smashed the objective - without a science book in sight.

DEEP DIVE

Intent

What is the overall purpose of your science teaching? Can your learners talk about what they are doing in science, and why? Are you making meaningful links with prior learning?

Implementation

Can you and your learners' work show how their conceptual understanding has developed? Are the learners aware of where their learning links to other subject areas? Are you using a range of enquiry types to allow the learners to develop all aspects of working scientifically?

Impact

How is the science work you are doing differentiated to meet the needs of all the learners? How is your assessment of science, both conceptual and enquiry work, informing future planning and outcomes? Is there evidence of any enhancement of the science curriculum provision through the learners' work and outcomes?

CHAPTER SUMMARY

This chapter has drawn together parallels between science and the arts in ways that we hope are interesting and novel. We suggest that while both subjects suffer at the hands of prioritising maths and English within schools, there is a great advantage to giving time and thought to the planning and delivery of science and the arts. They are not in opposition as some think, but rather work to support each other, and have shared attributes and characteristics that enable learners to achieve more by narrowing the dichotomy. In short, we are advocates for science *and* the arts, not science *or* the arts.

Further reading

Robbins, D. (2005) The origins, early development and status of Bourdieu's concept of 'cultural capital'. *British Journal of Sociology*, 56(1): 13–30.

8

POETRY – THE ART OF EXPRESSION

ALISON SILBY, SCARLETT MURPHY AND STEPHANIE SHARP

KEYWORDS: CULTURALLY SIGNIFICANT; EMBEDDED; EMPOWERING; EXPRESSIVE; IMMERSIVE; MULTISENSORY

CHAPTER OBJECTIVES

This chapter will help you to:

- understand how poetry develops children's understanding and love of English;
- appreciate how poetry evolves from early wordplay with rhythm and rhyme to creation and performance;
- consider the ways in which poetry can be embedded across the curriculum;
- learn how poetry can be realised through a school's curriculum offer;
- reflect on the ways in which poetry empowers children to explore our rich and varied literary heritage, as well as that of other cultures;
- explore the use of diverse spaces for experiencing poetry, as well as the impact that this has on interpretation and understanding;
- understand the part that poetry plays in unlocking potential in all children.

LINKS TO THE TEACHERS' STANDARDS

This chapter maps to the following Teachers' Standards:

TS1 Set high expectations which inspire, motivate and challenge pupils

TS3 Demonstrate good subject and curriculum knowledge

TS4 Plan and teach well structured lessons

See the Appendix for links to the ITT Core Content Framework.

Poetry's capacity to thrive depends on a wide community. Its 'power and scope for transformation' (Heaney) depends on poets, and how they make it happen in their lives. But it also depends on teachers, pupils, school and their communities, the connections they make with it and the determination and joy with which they share it.

(Dymoke et al., 2015, p211)

Introduction

In this chapter, we will investigate poetry as a form of expression that offers diverse opportunities for children to engage with a rich repertoire of texts across the early years and primary curriculum. Poetry is a powerful tool that allows children to experience different forms of language use and creates a platform to explore meaning through a range of responses. We will explore how being immersed in poetry empowers children to delve deeper into our rich and varied literary heritage, as well as that of other cultures. We recognise how the study of poetry enables children to appreciate that attitudes and societal constructs from the past have not always been what they perceive today in the twenty-first century. In addition, we illustrate how teaching poetry across the primary curriculum can help children to reach their full potential, as well as building a love of literature and language from an early age.

THEORY FOCUS: THE POWER OF POETRY

Poetry has an enviable position in today's curriculum because it is such a flexible medium that can permeate and enhance almost any subject encountered by young learners. Gamble (2019, p251) lists its many benefits, which range from the extending and enriching of children's vocabulary, to sparking their curiosity to look 'beyond the literal', to immersion in the symbolic. Poetry allows children to experience what it is to manipulate language beyond the formulaic. Dymoke et al. (2015) investigate how it supports the development of comprehension skills over time, as well as building resilience in both new and more experienced readers. Poetry offers children the opportunity to experience patterned language such as rhythm, rhyme and repetition, in addition to other language devices such as alliteration and assonance. This supports the development of auditory discrimination – the ability to detect similarities and differences in the sound structures of language (Buttriss and Callander, 2008). Children can map these auditory experiences and use them to explore wider encounters with language patterns. A poem can also evoke a wide range of emotional responses, allowing children to discover worlds both familiar and unknown (Wyse et al., 2018). Different points of view can be experienced alongside exploration of the challenges and injustices in the world.

REFLECTION

How much time have you spent engaging with poetry? Can you recall early interactions with rhythm, rhyme and wordplay? Do you associate your encounters with poetry as opportunities to view the world in a different way or as opportunities to express your own thoughts and ideas? Reflect on later experiences of poetry where a more analytical approach may have been adopted, and how this altered the way in which you perceived poetry.

No matter what your previous experiences have been, poetry has the potential to transcend being boxed off as a minor part of the early years and primary curriculum. As teachers, it is our responsibility to weave poetry into every part of curriculum design.

Poetry from the start: early encounters with poetry

Poetry should be viewed as an essential element of the early years curriculum as it offers diverse opportunities for children to engage with language in a playful way. From the earliest stages, language play allows children to explore the rhythms and patterns of both written and spoken language, facilitating connections that can be made between sounds and symbols. Therefore, it is crucial that early years practitioners use poetry to create language-rich classrooms.

Children who have been exposed to a broad range of nursery rhymes, songs and poetry in their early years are more likely to be successful when it comes to reading acquisition (Bradley and Bryant, 1983). These opportunities need to be created on a daily basis. Rhymes and chants such as the 'Clean Up' song (believed to have originated from a North American children's campfire song) can form an integral part of the school day, helping children to internalise pattern, rhyme and intonation while developing an understanding of roles and responsibilities in the classroom:

Clean up! Clean up! Everybody, everywhere.

Clean up! Clean up! Everybody do your share.

This understanding develops as young children experience a rich and broad range of poetry in all of its forms. Early encounters with nursery rhymes and even classic poetry support the development of narrative memory. Rhymes that can be recalled, such as 'Twinkle, Twinkle, Little Star' or 'Incy Wincy Spider', are highly memorable because of their melody and cadence, and they are often accompanied by actions. Such action rhymes are an excellent way to develop children's understanding of both the prosodic and paralinguistic features of language. The accompanying movements help children to realise the narrative structure as the actions often occur on the emphasised syllables, words or phrases (e.g. '*down* came the rain and *washed* the spider out'). Sense and meaning can be created through such intonation and action. In addition, musical elements such as dynamics and timbre allow children to develop a shared understanding of the narrative. Enjoyment is built through the anticipatory nature of both the rhyme scheme and the repetition of the spider's actions. These shared experiences of poetry develop a sense of community in the classroom as children's collective repertoires grow (Wyse et al., 2018).

Poetry, in its condensed state, allows children's understanding to develop and their vocabulary to expand (Benton, 1978). In terms of language acquisition, it is perfectly situated to develop strong foundations on which to build and broaden children's vocabulary. Consider this extract from Jan Ormerod's (2005) vibrant poetry picture book *Doing the Animal Bop*:

> *Put your heels together and waddle along.*
>
> *Go craak craak craak – it's the penguin song.*
>
> *High stepping knees and feather that bounce –*
>
> *Flim-flam flutter to the ostrich flounce.*
>
> (pp3–6)

Ormerod's writing introduces children to a delicious range of vocabulary that allows them to experience wordplay, building and storing descriptive language for future use. Lindsey Gardiner's accompanying illustrations lift the rhythm of the words off the page, allowing children to enjoy the richness of the text in visual form. This brings an additional layer of meaning, aiding interpretation. You can listen to and view the whole text at: **www.booktrust.org.uk/books-and-reading/have-some-fun/storybooks-and-games/do-the-animal-bop/**

Similarly, Joseph Coelho's (2020) collection *Poetry Aloud* offers diverse opportunities for very young children to experience musical devices in poetry, such as crescendo and diminuendo. His poetry allows children to hear the sounds that words can make as he manipulates dynamics and tempo to create meaning. Spend some time investigating his wider works at: **https://clpe.org.uk/poetryline/interviews/coelho-joseph**

REFLECTION

How will you go about equipping your early years classroom with a broad range of poetry texts? Consider exploring collections such as Michael Rosen's (2015) *A Great Big Cuddle*, which allows very young children to encounter and play with words and develop empathy skills through the depiction of shared experiences. Also, Julia Copus' (2015) *The Hog, the Shrew and the Hullabaloo* is a wonderful rhythmic story that supports children to hear rhyme in the text at the same time as sharing the characters' adventures. Children's natural affinity with music and the rhythms of language can be fostered through the sharing of patterned texts such as these.

Poetry as an expressive art form

When we think of using poetry as a vehicle for myriad outcomes, such as supporting children's understanding of their roles and responsibilities in the classroom, good behaviour management can also be a wonderful by-product. After all, when children are busy reciting from their narrative memory, they are practising experts, fully immersing themselves in the enjoyment of the sounds that they make and the 'say out loudness of a poem's music' (Agard and Nichols, 2004, p8). This leaves little space for children to become distracted.

Poetry can act as a stimulus for a range of topics to support the development of the soft skills that twenty-first-century employers are asking for. The Department for Education's report *An Unequal Playing Field* lists these higher-order abilities as the 'readiness to learn, problem-solving, and planning skills' (DfE, 2019a, p62), which echoes Bourdieu's theory that education can increase social mobility through employability (English and Bolton, 2016).

Children should be exposed to poetry regularly throughout the year, not simply during poetry week. A wide range of forms should be offered, from the acrostic and the kenning to humorous limericks and serious sonnets. It is essential that poetry is not 'dumbed down'; children should be allowed to access the breadth of the classics, as well as popularised, topical material.

As an expressive art form, poetry can be transformed through interpretation and reinvention. For example, while the idea of Shakespeare in the classroom can seem challenging, using texts where these stories are retold for children, such as *Shakespeare Stories* (Matthews and Ross, 2010), will allow these seemingly difficult classics to be accessible to all. After all, Shakespeare would have wanted his stories to be performed and remain contemporary.

Shakespeare's *The Tempest* begins right in the middle of the action: a ship is in the eye of a storm and the cast of characters are shipwrecked (Winston and Tandy, 2012). This teamed with the visual stimulus of J.M.W. Turner's painting *A Storm (Shipwreck)* (*c*.1822–1823), for example, allows a scheme of work to almost write itself. This would offer pupils a wide range of opportunities for poetry and drama activities and music and art compositions, as well as learning poetry by heart. Building objectives around soft skills such as speaking and listening will allow children to share their ideas and work in groups to organise their thinking. Going further, the blockwork print *The Great Wave off Kanagawa* (*c*.1829–1833) by Katsushika Hokusai would add another dimension to the production of haiku, for example. Sharing examples of storms from Shakespeare's other plays would also add depth to a collaborative creation or a school assembly to bring this work together, which would be an ideal showcase for assessing talk:

> ***King Lear*** (using a modern version of the text)
>
> Act 3, scene 2, lines 1–5
>
> *Blow, winds! Blow until your cheeks crack! Rage on, blow!*
>
> *Let tornadoes spew water*
>
> *until the steeples of our churches and the weathervanes are all drowned.*
>
> *Let quick sulfurous lightning, strong enough to split enormous trees,*
>
> *singe the white hair on my head. Let thunder flatten the spherical world.*
>
> *Pericles*
>
> Act 3, scene 1, lines 1–6
>
> *The god of this great vast, rebuke these surges,*
>
> *Which wash both heaven and hell; and thou that hast*
>
> *Upon the winds command, bind them in brass,*

Having call'd them from the deep! O, still

Thy deaf'ning, dreadful thunders, gently quench

Thy nimble, sulfurous flashes!

THEORY FOCUS: PLACING POETRY IN THE CLASSROOM

Poetry should be on display in the classroom at every opportunity, in a space that is made special by providing visual stimuli and examples of poetry, as well as poets who reflect the interests of the pupils in the class (Lockwood, 2008, 2011). Each child should see themselves represented in the books on display, on the shelves and in the book box. A classroom can be a lonely place if a child does not see characters or themes that reflect their own background or culture. In her article on developing a multilingual library, Sabine Little (2020) recognised that 'having a selection of multilingual children's books available normalises multilingualism in the school ... and raises its status' (p13). In this way, the school opens itself up to a wealth of resources, including knowledge of story and rhyme, shared by parents and other stakeholders, to strengthen the living language of poetry and the poetic forms of other cultures. Children should be encouraged to source poetry to add to this display; after all, 'the magic of the words and the wonder of shared ideas and impressions should never be forgotten' (Edwards, 2006). What better way to use those valuable minutes between taking the register and assembly, or getting ready for physical education (PE), than by reciting or reading poetry representative of the children in your class.

Building a community of global citizens

For older children, slam poetry is a vibrant poetic form building on the tradition of spoken and performance poetry. Nikita Gill's (2020a) anthology *SLAM!* brings diverse, modern writers together, which she describes as a 'manifesto for performance poetry' (Gill, 2020b). Tackling difficult subjects such as religion and culture, many young people will find themselves reflected in these words from 'Inheritance and New Ways of Learning' by Zainab Dawood (2020):

at home you placed a finger on the map and traced the

journey from here

to religion and further east to where you're finally just

another brown face in the crowd

another face in the crowd

and no-one looks at you funny when you eat with your

hands

(p4)

Slam is political – truths are told, and it can be bare. Performers are generally time-limited and are able to remould their poetry to fit the audience and the way that they are feeling at the time. Error is part of this truth. The Poetry Society website (**https://poetrysociety.org.uk**) offers poetry competitions and a useful teacher's toolkit for slam. It addresses the inclusion of pupils with English as an additional language (EAL) and suggests ways to support their creativity through experimentation, giving EAL pupils a real sense of control over their language through writing shared poetry with others. Using their mother tongue and translating their writing into English acknowledges the ownership of their home language, as well as giving them permission to play with it in a public forum. The Poetry Society suggests the following as a beginning to a shared understanding of different cultures in the classroom, where pupils are encouraged to write a list poem by writing:

Line in Ndebele (for example)

Line in English

Line in Ndebele

Line in English, etc.

This could be used as a stimulus for writing simple poetry in primary language learning to share the experience of all children learning a new language together.

Poetry for adults has always been presented as a crossover to the audience of children. Much like Shakespeare's plays, we would not necessarily wish to expose children to whole texts of poetry, but use our discretion in appropriating key passages and quotations. Personal experience and reflection are key when asking children to respond to their environment, as exemplified by Lemn Sissay (2008) in his poem 'Listener':

Imagination has a fingerprint,

Each dream is a new template,

Each emotion has contours;

Add inspiration and create.

Taking poetry outside

The outside is a rich source for the imagination – there are so many opportunities to take poetry out of the classroom setting. For example, the seasons provide ample space for a changing landscape to be observed, from the unfurling of a leaf in spring to the loss of the leaf in autumn. In *One Leaf Rides the Wind*, Celeste Mannis (2002) demonstrates the use of haiku by immersing the reader in Japanese culture:

One leaf rides the wind.

Quick as I am, it's quicker!

Just beyond my grasp.

Even in the most space-deprived schools, the long summer shadows and the short winter shadows can be seen and measured on the playground. The way that the sky changes from blue to grey, or the heat and cold of brick walls and metal railings, can all give rise to poetry creation.

First observations can be noted down in real time to capture first thoughts and feelings, rather than waiting to return to the classroom. These initial observations can be scaffolded using music, pictures, and even ideas from science to stimulate discussion about the facts of the observation, the feelings, and the part that the five senses have on these initial interpretations. This is particularly important for 'those that struggle with literacy ... or for whom English is an additional language' (Goodwin, 2011, p40).

Two examples of sensory-based learning are as follows:

- Pictures of ice sculptures accompanied by music, such as 'The Snow is Dancing' from Debussy's *Children's Corner* or 'Winter' from Vivaldi's *The Four Seasons*, would provide a rich working environment to inspire children.
- A video of water drumming on Banks Island, Vanuatu, could be used as a stimulus for percussion to replicate the sound of water: **www.youtube.com/watch?v=pEgJhfWKq4A**

Allow children the freedom to draw, paint, or use percussion instruments to express their inner thoughts and feelings. Display these creations or record them, and let children talk about and share their design choices. Through this process, the memory of the internal narrative will grow to support the child from shared composition to independent writing. If we want confident, independent young poets in the classroom, this cannot happen overnight or during one poetry week.

Teaching a sequence of poetry

The teaching of poetry requires careful planning not only to ensure that the relevant curriculum objectives are met, but that enough time is allocated for children to create, edit and perform. No matter the children's age range, teachers should aim to include some time in the day when children have the opportunity to hear poetry being read aloud. This provides the platform for children to experience poetry being read for pleasure.

Dymoke et al. (2015) offer practical suggestions for creating poetry-friendly classrooms, but it is ultimately down to the teacher to ensure that poetry is given the time it deserves.

When planning a poetry sequence, teachers need to consider the following:

1. *Immersion*: How will the children be exposed to poetry? What opportunities will there be to hear it being read aloud? How will they be involved in choosing the poems shared? Consider these opportunities:

    - A poem a day – chosen by the teacher or the children.
    - Singing/rapping with the children – start with a simple chant with actions, such as 'Banana Splits' (see Sanderson, 1995).

- Use Perform a Poem (**https://performapoem.lgfl.org.uk**) for the children to watch poems being performed.
- Swap poems (see Rosen, 2011).
- Talk – share your thoughts about poems. How did the poem make the children feel? What affect did the poem have on the reader?

2. *Curriculum*: What objectives will be covered? Poetry not only addresses the writing objectives of drafting, editing and publishing, but also speaking, listening and performing. Spend time considering the topics covered across the curriculum before considering the following:

   - Look at the different language features of poetry (e.g. similes, metaphors, alliteration, different forms such as calligrams and kennings). How many of these have been shared with the children? Which is most appropriate for the topic?

3. *Purpose*: Be clear about purpose and expectations from the beginning. Children may not want to share their poems with a wider audience if they are personal in nature. However, if comfortable, encourage them to read aloud or 'perform' their poetry. Hearing poetry read aloud allows children to understand how performance aids understanding, how emotions are expressed, and how language patterns are utilised. In addition, performance develops greater understanding of rhyme and rhythmic patterning. Consider the following ideas:

   - Perform to other classes, teachers, parents or the wider community – providing this type of platform enables children to understand the value of their work.
   - Create a poetry anthology and publish it in e-book form – this can be shared with a wider audience.
   - Put on a play – patterned language is integral to performance and sits well inside a narrative.
   - Compose a class song – draw on known melodies in the initial stages, such as setting words to a familiar tune or an ostinato pattern.

4. *Using a model*: This can act as a template in the initial stages of immersion when the children engage in learning poems by heart and subsequently explore imitation. This can work well for the exploration of poetic features such as alliteration and imagery, but care should be taken not to stifle creativity due to children being restricted by structure. However, templates or models can work to support those with English as an additional language or assist those with any barriers to learning. The poem below shows an example of a poem written using 'Recipe to Make a Wolf' by Pie Corbett (Teach Primary, 2011).

   To make a deep cavern knocker

   Take,

   The bat's ears as they twitch in the dark

   The unicorn's horn as it uses its magic powers to set itself free from hunters

For its ears.

Take,

A magic mirror as it forms into the picture you want

The swirls from a cauldron getting mixed

For his eyes.

Take,

The letter 'm' and duplicate it smaller

An old wrinkly hand of an elderly witch as it gets older by the minute

For its neck.

(Lee, age 10)

The poem was innovated by a lower-attaining child in Year 6 who used the model to write his own version of the poem. Pie Corbett's *Talk for Writing* books provide further examples for children to innovate (see Corbett and Strong, 2020), and BookTrust offers recommendations for different age ranges (**www.booktrust.org.uk**). Rhythms from songs, raps and jingles can also be imitated to help children create their own poems.

5. *Analyse*: This can be a rewarding element of the learning and teaching process, and an analytical approach can be embedded within the creative exploration of poetry. Overanalysis can reduce enjoyment, diminishing poetry to a collection of literary features. Discussing the impact of a poem on the reader and how the features affect meaning will enhance children's criticality and ability to manipulate features independently. It is important to ensure the following:
   - Open communication and discussion of thoughts and feelings, as well as how these may vary depending on the reader or writer.
   - Children are provided with opportunities to explore and create similes and metaphors as building blocks for poetry. Explore substituting these with literal phrases. Engage in the explicit teaching of any new features or types of poetry.
6. *Plan, write and edit*: It is imperative that time is given for these stages. Remember how personal poetry is – it should not be rushed. What opportunities for feedback will there be? Planning a poem may include:
   - Lesson warm-ups and plenaries – think about ways to practise the skills that children will use. *Jumpstart! Poetry* by Pie Corbett (2018) contains some engaging poetry warm-ups for all age ranges, as does the Centre for Literacy in Primary Education (CLPE) website (**https://clpe.org.uk**). Consider the ways in which children can reflect on what they have written, going back to those questions about feelings, emotions and comparisons.
   - Warm-up words – encourage children to co-construct ideas for single words or phrases related to the poetry topic or stimulus (e.g. song, picture, emotion, theme), identifying potential rhymes and playing with words before a more formal generation of ideas. Allow

children the freedom to work within the topic or broaden their ideas using a different stimulus. The poem below was written in response to a photograph of children in a warzone. Such thought-provoking images can provide a powerful stimulus for writing.

- Reordering words, extending them and beginning to form verses using conjunctions.
- Imitating rhythms found in language, using musical instruments to explore syllables in words and the melodies created through intonation.

Discovery

Earth
burnt to black,
like an unwanted piece of toast,
ruin, destroyed, all because of him.

Heartbroken,
rivers of tears, memories created and forgotten,
numb fingers,
slumped over,
searching for a glimpse of happiness.

Crying,
crumbling, tumbling bricks and crushing dust,
hurting me, comforting me – my new home.
A black hole of darkness. Despair. End.

Pain,
physical, emotional, everywhere,
threatening to smash my heart,
like it has my world.
Why?

(Ania, Year 6)

7. *Perform/publish*: This is a vital step for all writing. Giving children a reason to write results in heightened engagement. It is essential for children to see the finished product realised in published form, such as a printed book or e-book, work of art, or media production.
8. *Reflect*: How did the children find the experience? Did they enjoy it? Did you, as a teacher? By working alongside the children, you may discover a new-found appreciation for poetry, and you will be modelling how to read for pleasure and how to become a writer.

CASE STUDY: BECOMING A POET

Anisha is a newly qualified teacher (NQT) working in Year 2 in a mainstream primary school. She did not study English at A level, and it has been a while since she has read or written any poetry. She would describe herself as 'lacking confidence' in regard to teaching poetry.

Working with her mentor and partner teacher, Anisha discovered that her lack of confidence meant she had not been sharing poetry with the class and had not been planning sufficient time to teach it. Working with her mentor and partner teacher, she discovered how to engage the children and build a love of poetry.

Lack of confidence can often be the primary reason why teachers - both new and experienced - do not teach poetry at all, or allocate it a few days at the end of term as a time-filler. If a teacher has had a bad experience or no experience with a subject, it can be easy to let that affect how they teach it. It is essential for teachers to consider the benefits of teaching poetry, as well as how to develop an atmosphere of creativity, openness and expression in the classroom.

Anisha worked through the following steps to create a poetry-friendly classroom and build her own confidence:

1. *Immersion*: Anisha ensured that she exposed her class to poetry on a regular basis. At the end of each day, during uniform changes, and while lining up for lunch, she began to read poetry to the children. For three days a week, she chose the poem; and on the other two, the children did. Slowly but surely, the children began to request their favourite poems and started reading along with her. Anisha built her confidence in performance by using any type of poetry she could find from songs, raps, sonnets and anthologies. The children soon became familiar with a wide range of poets. She sang nursery rhymes with the children, who enjoyed performing these as they had already learned them by heart in their earlier years. By hearing poetry aloud, the children were able to experience the rhythms and rhymes rather than being asked to analyse devices and meanings on initial exposure.
2. *Discussion*: As the children began to experience more poetry, Anisha began to ask them how poems made them feel, as well as what their favourites were, and why. Anisha slowly realised that many of the children had different experiences of the nursery rhymes and expressed different emotions - no single emotion was labelled as being 'correct'.

Anisha's questioning was based on Amy L. Eva-Wood's (2008) four affectively based strategies, which covered:

1. responding to key words and phrases;
2. visualising and using the senses;
3. relating the text to personal experiences;
4. identifying with the speaker.

(Continued)

(Continued)

All of this occurred before the children had even discussed a simile or metaphor.

3. *Know your children*: Anisha's class had begun to struggle with gender stereotypes when displaying their opinions on what they wanted to be when they grew up. She discovered that her class lacked self-efficacy, and many did not believe they would be successful when they were older. Anisha decided to link their poetry to their personal, social, health and economic (PSHE) education lesson, and used the song 'Unwritten' by Natasha Bedingfield as a prompt. Rather than showing the children the song written down, the children learned it and sang it whenever they could. Through this, Anisha chose the start of each child's poem:

I am a book, the pages are unwritten. I am who I want to be.

4. *Relating to personal experiences*: Through discussion in a PSHE education lesson, Anisha discovered what the children really wanted to be when they grew up, if there were no barriers. She was shocked. The answers varied from astronaut to rapper, blogger and ballet dancer. What would they need to do to get there, or what skills would they need to have? Anisha wrote these down with the children: super-fast feet, the ability to jump high in the air, patience, being able to tell the time. It was only here that Anisha began to discuss the typical 'features' of poetry. How could they turn their ideas, their words, into similes?

Feet faster than a plane ...

A jumping gazelle ...

Super star soaring through the sky ...

5. *Create and perform*: By writing her own poem, Anisha showed the children how to write theirs. Modelling how to turn their ideas into a poem that was personal to them enabled them to feel the freedom of poetry. By having an example to use, they were able to imitate the layout and structure rather than the language or features used. Anisha gave the children the opportunity to perform their poems, if they wanted to, in an assembly. The purpose was there. Every single child chose to perform their poem to an audience of peers, teachers and family members.

I am a book, the pages are unwritten. I can be who I want to be.

My feet are faster than a plane, soaring across the field

Leg muscles bulging, eyes looking, football flying

I shoot, I score!

I am who I want to be.

(Sanjay, age 6)

REFLECTION

How has this case study changed the way you might approach the teaching of poetry in your classroom? Consider how immersion in poetry can increase children's engagement and enjoyment. Think about the way in which your practice can be transformed as a result of using poetry more frequently.

DEEP DIVE

Intent

It is important to ensure that poetry is embedded in your school's curriculum offer. Opportunities for engagement need to reach wider than communication and language for the early years foundation stage (EYFS) and the Key Stage 1 and Key Stage 2 objectives for English. Is planning still progressive while also allowing children to explore poetry through expressive mediums other than writing? Poetry throughout any school needs to be ambitious in approach and fully inclusive in form.

Implementation

How are you going to engage children in a subject that they may have limited experience of or lack confidence in? How will you ensure that you are confident in your subject matter? Poetry can be overlooked within the timetable, but it is vital in giving children a chance to express their thoughts, feelings and emotions in a format where they are free to create. What will your approach be? Think about how you will timetable poetry sessions to ensure that enough time is given to children to explore, write and present their work.

Impact

Review the impact of the teaching of poetry by evaluating outcomes related to the range of opportunities offered across the school. Do children apply their growing knowledge of poetry across a variety of forms?

CHAPTER SUMMARY

Poetry, in all its rich forms, can transform the way that children view the world around them. It is an integral part of our cultural heritage and has the power to strengthen classroom communities. Exposure to poetry from an early age is essential in developing children's awareness of language and meaning. It provides a platform for expression and can extend the imagination far beyond that of conventional narrative. Poetry offers the opportunity to explore different experiences and develop new ways of thinking, seeing and understanding the world. Its versatility is simply immense. It can be transformed and interpreted through multiple modes, situating it as one of the most powerful forms of literature in our classrooms today.

Further reading

Dymoke, S., Barrs, M., Lambirth., A. and Wilson, A. (2015) *Making Poetry Happen: Transforming the Poetry Classroom*. London: Bloomsbury.

Gill, N. (2020) *SLAM! You're Gonna Wanna Hear This*. London: Macmillan Children's Books.

Lockwood, M. (2011) *Bringing Poetry Alive: A Guide to Classroom Practice*. London: SAGE.

9

DIGITAL MEDIA AND PRIMARY COMPUTING

MILES BERRY

KEYWORDS: CODING; COMPUTATIONAL THINKING; COMPUTING; CREATIVITY; DIGITAL MEDIA; PROGRAMMING

CHAPTER OBJECTIVES

This chapter will help you to:

- appreciate the difference between using technology and understanding the principles which underpin its development and impact;
- consider common characteristics of creative work across digital media;
- understand the place of computing in the national curriculum;
- consider the ways in which artists' thinking style can be linked to creative work in computing;
- link computing to work in art and design, music, poetry, drama and dance;
- consider how the arts can be an integral part of creative work in programming.

LINKS TO THE TEACHERS' STANDARDS

This chapter maps to the following Teachers' Standards:

TS1 Set high expectations which inspire, motivate and challenge pupils

TS3 Demonstrate good subject and curriculum knowledge

TS4 Plan and teach well structured lessons

See the Appendix for links to the ITT Core Content Framework.

Introduction

From an early age, digital technology is a part of almost every child's experience. For example, many young children learn to interact with touchscreens before they learn to speak, draw or write. While teachers might object to the increasingly dominant role of technology, few can argue about its near ubiquity (Ofcom, 2020).

There are differences, however, between passively watching digital media and actively creating media; between using digital technology and having an understanding of how such technology works and is programmed; between uncritically consuming digital content and acting as an empowered citizen in a digital world. The programmes of study for computing in the national curriculum begin with the ambition that 'A high-quality computing education equips pupils to use computational thinking and creativity to understand and change the world' (DfE, 2014b).

The hope is that through learning computing, pupils will come to understand something about how digital technologies and media work, as well as how they are made. Children will be empowered to make a positive difference to their worlds through creating new media of their own.

Teaching computing at primary school puts a lot of demands on teachers. It involves a complex weaving together of transferable pedagogical skills to inspire pupils, building up pupils' prior skills and knowledge, as well as assessing their progress. This is all alongside developing new subject knowledge (which few primary teachers learned while at school themselves) and acquiring the technical skills that are needed to demonstrate and support pupils using hardware and software (Koehler and Mishra, 2009).

With a crowded curriculum and many demands on teachers' time, it can be all too easy to lose sight of the overarching aims for pupils' progress in computing, making do with undemanding work, where pupils do little more than follow instructions or receive repeated practice in already familiar technical skills. Such an approach seems ill-suited to developing a more critical understanding that a creative approach would support.

REFLECTION

How are primary school pupils' experiences of technology different from your own? To what extent does children's apparent familiarity with digital media ensure that they understand these technologies? What place does assessment of prior learning play in delivering an engaging computing curriculum?

Creative work in digital media

The early years and primary curricula offer so many opportunities for pupils to work creatively in traditional media. There is no reason to limit the media of their creative expression to analogue forms as modern digital technology makes it possible for primary school pupils to produce a range of products and engage in learning opportunities, including on-screen or printed text; to work with multimedia as web pages, presentations or video; to record and compose digital audio; to take digital photographs and create 2D digital images and 3D scenes, including in virtual or augmented reality; to create stop-motion and scripted animations and record and edit live video; and to make interactive media, such as simple computer games or 'choose your own adventure' stories. With hardware such as handheld devices and free or low-cost 'apps', the tools needed to work across all of these media are readily available and often easily accessible to primary pupils.

Over and above the specifics of particular media, devices and software are a number of broad general principles that offer a framework for developing creative work in digital media. Common to creative work across all digital media are five key elements: making, originality, quality, fluency and culture.

Making

If teachers are to develop pupils' creativity in digital media, then pupils must have repeated practical opportunities to *create* things. We might describe this as 'digital making': the things that they make can be entirely within the digital realm, such as visual art or scripted (i.e. programmed) animation or games, or they can combine the physical and the virtual, such as recording and editing audio and video. In whichever case, the thing made is not merely an end product that demonstrates – and allows assessment of – the skills and knowledge acquired; rather, it is *through* the process of making that the learner acquires skills. While we can teach pupils how digital images are formed and processed, it is through direct experience of making such images that this knowledge becomes real for them. Seymour Papert coined the term 'constructionism' for this philosophy of learning, building on Piaget's constructivism:

> *Constructionism shares constructivism's connotation of learning as 'building knowledge structures' ... It then adds the idea that this happens especially felicitously in a context where the learner is consciously engaged in constructing a public entity.*
>
> (Harel and Papert, 1991, p1)

Originality

Creative work has some element of originality to it. While the genuinely innovative would be exceptional in the primary classroom, it is common for pupils to create something unique to them. We would expect that a particular artefact be original in the sense that nothing exists which is *exactly* the same as the thing that the child has just made. If creative computing is our goal, there should be the opportunity for children to weave in something from their own experiences, imaginations or interests. For teachers, open-ended opportunities for pupils to explore their own particular ideas or enthusiasms can be hard to manage, but it is quite practical to set tasks that give some opportunity for children to express themselves.

Quality

Ken Robinson's preferred definition of creativity starts from the premise of originality but adds to this an aspiration that work is of value (Robinson, 2009). In practical terms, this means attention to the quality of work that is produced, being willing to draft and redraft, to explore and experiment until the result is as good as it might possibly be. Digital technology makes this somewhat easier than traditional analogue media, allowing changes to be tried out and modifications to be undone if they do not improve the quality of the work. The heavy lifting done by the software makes high-quality production accessible to even young children, at least if they are willing to persevere and use iterative approaches to make changes to their work. To do this well, pupils need some appreciation of what quality work looks like in the particular medium in which they are working. Teachers have a role to play here in sharing inspirational examples and providing constructive, critical feedback on pupils' work. This sort of inspiration and feedback can come from pupils' peers, both within and beyond the classroom.

Fluency

Creative work of high quality requires a degree of familiarity, fluency or mastery of particular tools. While technology developers have done much to make their platforms and tools as accessible as possible to a broad community of users, it takes some practice – and often some instruction – to be able to use these without tools being the main focus. There is a place for lessons focusing on developing a basic familiarity with the particular platform and software, but the risk for creative work in digital media comes when such lessons are the limit of pupils' experiences – where all pupils do is engage in short, skills-focused exercises without applying the skills to more open-ended projects that allow some form of creative expression.

Culture

Finally, we should recognise that creative work does not take place in isolation. 'Original' work is almost always inspired by other creative work in the domain, whether that of artists, teachers or other pupils in the class. Work that pupils create deserves an audience which is able to offer encouragement and constructive advice, as well as providing a sense of purpose for the work in progress. Pupils learn techniques by watching how teachers and peers approach their work and have far more sense of purpose to what they are learning by having an audience with whom to share their work. The internet has made it possible for pupils to take inspiration from, to work alongside, and to show their work to a global audience, although many are rightly concerned that this might lead to additional risks such as exposure to inappropriate content, unwanted contact, and potential online bullying.

REFLECTION

Are these five elements equally important? Where would you place the emphasis? Are there other elements that you would add to this list? Do these apply to all creative work, or are they specific to work with digital media?

Computing in the national curriculum

Many of those training to teach now will have been taught according to the 1999 national curriculum programmes of study for information and communications technology (ICT) (DfEE and QCA, 1999), which focused on developing pupils' skills in using a range of different applications. By 2011, many had expressed concerns over the adequacy of this approach. The 2013 national curriculum replaced ICT with a new subject: computing. This followed recommendations from the Royal Society (2012) to address digital literacy and computer science alongside information technology (IT). While the 2014 programmes of study place more emphasis on programming than ever before, core IT competencies remain important. While relatively few pupils will eventually get jobs in the software industries, many will find themselves developing digital content in the workplace or in their personal lives.

REFLECTION

Do you think that the government were right to include computer science and digital literacy alongside IT skills at primary level? Where do you think the emphasis should lie in computing lessons? Do national curriculum requirements give enough detail on the sort of IT that could be taught in and beyond computing?

Thinking like an artist in computing

Programmers and those working in digital media more generally often approach their work in an exploratory, experimental way that has close parallels with the sort of artistic thinking which Ogier and Tutchell describe in Chapter 1 of this book. If pupils are to learn something of how computing professionals think, then the logical, analytical aspects of 'computational thinking' should be taught in parallel with the more creative, playful approaches that characterise thinking in the arts.

Software engineering used to be seen as a design process of developing and implementing a programmed solution to satisfy a detailed specification. This might be seen as rather removed from creative work by producers, composers and artists working in digital media. Digital media, however, is highly malleable: ideas can be easily tried out on a provisional basis, with changes quickly undone or revised if they do not work out.

Dialogue with a wider community can be found in both programming and digital media more generally. Open-source development, in which the source code for software is shared with the public, has resulted in much of the software on which we have come to rely. By releasing the source code, a program's users can spot bugs, make improvements and develop additional features. Even where the source code for software is not released, developers are open to bug reports and feature requests from their users, with many projects drawing on a small community of invited beta-testers to try out new versions of their code before public release.

Dialogue with an audience is evident in more general digital media work, where the internet has made it possible for creative work to be shared by any with a global audience. While 'likes' and subscriber counts are a superficial way of gauging an audience's reaction to work, and risk compromising artistic intent for mere popularity, these metrics can offer some motivation by demonstrating that there is a public 'out there' who are receptive to the artist's work. Perhaps more meaningful are the comments written in response to work, whether appreciative affirmation or constructive criticism. The Creative Commons licencing framework moves beyond the usual 'all rights reserved' copyright protection to allow others to reuse, revise and remix work without the need for additional consent. Similarly, open-source software licences allow developers to reuse code from others' projects.

Working in new media and on digital platforms is by nature open-ended and creative: new versions will build on what is already there through experimentation with tools and techniques – sometimes aiming for more sophistication, but equally striving for simpler, more elegant approaches.

REFLECTION

Do software engineers really think like artists? Do digital media creatives think differently from artists working in traditional media? How can pupils best be exposed to these approaches in school?

Computing and the arts

Incorporating the use of digital media into learning in arts subjects should be a natural part of any project. Such approaches in school link together the analytical, problem-solving approaches of computational thinking with the more exploratory, open-ended and creative approaches that characterise an artist's thought processes. They extend the range of techniques, materials and tools on which pupils can draw in their work, giving this a more contemporary aspect in an increasingly digital world. They also, through the provisional nature of digital media, encourage experimentation and iterative approaches.

From the computing perspective, linking computing with arts subjects provides a motivating context for many pupils, again making the subject seem more relevant by focusing on digital media with which many pupils are familiar. It also moves computing from the relatively dry realms of solving problems and developing products to one of creative exploration. It moves computing from a focus on making things work to making things that are engaging or challenging – the things that pupils create in computing can be beautiful as well as useful.

Art and design

Digital technology can be easily incorporated into art and design lessons through 'finger painting' on a tablet screen, for example by looking at the work of David Hockney for inspiration. Apps such as *Brushes Redux* provide an uncluttered interface for users to draw or paint, with the ability to zoom in to add detail and to undo changes when things do not work out as planned. These programs typically allow paintings or drawings to be made using multiple layers, and so users can start with a base image such as a digital photograph and then add their own layer on top of this. While accessible to even very young children, such programs are often the medium of choice for professional artists and illustrators (Gayford, 2016).

Smartphones and tablets have made photography a more accessible medium, doing much to encourage users to take many photographs of the same subject before eventually selecting an individual image for further work and eventual distribution. While very young children know how to take photographs on their parents' smartphones, few will have been taught how to take *good* photographs, or to have experimented with the different filters and effects that can be applied to the images. Digital photography lessons might start by using image search engines such as Google Images or Pixabay for inspiration, before considering as a class what makes for particularly effective, stunning or beautiful photographs on a given theme. Pupils might then be encouraged to take their own photos, carefully framing their chosen subject and experimenting with different approaches. Back in the classroom, they might review with a partner which photographs worked best, before applying filters and effects to these, learning that often more subtle enhancements work more effectively than dramatic ones. Pupils might then share their images with a wider audience, perhaps via a gallery on the school's website or by uploading their images under a Creative Commons licence back to Pixabay for others to use.

Music

One approach to using digital technology within music is simply to record sounds in the environment using tools such as the voice memos app on a handheld device or *Audacity* on a PC. Audacity allows multiple tracks to be recorded, allowing a composite recording to be built up one sound or voice at a time, as well as rerecording a track if it does not work as a part of the whole. Effects can be applied to individual tracks, perhaps increasing the volume of one, changing the overall pitch of another, and shifting the left/right stereo balance of a third. While much of the joy of a music lesson happens in performance, the opportunity to quickly review and learn from that performance can support assessment for learning in music.

Other music software, such as Apple's *GarageBand*, makes it possible to compose and perform music digitally rather than using traditional instruments. *GarageBand* is complex software, but thoughtful scaffolding can make it accessible to primary school pupils, as well as offering a great sense of achievement in creating high-quality musical compositions and performances. Like *Audacity*, *GarageBand* can be used as an audio recorder to capture and then edit vocal or instrumental sounds, layering multiple tracks together, but its potential is only realised when used directly for performing or composing. In tracks mode, individual tracks are recorded or composed using interfaces appropriate to the virtual instrument involved, building up layers of sound. Experimentation is key here. Pupils might start by laying down a percussion track, either through playing a virtual on-screen drum kit or creating a planned repeating pattern of beats using untuned percussion instruments in a beat sequencer. The former is closer to the experience of playing percussion, whereas the latter is composition, making it easier to experiment with the pattern to be played. There is also a smart drums instrument that automatically creates a percussion track according to parameters under the user's control. Pupils might then add on a track for the melody of their composition. For example, this can be done using one of the functions for strings or keyboard, or by writing elements such as note, pitch and duration into a 'piano roll' programme. Pupils who are already familiar with traditional instruments can play their virtual equivalents or can connect an electronic version of the instrument via a Bluetooth MIDI interface. They and others can experiment with composing using the 'piano roll' visual representation of the music. The sound associated with the notes written or recorded can be modified, so pupils can explore how a particular tune would sound if played on a different instrument or with audio that they sample themselves.

Once again, pupils' compositions and performances can be exported and shared with a wider audience, perhaps on the school website or learning platform, or on the open web.

Poetry

Poetry provides an opportunity for pupils to develop their skills in and knowledge of word-processing software and desktop publishing. As well as concern over the words they use, many poets take a particular interest in how their work is displayed on the printed page (Pacheco, 2006). The 'concrete poetry' genre takes this to extremes, where the typographic presentation of the poem becomes at least as important as its verbal form (Solt, 1968).

Poetry work might begin with a familiar poem or poems written by pupils themselves. Poems with made-up words, such as Lewis Carroll's 'Jabberwocky', can be particularly interesting to word-process as they typically will defeat the built-in spellcheck tools. Pupils can experiment with font options and effects, including leading and kerning settings, as well as experimenting with paragraph spacing and document margins, to produce a poem that looks beautiful when printed. Shape poems in the children's book *Apes to Zebras* by Liz Brownlee et al. (2018) is a good example to use to illustrate this.

Taking the idea further, pupils might experiment with adding appropriate images to their poems to produce illustrated versions of them, perhaps reminding them of children's picture books.

Drama

Drama and art can be combined through the technique of stop-motion animation, similar to that used by Aardman Animations for the *Wallace and Gromit* films. In stop-motion animation, a sequence of still images is taken of a scene and characters. These are slightly moved from one frame to the next so that when the images are shown in quick succession, an illusion of smooth movement is created. This approach to animation is time-consuming, but can produce high-quality results and gives an insight into how traditional cartoons are created. Stop-motion can be filmed in 2D using drawings or jointed figures, or 3D using modelling clay, small toys or LEGO models. It allows scope for creativity in designing figures and sets, scripting action and dialogue, and experimenting with camera angles and effects. The best results are achieved by placing the recording device on a tripod and ensuring that the scene is well lit.

Another approach is to create a scripted animation using a tool such as MIT's Scratch programming language, where characters ('sprites') are given sequences of instructions to follow on a stage. Careful timing or 'broadcast' messages can be used to synchronise dialogue and action between multiple characters, and there is a built-in image editor for creating backdrops and costumes. Audio can also be recorded, and thus the on-screen characters can be given a voice.

Dance

Computing can be brought into dance lessons through the use of video to film dance, perhaps simply to create a record of a particular performance, but also to provide a way to review that performance, looking for ways in which it might be developed.

The use of video in dance need not be limited to a simple recording of the performance. Multiple devices might be used together to create footage of the performance from different perspectives, subsequently using the *iMovie* app or similar video-editing software to synchronise the footage and produce a much more engaging film of the performance. Using tripods to support the tablets, as well as good lighting, makes it easier to obtain high-quality footage, although it can be interesting to break the rules, such as incorporating one or more devices into the dance or using handheld torches in a darkened room to show movement. *iMovie* and similar software provide filters, effects and transitions, making the recording of the performance as much a creative work as the performance itself. The music used in the dance can be added to the movie as a soundtrack, replacing the typically low-quality audio recorded through built-in microphones.

Another approach in dance might be to log movement data from the accelerometers built into micro:bit single-board computers, importing the numeric data collected during the dance as the basis for a more abstract visualisation of the dance using the computer.

REFLECTION

How have you used digital technology for creative work in the arts? What is gained, or lost, through using digital media rather than more traditional forms? What would you see as challenges to making use of digital technology in arts lessons? What lesson ideas would you wish to pursue?

The arts and programming

The above ideas focus on the creative development of digital media using traditional 'arts' subjects as a starting point. The new emphasis on 'computational thinking' and computer programming in the national curriculum opens up other approaches, including seeing code as a medium for creative expression. In Key Stage 2, this might involve creative work using the Scratch programming language from MIT (Maloney et al., 2008). Creative projects might involve geometric patterns using Scratch's pen library for 'turtle' graphics, drawing on the ideas of the Logo programming language from the 1970s and 1980s (Papert, 1980); musical composition using pre-recorded sampled notes or Scratch's MIDI-like music extension; scripted animation to act out stories; or interactive media in the form of video games.

DEEP DIVE

Intent

- How does your curriculum support progression in computing?
- How much time is given to computing? Is this enough?
- Are there areas where you expect to go beyond the programmes of study with some or all pupils?
- Are there areas where you expect not to fully cover the programmes of study with some or all pupils?
- Explain how you have constructed your scheme of work for computing. Why did you sequence topics in this way?
- How do you ensure that there is a good balance across the different elements of the computing curriculum?

Implementation

- What have you found to be effective in the teaching of programming?
- Give some examples of projects that have helped pupils to develop their creativity in computing. What knowledge and skills have they drawn on, and how do you expect these to develop further?
- Are the resources you have, including IT equipment, sufficient for delivering the curriculum?
- What do you do to help pupils see connections across all curriculum subjects within computing? Do they use computing skills and knowledge elsewhere in the school's curriculum?

Impact

- How is computing assessed? How do you ensure reliability, validity, equity and manageability of this approach?
- What proportion of pupils meet the expectations of the statutory attainment target, 'By the end of each key stage, pupils are expected to know, apply and understand the matters, skills and processes specified in the relevant programme of study'? How do you know?
- What computing-specific professional development have teachers undertaken in the last 12 months? How effective was this? How do you know?
- Are there pupils, or groups of pupils, who find computing uninteresting or challenging? What are your strategies to engage or support them?
- Are there pupils, or groups of pupils, who find computing particularly exciting or easy? What are your strategies to nurture their love of the subject or challenge them?

CHAPTER SUMMARY

In this chapter, we have considered the apparent familiarity of young people with digital technology. We have considered how principles such as making, originality, quality, fluency and culture can underpin creative work across digital media. We explored the parallels between artists' thinking and that of software developers and digital creatives more generally. We considered some of the advantages of linking computing more closely with arts subjects, and explored ways of doing this for art and design, music, poetry, drama and dance. We also considered ways in which programming might be linked to the arts.

Further reading

Berry, M. (2015) *QuickStart Computing: A CPD Toolkit for Primary Teachers*. Swindon: Computing at School.

Papert, S.A. (1980) *Mindstorms: Children, Computers, and Powerful Ideas*. New York: Basic Books.

Resnick, M. (2017) *Lifelong Kindergarten: Cultivating Creativity Through Projects, Passion, Peers, and Play*. Cambridge, MA: MIT Press.

10

DANCE: THE ART OF MOVEMENT

VICKY RANDALL

KEYWORDS: CROSS-CURRICULAR LEARNING; MOVEMENT; MOVEMENT SKILL LEARNING; PHYSICAL EXPRESSION; STIMULI; WELL-BEING

CHAPTER OBJECTIVES

This chapter will help you to:

- understand the unique and important role of movement in the arts;
- explore different stimuli to inspire movement through dance;
- recognise the wider role that movement has in the broader primary curriculum to develop young people's imagination, expression and creativity;
- consider how language can inspire creative movement;
- develop dance ideas for inclusive practice.

LINKS TO THE TEACHERS' STANDARDS

This chapter maps to the following Teachers' Standards:

TS3 Demonstrate good subject and curriculum knowledge

TS4 Plan and teach well structured lessons

TS7 Manage behaviour effectively

See the Appendix for links to the ITT Core Content Framework.

Dance encourages children and young people to express themselves. It promotes physical interaction, and allows children and young people to communicate their ideas, emotions and thoughts through performance.

(DCMS and NDTA, 2005, p1)

Introduction

Movement is a fundamental part of what it means to be human (Doherty and Brennan, 2014). Before we could talk, movement helped us to express our feelings and communicate our needs. Through gesture, we learn to convey our emotions; and as our bodies grow, movement helps us to go about our daily lives. From childhood into adulthood, we hope that our body enables us to engage with the wider world, perhaps for the purposes of adventure, hobbies, social engagement and enjoyment. However, in recent times, we have sadly come to see the stark reality of how a lack of movement can lead to poor health. Before children have even developed the most functional of movement skills (e.g. walking, jumping, climbing), sedentary behaviour can limit their movement patterns – and ultimately their physical endeavours.

While these illustrations show the unquestionable importance of why we should encourage movement in childhood, movement is much more than just a functional task or a means to keep us physically well. We can use our bodies to explore ideas, express feelings and emotions, create images, and make sense of our complex world, but we can also use movement to connect us to the arts.

In this chapter, I draw upon children's natural propensity for movement to nurture expression and imagination. I present movement as an art form for powerful and inclusive learning. I will position dance as having a unique place in the primary curriculum whereby children can achieve movement competence and develop a growing respect for and confidence in their body. Finally, this chapter will offer support and practical ideas to help create simple and engaging dance experiences for young people.

The importance of dance in the primary school

In a congested and busy primary curriculum, it might be asked, 'Why do children need dance?' Beyond the health benefits associated with being physically active, dance can provide children with a medium for learning in and through the social, personal and cognitive domains, building upon a natural curiosity for play (Pickard and Maude, 2014), as well as contributing to the all-round development of an individual (Smith-Autard, 2002). Dance, as an art, provides children with the opportunity to exercise their initiative, creativity and adventurous mood (Lykesas et al., 2014).

Movement forms part of what it means to be human, spanning across generations, cultures, traditions and time (Doherty and Brennan, 2014; Paine, 2014). Through movement, we learn not only *how to move*, but how we can use the body *to learn*. Paine (2014) further suggests that when taught well, dance can:

- give children unique forms for communication and expression;
- put creative thoughts into action;
- promote appreciation of and interaction with other art forms (e.g. literature, art, music, the natural world);
- develop physical coordination and fundamental movement skill competencies;
- make connections between the mind and body through physical and emotional well-being;
- provide opportunities for children to respond imaginatively to different sensory stimuli;
- create an awareness of and respect for the body.

While this list is by no means exhaustive, it offers a starting point to consider how dance can enrich a child's education. At the same time, it is also useful to consider what primary dance *is not*. Lavin (2008) acknowledges that teaching dance can be a stressful experience for teachers who lack confidence and believe they require specialist dance 'know-how'. This belief can stem from a preconceived idea that teachers must create and teach dances that focus on 'performance' alone, where children copy a set of orchestrated movement patterns, or that dance must be linked to forms of popular dance culture in order for it to be enjoyable. Chappell (2007) cautions that a focus on teaching dance through formulaic choreographic processes and products alone can endanger the creative contribution which dance can make.

No doubt many children will find learning and replicating dances enjoyable, but they will not necessarily connect any meaning to the movement or feel that they have contributed their own ideas to what their bodies are doing. Once we remove the barrier of having to teach a 'ready-made dance', there are endless possibilities as to what children can create with the adult or teacher as a guide.

REFLECTION

If you had to justify the place of dance in the primary school curriculum, what key messages would you advocate for? From the ideas offered above, what would you want to promote within your own dance teaching, and what might you want to avoid?

THEORY FOCUS: DANCE AS MOVEMENT LEARNING

Quality dance education is understood to include three key components: composition, performance and appreciation (Smith-Autard, 2002). Through exploration and play, there are endless possibilities for children to create dances and sequences of movements. Similar to other art forms, children can learn how to formalise their movement experiences to create 'motifs', where they represent an idea, image or design that can then be repeated or developed (Paine, 2014).

The seminal work of Rudolph Laban has provided dance with a framework for movement exploration, but with a focus on movement quality through body actions, space, dynamics and relationships. By using this framework, links can be made to language learning. For example, body actions are verbs, describing what the body is doing. These actions also share a close relationship with a broader understanding of fundamental movement skills in physical education (PE) as they connect to functional ways that the body can travel (e.g. hop, run, skip, leap, jump) and balance (e.g. turn, twist, land, stop). Laban's placement of relationships makes further connections to fundamental movement skills through object control as children are introduced to moving with props/objects to develop their dance ideas. George Graham et al. (2020) argue that developing technical body actions alone is not sufficient to achieve movement competence; therefore, children need to be able to explore the fundamental skills of travel, balance and object control through movement concepts such as space, effort and relationships. The alignment to broader thinking of movement development is further evidenced in Laban's (1948) framework, with the key elements of space and dynamics requiring children to consider not only what movements to perform, but the many ways that movement can be performed.

Figure 10.1 outlines the key headings from Laban's (1948) ideas around movement notation to create a simple framework whereby movement can be explored and used to form dance motifs. These headings can be shared simply with children to understand that movement is about the what (of movement in action), the where (movement takes place), the how (movement is experienced), and with whom (the movement is performed).

Body actions (what) Travel Turn Gesture Stillness Transfer of weight Elevation	**Space (where)** General/personal space Size Position Pathways Levels Direction Formation Shape Symmetry/asymmetry
Dynamics (how) Time Weight Space Flow Rhythm	**Relationships (who)** Contact Devices Number and groups

Figure 10.1 Movement framework (adapted from Paine, 2014)

Laban's principles of movement notation still underpins modern educational dance today. Through its creative and movement-based focus, it provides important content for both primary PE and the arts curriculum. By developing the vocabulary associated with moving, children can create a greater repertoire of ways that their bodies experience movement, and ultimately provide richer content to draw upon when creating movement phrases.

The list of words below was drawn up by children in a reception class after listening to the song 'Mess Around' by Ray Charles. These words were then explored physically using their bodies. Some of the words were already familiar to the children, such as 'run', 'slide' and 'spin', and were likely to have already been experienced in other movement contexts such as play and games. Other words were made up by the children to express what the music meant to them, such as 'twizzle', 'flurry' and 'pop'.

- run
- spin
- twizzle
- pop
- whizz
- flurry
- slide
- shake
- wobble

Much movement exploration can come from a single stimulus such as music. Children from a young age can have fun with their movement using the ideas from Laban's framework (see Figure 10.2).

Try this out:

1. Link movements together (e.g. 'What does a "running twizzle pop" look like in action, or a "sliding flurry shake"?') (*body actions*).
2. Copy your partner's actions (*relationships*)
3. Explore body actions in contrasting ways (e.g. fast and slow, high and low) (*dynamics and space*).
4. Choose your favourite action and see if you can perform it forwards, backwards and sideways (*space*).

Figure 10.2 Exploring movement in the early years

Figures 10.3–10.5 are drawings from reception-aged children reflecting upon their dance lesson using the fairy tale 'Jack and the Beanstalk' as their stimulus. In the lesson, children explored the actions of Jack and the giant, as well as how their own bodies could take on the shapes of the beanstalk. The drawings illustrate the children's understanding of the lesson by showing contrasting body shapes (i.e. big/small, wide/narrow, low/high) and movement actions such as walking, balancing and jumping. Drawing when reflecting on the lesson can be a simple way for children to capture their movement learning once they have transitioned back to the classroom.

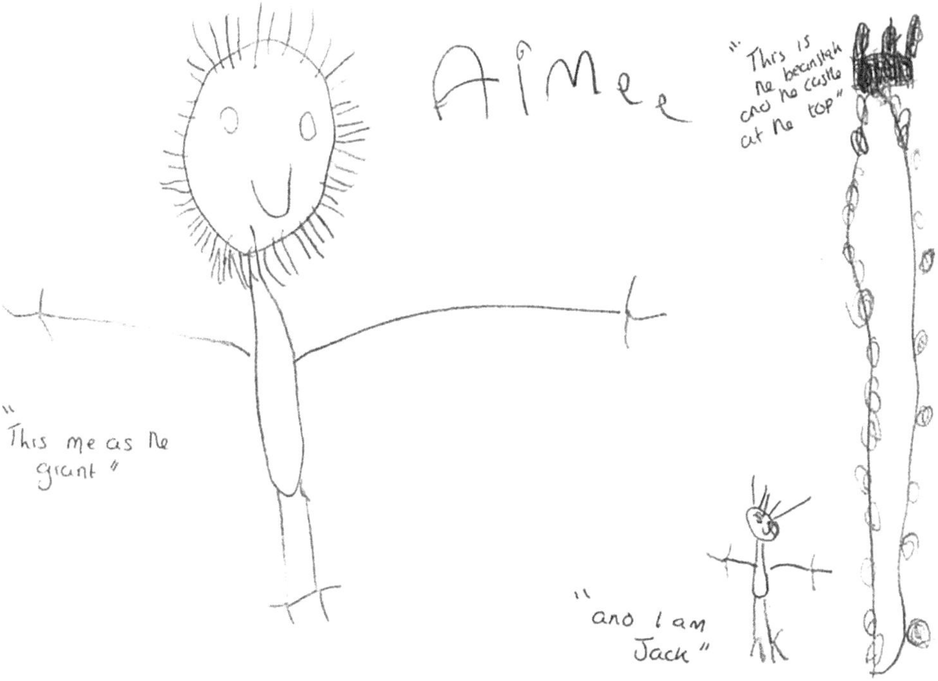

Figure 10.3 *Aimee's picture of herself being Jack next to the contrasting size of the giant*

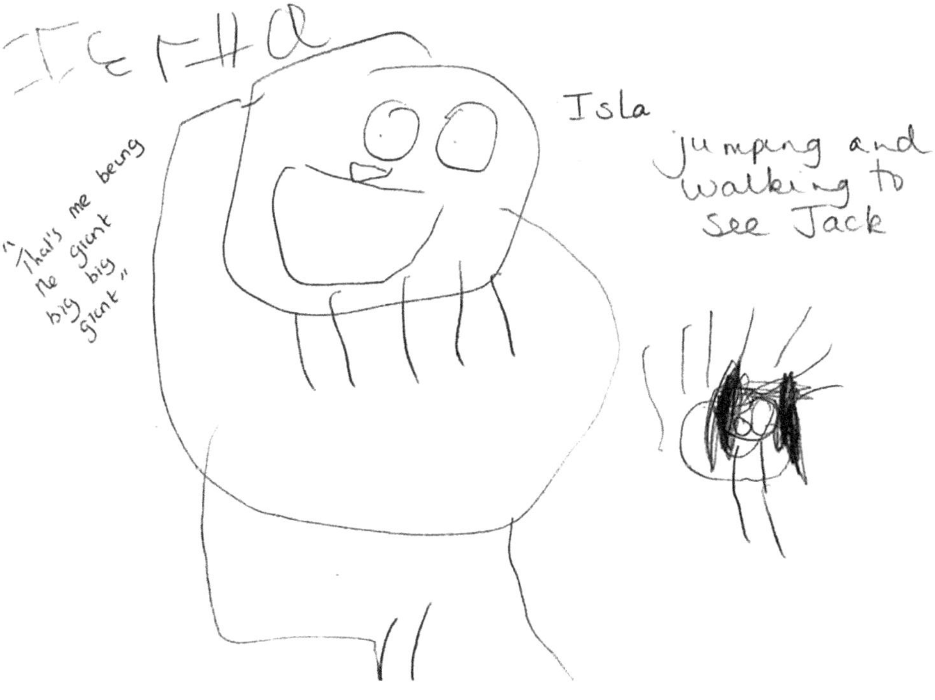

Figure 10.4 *Isla's picture, depicting the characters of Jack and the giant from the dance lesson*

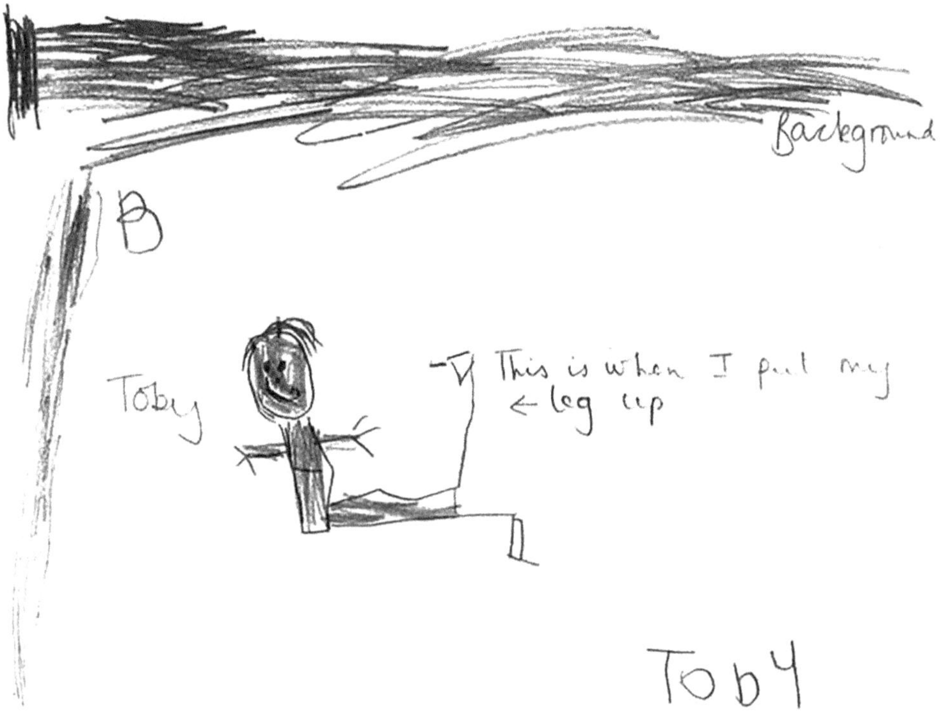

Figure 10.5 *Toby's picture, showing his favourite 'balancing beanstalk shape'*

Lessons that explore, create and perform

As children develop their movement vocabulary, they will start to increase the content on which they can draw upon to compose, perform and evaluate dances. The following teaching activity is another example of how using Laban's framework can be adapted for all primary-aged children to explore and create motifs.

Roll it, chance it, dance it

Table 10.1 *Movement framework for creating dance motifs*

	Body actions	Space	Dynamics	Relationships
1	Jump	Wide	Fast	Mirror
2	Roll	Low	Heavy	Cannon
3	Spin	Narrow	Jerky	Back to back
4	Run	Forwards	Smooth	Near
5	Leap	Curved	Light	Follow
6	Freeze	Backwards	Slow	Unison

1. In pairs, roll a die for each column from Table 10.1 to create a random movement action (e.g. rolling 1, 6, 2 and 2 would produce a 'jump backwards heavy cannon' action). Combining all of these together would become your first movement.
2. Repeat the activity four more times to produce a series of other random movements (see Table 10.2).

Table 10.2 Example dance motifs to create dance actions

Action 1 (1, 6, 2, 2)	**Action 2 (4, 4, 6, 5)**	**Action 3 (2, 1, 2, 1)**	**Action 4 (3, 2, 5, 6)**	**Action 5 (5, 3, 5 & 4)**
Jump, backwards, heavy in cannon	Run, forwards, slow while following	Roll, wide, heavy and mirroring	Spin, low, light and in unison	Leap, narrow, light and near

3. Once the children have explored all five different movements, ask if there are any elements of these movements that they would like to change. For example, in action 3, they might want to swap 'mirroring' with 'back to back'.
4. Children can then play around with the order in which the actions are performed to create a sequence of movements (motifs) (e.g. action 1 is then followed by actions 2, 5, 4 and 3).
5. Each pair then performs their chosen sequence of movements to another pair. The observing pair then provides ideas regarding what they liked about the performance and one way it could be made even better/different.

Similar to the early years example, the above activity introduces children to all three dance elements of composition, performance and appreciation in one learning task. This is done with minimal teacher input and in a way that encourages children to have fun with actions without the pressure for movement to look a particular way. As children develop their movement vocabulary, they might like to create their own content for Table 10.1, perhaps linked to a topic, theme or stimulus (for further ideas and examples, see the rest of this chapter).

Figures 10.6 and 10.7 show a different way for children to explore movement content through language, connecting movement vocabulary to emotions and feelings.

In these pictures, Annabelle and Emily have used written words to explore how they might feel from one day to the next or in response to a given event. From this, they have chosen a word that best fits how they feel on that day and then drawn a picture of a movement which illustrates that emotion. For Annabelle (Year 3), her chosen word of 'excitement' was depicted through the body action of jumping. From her picture, she has been able to describe what her body is doing in the action (e.g. 'stretched', 'tuck', 'jump'). For Emily (Year 5), her chosen word of 'happy' was associated with a cartwheel. When describing what her body is doing, she is able to recognise this as a 'rotation' and an 'upside-down movement'.

In the examples illustrated below, the children have turned words into movement by the simple process of using vocabulary to express emotions. The next section will look at how different environments and stimuli can be drawn upon to inspire children's movement further.

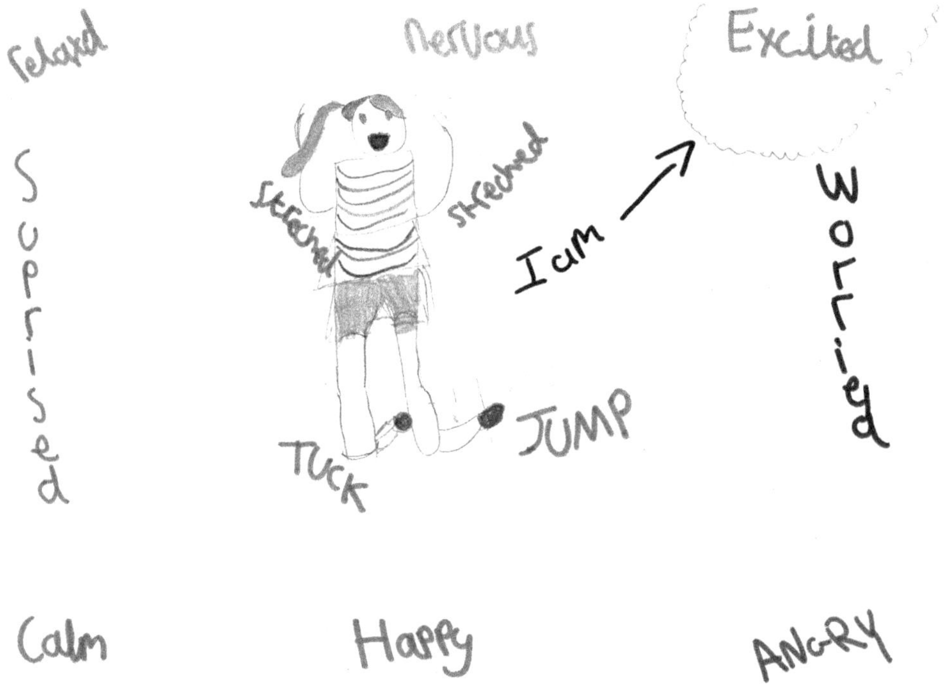

Figure 10.6 Annabelle (Year 3)

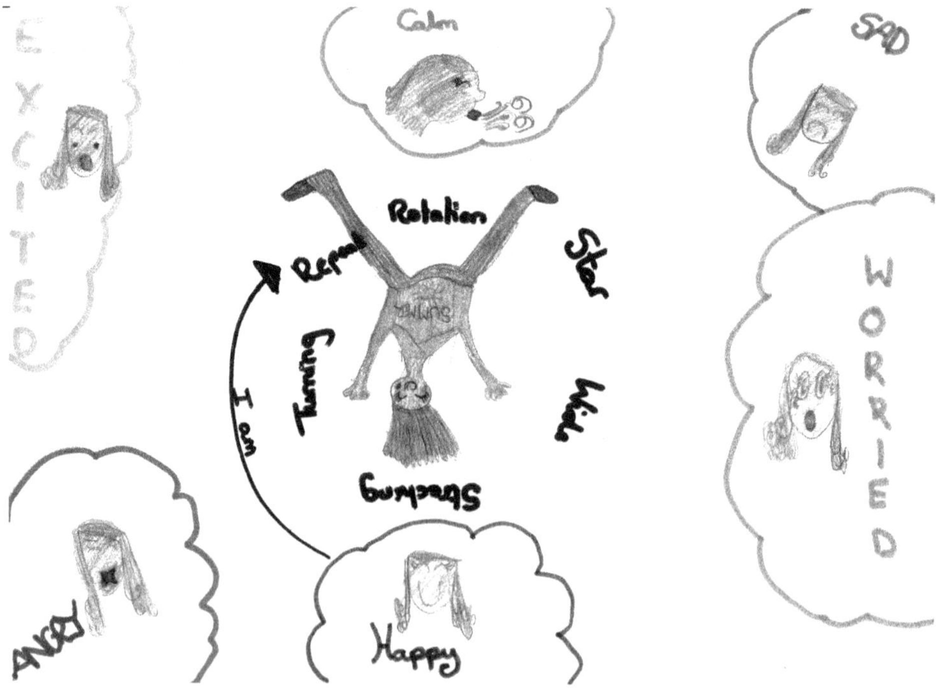

Figure 10.7 Emily (Year 5)

Dance spaces: exploring different environments and stimuli for dance

We might be forgiven for thinking that dance in the primary school must be taught in either the school hall or an inside space; however, the environment for learning dance can be experienced anywhere that it is safe to do so if we are imaginative about it. Although it might not be possible to venture outside of the school grounds, stimulating children's imaginations can also inspire dance movements in many ways. Table 10.3 explores five environments that engage the auditory, kinaesthetic and visual senses through different stimuli.

Table 10.3 Five environments that engage the auditory, kinaesthetic and visual senses

Environment	Auditory	Kinaesthetic	Visual
The seaside (reception)	Picture books such as *Sharing a Shell* (Donaldson and Monks, 2005) Beach sounds	Shells and other seaside finds	Photographs Videos of birds and sea creatures Videos of the sea and waves
The city (Key Stage 1)	Music (e.g. city sounds)	Films and animations (e.g. action heroes, comics)	Television adverts of city driving (see car advertisements)
India (lower Key Stage 2)	Books such as *Footprints in the Forest* (Ghazi, 1999)	Practising and mirroring mudra hand gestures	Pictures, artwork and sculptures of Indian landscapes, flowers and nature
The school playground (upper Key Stage 2)	Poems and stories such as 'The Loner' by Julie Holder (see Paine, 2014)	Explore playground games (e.g. tag, hopscotch, skipping, hula-hooping, throw and catch)	Compare pictures of playground games from different eras (e.g. a contemporary school playground versus one from the 1950s)

REFLECTION

Using Table 10.3, what sort of teaching activities do each of the stimuli inspire? Can you think of any additional environments (real or imagined) and related stimuli for each of the senses and for each Key Stage?

Dance across the curriculum

Connecting dance to the broader early years and primary curriculum can provide meaningful links to be made between subjects, where children can strengthen their learning while also respecting the equal contribution that each subject can have (Paine, 2014). In order for this to occur, the teacher needs to plan and recognise the unique, as well as shared contribution of each subject, to avoid only superficial links being made.

This chapter has already illustrated where links to the broader curriculum can be made possible through dance, specifically how different forms of the written word can be a useful tool to support

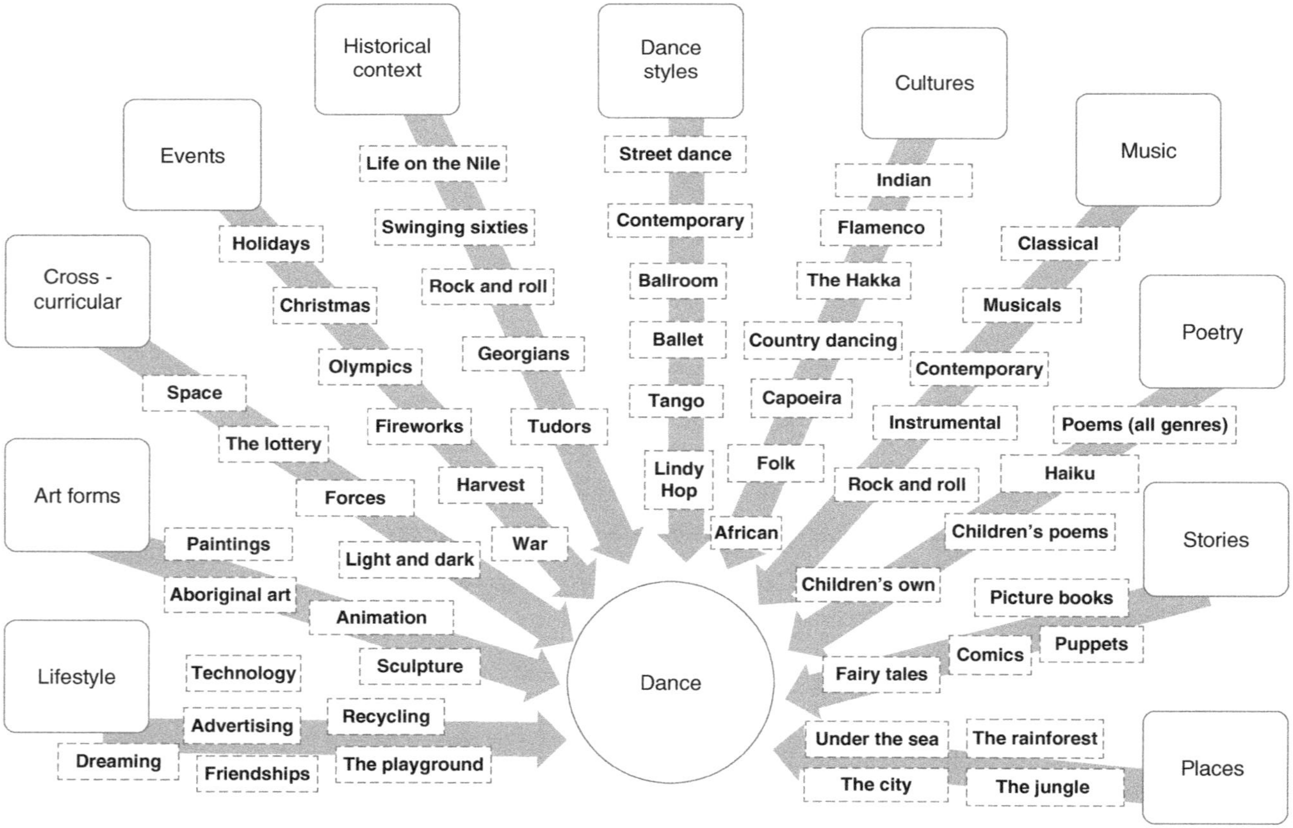

Figure 10.8 Dance ideas

the exploration of movement. Stories, poems, prepositional language, verbs, adjectives and creative language can help to bring movement to life.

Figure 10.8 provides an illustration of how 'dance ideas' can be connected to the broader primary curriculum. Teachers and children might have fun exploring how different strands of this diagram can be used to create unique and meaningful dance experiences.

The case study below provides a further example of how linking dance to the wider primary curriculum can not only encourage children's ownership of their learning, but support teacher confidence in teaching dance as an art. In this example, the following strands from Figure 10.8 were drawn upon to create a cross-curricular learning context, as well as using the teacher's existing confidence in teaching literacy and history to build confidence in teaching dance too:

- *Events and historical context:* The First World War.
- *Art forms*: animation.
- *Dance styles*: contemporary.
- *Music*: world music (France).

CASE STUDY: DEVELOPING TEACHER CONFIDENCE TO TEACH PRIMARY DANCE BY LINKING LEARNING TO THE WIDER CURRICULUM

The teacher in this case study worked alongside a tutor from the University of Winchester to develop her confidence in teaching dance by drawing upon existing knowledge of the English and history curricula.

During 2014, the school commemorated the start of the First World War across their curriculum. The Year 3/4 class teacher and children took inspiration from a short animation called *The Piano* by Aidan Gibbons (2011) to develop a sequence of dance lessons (see https://vimeo.com/200936986). The dance unit required children to consider the feelings, emotions and importance of relationships for the characters in the animation. The children also considered the impact of war on people's lives. They drew upon images and music that related to the animation and used these as the stimuli for their dance.

A dance was created by adapting and replicating core movement phrases (motifs) with a particular focus on the characters in the story (the old man, the wife and the child) and by adapting their ideas through the movement concepts of relationships, dynamics and space. Children considered the way that these concepts related to the story, such as 'slow' and 'graceful' for the old man, 'shadowing', 'mirroring' and 'matching' for the wife, and 'quick', 'lively' and 'playful' for the child.

(Continued)

(Continued)

To begin, children watched the animation. As a class, they discussed their ideas about what they thought the story was about. The class then agreed on four parts of the story that would eventually become the structure of their dance:

Part 1: The old man and his wife (perform in pairs).

Part 2: The Great War (perform as a whole class).

Part 3: The playing child (perform as an individual).

Part 4: Closing scene - contrasting the characters of the child and the old man as two distinctive groups of performers (action/reaction) (half of the class at a time).

For each of the sections above (Parts 1-4), children created word walls (verbs and adjectives) that depicted what they thought each section of the story/dance was about. They also decided how each section would be performed and with whom (relationships). Each lesson then focused on developing and performing each of the sections. In pairs, children explored as many of the words from their word walls as physical movements and then selected their favourite three or four actions to link together to create a simple motif for the section. Children were then asked to repeat the movement sequence three times, changing it each time (see Figure 10.1):

- mirror/matching;
- unison/cannon;
- near/far;
- speed;
- direction.

When all of the sections had been developed, children then practised and created success criteria, as well as performing, recording and evaluating their work. The final piece was shared in a commemorative assembly with children, staff and parents.

REFLECTION

How has this case study made you think about how dance can be connected to the wider curriculum and wider school life? For example, what topics or themes do you think would motivate children to learn? What different stimuli could these topics include (e.g. images, music, artefacts, animations, stories)? Are there particular topics that children find difficult, where exploration through movement might help them to make sense of or communicate ideas in a different way (e.g. concepts of space, forces, emotions, prepositional language)?

DEEP DIVE

Intent

How is movement experienced and communicated in your setting? What importance is given to movement beyond the functional and practical when children engage in dance? What ways can movement be used in conjunction with other art forms to communicate feelings, expression or ideas? What conversations can be had, and what language skills can be developed, when children move or observe movement?

Implementation

Using a variety of stimuli (visual, auditory and kinaesthetic), create different ways to inspire movement. Allow children to create stories linked to different stimuli that can then be shared through dance. Map the curriculum and explore where natural links to dance and movement can occur, as well as what topics children have been motivated to explore further.

Impact

Observe where children use movement to express ideas outside of dance. What language do children use when observing and evaluating their own and others' performances? How do children emotionally respond to movement and dance? Do their confidence and control of movement progress over time?

CHAPTER SUMMARY

Dance holds a privileged and important place in the arts curriculum, contributing to learning through and about movement in creative and expressive ways. By recognising movement as an art, and more than just having a functional role for daily life, children can help to nurture important physical and social skills, as well as learning about their own emotions, likes and dislikes. Through dance, the body can be respected and appreciated, seeing that each and every body is unique and special. In this chapter, practical illustrations have been given to provide inclusive and simple approaches to planning and teaching dance. Links to the wider curriculum have been made to show how broader learning contexts and a range of stimuli can enrich a child's dance experience. A key message from this chapter is to present movement as an experience for everyone, as well as an art form that can offer children meaningful and purposeful learning.

Further reading

Gibbons, A. (2011) *The Piano*. Available at: www.youtube.com/watch?v=0uHCMt3wm04

Jefferson-Buchanan, R. (2012) Dance teaching and learning possibilities within the early years and primary school context. In G. Griggs (ed.), *An Introduction to Primary Physical Education*. London: Routledge, pp135–50.

One Dance UK (2010) *Dance in and Beyond Schools*. London: One Dance UK.

11

THE ARTS AND MATHEMATICS

NASREEN MAJID

KEYWORDS: ARTS; CREATIVITY; GEOMETRY; MATHEMATICS; PROBLEM-SOLVING; REASONING; THINKING

CHAPTER OBJECTIVES

This chapter will help you to:

- explore a range of ways to develop links with mathematics and the arts;
- know how many aspects of the arts are inspired by mathematics;
- draw on artists who have used mathematics as inspiration for their work;
- see mathematics in nature, as well as how patterns are used to develop mathematical thinking;
- draw upon geometry as an art form to develop patterns inspired by nature;
- share worked examples of how mathematics and the arts can be developed in primary schools.

LINKS TO THE TEACHERS' STANDARDS

This chapter maps to the following Teachers' Standards:

TS1 Set high expectations which inspire, motivate and challenge pupils

TS3 Demonstrate good subject and curriculum knowledge

TS4 Plan and teach well structured lessons

See the Appendix for links to the ITT Core Content Framework.

The system is the work of art; the visual work of art is the proof of the System. The visual aspect can't be understood without understanding the system. It isn't what it looks like but what it is that is of basic importance.

Sol LeWitt

Introduction

Mathematics has a long-established heritage in the arts; however, this is very rarely discussed or featured in the primary mathematics curriculum. One of the major factors driving this is the dense curriculum and demands on teachers' time to deliver all aspects, leaving little time to plan and deliver activities that make connections with the richness of mathematical ideas and their links to the arts.

At the heart of mathematical thinking lies the notion of patterns. Our lives are driven by patterns. We may not think about them explicitly, but implicitly they are there (e.g. our daily routines are determined by patterns). Pupils as young as nursery age know the structures of their school day and hence the pattern to their day. Goldin (2002) simply describes mathematics as 'the systematic description and study of pattern' (p197). Mathematics is the science of patterns, and Steen (1988) describes mathematicians as people who seek patterns 'in number, in space, in science, in computers and imagination' (p616). The idea of mathematicians seeking imagination is an important one, as the imagination drives creativity and creativity drives the arts. Therefore, pupils in primary schools would highly benefit from a range of approaches in building mathematical understanding through the different art forms, thus fostering the thread of creativity through their mathematics learning (Mann, 2016).

The work of Jerome Bruner is a vital component in how pupils develop their mathematical thinking (e.g. Bruner, 1966). His modes of representation, from the concrete, to the pictorial, to the abstract (CPA), form the foundations of how mathematics is taught not just in the English mathematics curriculum, but also around the world. The English mathematics curriculum is designed and developed with these underpinning principles. Therefore, when pupils start to learn mathematics, they are given opportunities to experience it through a range of sensory approaches using manipulatives and the physical space to develop understanding. For instance, music can be used to build mathematical understanding through the use of patterns within a sequence of music, and dance sequences can be developed by giving pupils instructions on the number of movements involved within a set sequence. Furthermore, rhyming patterns are used regularly to develop language, but they have a distinctive meter pattern shaped by the repetition of the number of syllables used to develop the rhyme. This informative, arts-based, early concrete and sensory experience supports the holistic development of pupils' insight into the beauty of mathematics.

PRACTICAL POWER

Did you know that the now embedded mathematical resource of Cuisenaire rods was developed by a primary teacher who created the resource to make the learning of mathematics a more hands-on, sensory experience? Georges Cuisenaire was a music and mathematics teacher at a school in Thuin, Belgium. While teaching music, he noted that pupils benefited from learning music through an instrument, thus making the learning a practical experience. Furthermore, listening to musical keys on a keyboard and understanding the relational distance between the keys aids learning. He decided to develop a set of ten differently coloured rods to represent numbers, thus supporting and enhancing his pupils' visual understanding of the numbers 1 to 10 (ATM, 2020) (see Figure 11.1).

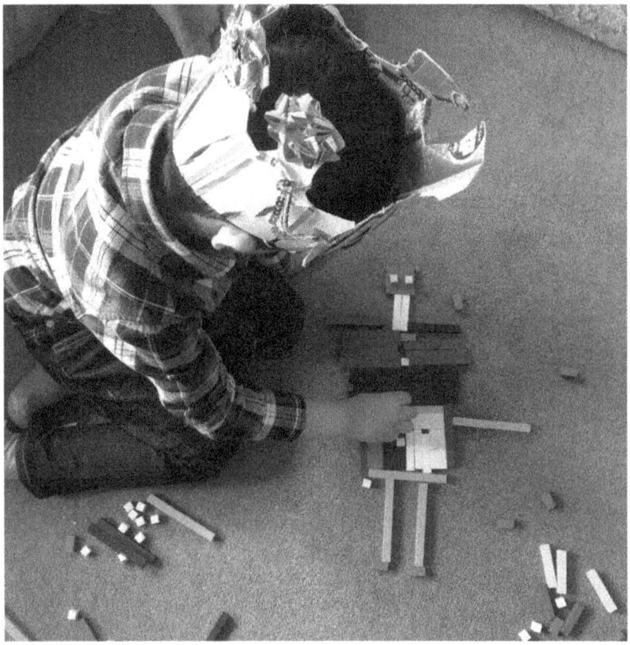

Figure 11.1 Shahzaib, a reception pupil (age 5 years), creating images and patterns with Cuisenaire rods

Cuisenaire rods are introduced to pupils as young as reception class. Pupils are encouraged to use the rods to make patterns. The handling of the rods supports pupils to become familiar with and relationally aware of the different sizes. This builds an early foundation in their use of rods as mathematical tools for learning and reasoning.

REFLECTION

How do you use Cuisenaire rods for your mathematics learning? How can you use the rods to build creativity within your mathematics teaching?

Examples of good practice: case studies/ interviews/personal stories

Geometry is an area of mathematics that artists have been fascinated with and used across millennia to develop their work. Artists such as Wassily Kandinsky, Sol Lovett, M.C. Escher and Anni Albers – to name a few – have all taken inspiration from geometry to develop their work.

Islamic art, as a discipline, uses the principles of geometry to develop intricate patterns. The principles of the golden ratio, as well as how it applies to symmetry, are commonly applied to develop intricate geometric patterns. The Alhambra palace in Granada, Spain, has complex geometric patterns developed by artisans both on tiles as well as stone and wood carvings. The palace was the inspiration for M.C. Escher's work. Escher used the principle of tessellation, where differently shaped tiles can fit together without overlapping (Bachmeier, 2016). He studied the shapes and patterns and used them to develop what we now know as his distinctive art form. The mathematical principles of tessellation can be used to develop a project with upper Key Stage 2 pupils. This can be further enhanced by sharing the work of Escher and for pupils to develop a final piece in the style of Escher (**www.tessellations.org/tess-what.shtml**). The box below provides a step-by-step sequence (illustrated with photographs) to develop this project.

RUN YOUR OWN TESSELLATION PROJECT

Different shapes can be introduced to pupils to examine and decide which shapes tessellate. Pupils can be encouraged to look at the similarities and differences between the shapes, hence exploring the properties of shapes that tessellate (see Figures 11.2 and 11.3).

Follow these steps to success for developing this activity:

1. Share a range of images of the Alhambra palace. You can find a selection on its website (**www.alhambradegranada.org/en/info/galleryofphotographs/tiles.asp**). Feel free to copy these images to share with pupils to facilitate the next stage of this activity.

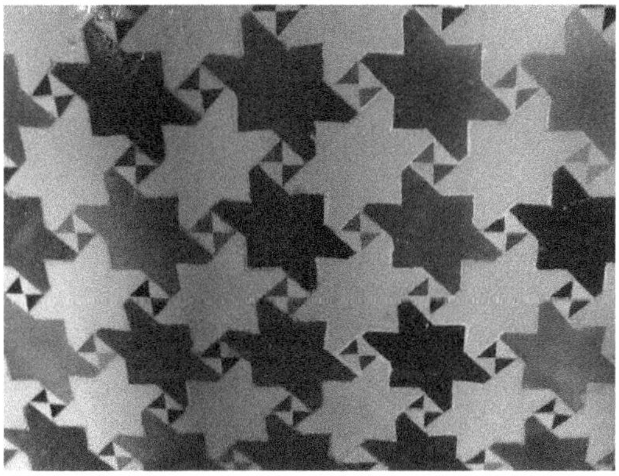

Figure 11.2 Tessellating patterns at the Alhambra palace

(Continued)

(Continued)

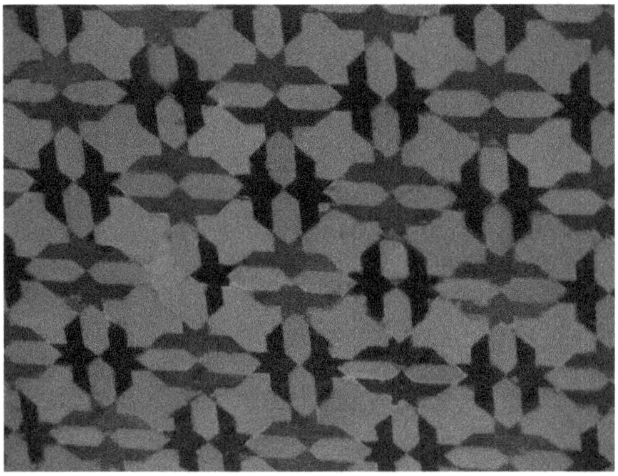

Figure 11.3 Tessellating patterns at the Alhambra palace

2. Encourage pupils to see the patterns and where the principles of tessellation occur.
3. Share some images of Escher's work (**https://mcescher.com/gallery/symmetry/**; **https://mcescher.com/gallery/mathematical/**) and get pupils to compare and contrast the work with the images of the Alhambra palace.
4. Pupils should design their artwork representing tessellating patterns in the style of Escher (see Figure 11.4):
   (i) Start with a shape that will tessellate (e.g. a square).
   (ii) Cut out a shape from one side of the square and fix it to the other side.
   (iii) Now you are ready to use this as a template to develop your tessellating pattern.
   (iv) Use the template to develop your pattern.

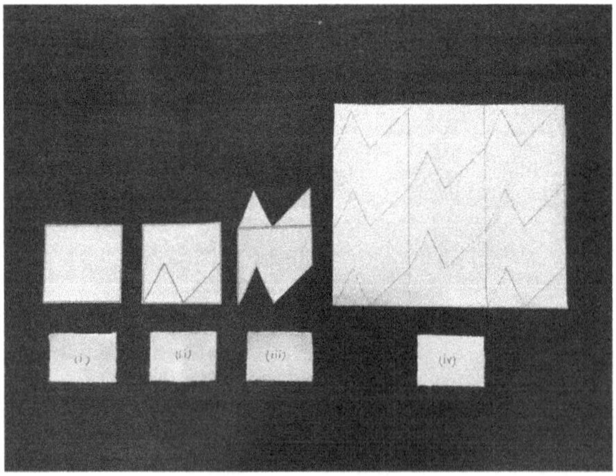

Figure 11.4 Using the principles of Escher to develop a piece of art

CASE STUDY: A TRAINEE TEACHER DEVELOPING THE ARTS WITH HER YEAR 5 PUPILS

Saffron was a trainee teacher undertaking a PGCE. She was on her final teaching practice. Her confidence in teaching the arts was rooted in her own experiences of learning in school.

The class had developed a project on India as part of their summer learning. Saffron had been given the task of teaching a sequence of lessons incorporating aspects of geometry and art. Although she perceived herself to be a reflective learner, open to new ideas, this task had created a sense of anxiety. Her anxiety stemmed from not being able to see the links between mathematics and the arts, or a place for diversity in order to create an inclusive space for all learners. After careful thinking, research and planning, she developed a sequence of lessons that represented and developed the ideas of geometry and art, with the pupils' ideas as her starting point.

Saffron first asked pupils to bring along items from their homes that represented aspects (e.g. patterns, shapes, imagery) from their cultures. These could be artefacts or images from the internet. This formed the basis of the first lesson, where experiences were shared of how patterns and shapes were evident in artefacts from around the world, as well as their cultural significance. The remainder of the lesson used the stimulus of the Taj Mahal and the geometric patterns within it. Pupils studied the patterns and looked out for their properties (e.g. tessellation, size, mirror symmetry). Saffron shared a range of patterns from the Taj Mahal to get pupils to develop a shared collage of their work. Pupils used their knowledge and understanding of mathematics learning and patterns at the Taj Mahal to develop their unique geometric patterns. Their patterns showed mirror symmetry and were designed to be set on a 16 cm ÷ 16 cm tile. Pupils used the ideas to develop their patterns, which they added to a ceramic tile as part of their final piece. The final piece of art was a collaborative effort by Saffron's class that went up on the 'wall of diversity', representing a community of individual and collective learners.

An additional aspect of work that Saffron went on to develop was looking at the tradition of dance in India, as well as developing a sequence of dance moves with pupils to perform in a class assembly. Saffron drew on mathematical concepts of developmental sequences in pentagonal and hexagonal patterns and the repeated patterns in sequences of two and three. Principles of traditional music, musical instruments, the patterns in each sequence of dance moves, and bringing the class together in a collective dance sequence enabled Saffron to incorporate aspects of the arts, mathematics and cultural diversity into her learning. This work was showcased at a class assembly to children's families and was celebrated by the whole school community. Saffron was highly commended by the headteacher and the parents.

Reflective questions

- How would you tackle a challenging situation if you were asked to develop a sequence of learning incorporating the arts into your teaching?
- What would be your starting point?
- How would you involve your learners and incorporate their heritage in developing the learning?

Analysis

Confidence develops with experience and a belief that there is value in what you are trying to achieve. Creative and arts-based approaches to teaching extend one's repertoire as a teacher but also enable learners to understand subject interconnections. It is wonderful to think that some of the fundamental principles of artists' thinking are rooted in mathematics. Furthermore, enabling exploration at this level broadens insight into different cultures, thus developing engagement in meaningful, diverse activities and learning opportunities within the primary classroom.

The early years and Key Stage 1: mathematical development through the arts

Pupils in the early years are immersed in their environment and encouraged to make links that help to develop their understanding holistically. Nature trails form a key part of pupils appreciating their spaces, and linking learning through these walks creates a fun way of facilitating all aspects of learning. Mathematical development can be accelerated through this immersion, with an emphasis on observation, questioning and discussion of what is observed through these immersive experiences in nature. Ann Montague-Smith et al. (2018) discuss the nature of learning mathematics as well as the importance of making connections and understanding the relationship between the connections being made. Hence, it is important to support pupils from a young age to see how their living and learning spaces enable them to see patterns creatively. The connections between those patterns form a vital step to the early development of mathematical creativity.

The outdoor space is a rich environment for learning, and there are many opportunities to link mathematics and mathematical thinking while being immersed outdoors. One obvious way to do this is via the use of maps and developing mapping skills with primary-aged pupils (RGS, 2020). Mapping skills allow pupils to engage in a range of ways with the outdoor space. First, reading maps is a key skill, and developing this skill early in primary school supports pupils with their problem-solving skills and spatial reasoning. Pupils in primary school are introduced to maps by sharing different types of maps to understand that they come in a range of representations (e.g. globes, world maps, Ordnance Survey maps, local town maps, school site maps). Allowing pupils to explore the nature of maps and understand their variety is the first step in learning the language of mapping, as well as how they are pivotal tools for navigation. These are also key skills in mathematical thinking and developing mathematical language, such as positional vocabulary.

Activities to explore the outdoor space and mapping skills

Pupils in Year 1 should explore an outdoor space familiar to them (e.g. playground, local woodland) and then be encouraged to observe what is in the space, as well as how this could be represented on a map. The four compass points are also introduced at this point, and pupils are encouraged to work in pairs to give each other directions to follow. This can be extended into a treasure hunt to creatively explore spaces and areas for ideas – the pair who find the most objects win the treasure! Allow the pupils to take photographs of the area being explored. These can then be used as a whole-class follow-up activity to draw a map of the area explored, containing both the found objects and compass directions.

Developing outdoor trails is an excellent way to incorporate mathematical thinking with primary pupils. These can be exploratory, where pupils are encouraged to look out for items that they can collect along a walk. The collection of items can be used to develop mathematical thinking (see Figure 11.5), or they can be more structured and incorporate a trail where questions have already been set and placed in an outdoor space that you would like the pupils to explore. For example, if

Year 2 pupils have been working on fractions, one of their learning activities could be to develop a set of questions for an outdoor mathemetics trail. This will not only provide a purpose for the learning happening in class, but also have the added value of exploring the outdoor environment by taking part in the mathematics trail. Both activities have merits in supporting mathematical learning in a creative and imaginative way for primary pupils.

Activity 1

Nature trails are a fun and creative way for pupils to make sense of their surroundings. While on a walking trail, pupils can be encouraged to pick leaves and other natural materials (under the guidance of an adult). During the walk, questions such as comparison of the sizes of materials and shapes of the items gathered can be asked to facilitate mathematical thinking. These items are then brought back to the learning space and used to further discuss the properties of the shapes. More mathematical concepts can be developed by grouping the objects using criteria such as colour, size, shape, and so on. The final piece, with all of the materials gathered, would be a class collage. This can be added to a large piece of paper, such as a paper roll, to be displayed in the class.

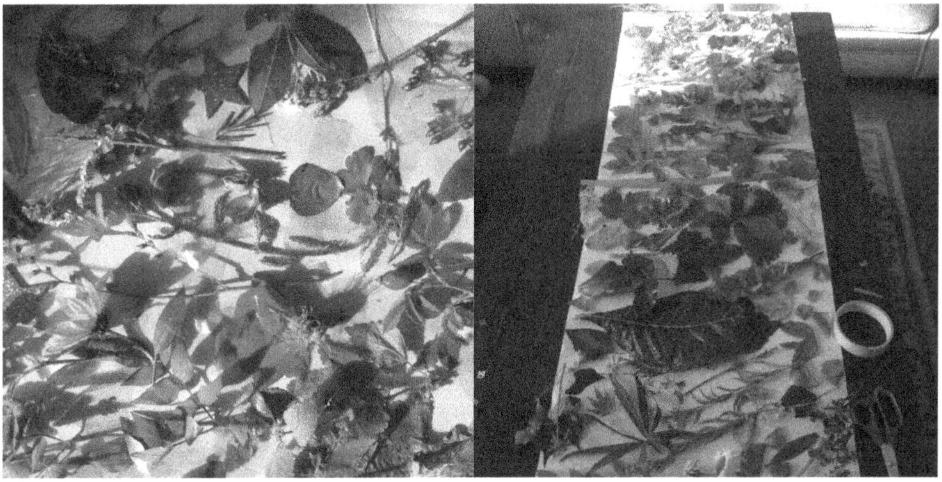

Figure 11.5 These two images illustrate the development of a nature trail collage (created by Shahzaib, age 5).

Activity 2

Using the outdoor space, pupils can be encouraged to create a dance sequence by sharing the number of steps within the sequence with another child or small group. This would work well with children working in pairs so that pupils would develop both their language and listening skills. When one pupil is sharing their dance sequence, the other listens and follows the instructions to try it out. The activity is then repeated to ensure that both pupils have a go at interpreting and developing the dance sequence of their partner. The activity can be scaled up by asking two pairs to join up and share their dance sequences, and then challenging them to blend their dance moves together.

The blending would involve the pupils thinking about the sequencing of their moves and how this would play out with the merging of two distinct sets of sequences. The activity can be further extended by providing a set of rules that represent sequences of numbers, and pupils then use these rules to develop their dances. For instance, 'In your dance moves today, we would like to see four hops, five jumps, two shuffles, six steps', and so on. Pupils would then create their sequence with these criteria, but how a sequence is arranged is up to each individual or pair of pupils. Pupils could be further challenged to develop a dance sequence to a piece of music where a set of numerical criteria are shared. This creates a more open-ended activity, thus fostering further creativity, reasoning and problem-solving.

REFLECTION

Think about the activities that you do regularly which develop both mathematics and the arts together.

- How do you visualise the use of the outdoors to facilitate learning in mathematics and the arts?
- Can you think of new and creative ways to teach mathematical concepts through the arts?
- What ideas will you take away from these examples to develop with your pupils?

DEEP DIVE

Intent

Have a thorough look through your mathematics provision and reflect on where the arts already exist. How can this be further enhanced within the teaching and learning of mathematics? What aspects of incorporating the arts within the teaching and learning of mathematics link to issues of cultural capital (Bourdieu, 1973), and hence furthering aspirations and opportunities for all pupils?

Implementation

Where is the evidence within your long-term planning of a creative approach so that you can incorporate the arts within your mathematics provision? How can your mathematics lead and school leaders support weaving the arts into the teaching and learning of mathematics? What type of professional development learning opportunities can be implemented in your school to facilitate the teaching of mathematics through the arts?

Impact

What is the impact of this work on pupil outcomes? How do you measure this?

CHAPTER SUMMARY

This chapter has aimed to demonstrate how creativity within mathematics can be utilised to incorporate the teaching of mathematics through the arts. It is rare to see the marriage of the arts and mathematics in schools being utilised to a full extent, yet at the heart of mathematical thinking is the notion of creativity and making connections. The chapter has supported you to understand how key theories link with mathematical knowledge and understanding, as well as seeing the connections with the arts. There has been an emphasis on practical, measurable activities that can be developed with little resource implication to support teachers in achieving high gains in learning outcomes. The chapter has intended to inspire the reader to look at mathematics more holistically so that the learning approaches can facilitate the promotion of the arts, as well as deepening children's knowledge and understanding of mathematics in accessible and inclusive ways.

Further reading

Escher In Het Paleis (n.d.) *About Escher*. Available at: www.escherinhetpaleis.nl/about-escher/?lang=en

Gutstein, E. (2006) *Reading and Writing the World with Mathematics: Toward a Pedagogy for Social Justice*. London: Routledge.

12

WRITING AS AN ART: ENGAGING CHILDREN IN CREATIVE WRITING

KERENZA GHOSH

KEYWORDS: COMICS; DRAWING; MULTISENSORY APPROACHES; MUSIC; PICTURE BOOKS; VISUALISATION

CHAPTER OBJECTIVES

This chapter will help you to:

- reflect on the connection between writing and the arts;
- engage children in writing through multisensory approaches;
- create motivating and meaningful opportunities for children to write;
- understand the key role of illustrated texts and picture books in developing immersive and imaginative ways into writing for children;
- consider how creative writing involves teaching approaches and contexts that are more traditionally associated with the arts.

LINKS TO THE TEACHERS' STANDARDS

This chapter maps to the following Teachers' Standards:

TS1 Set high expectations which inspire, motivate and challenge pupils

TS3 Demonstrate good subject and curriculum knowledge

See the Appendix for links to the ITT Core Content Framework.

Art frees us; and the art of words can take us beyond anything we can say in words. I wish our teaching, our reviews, our reading would celebrate that freedom, that liberation. I wish, instead of looking for a message when we read a story, we could think, 'Here's a door opening on a new world: what will I find there?'

(Le Guin, 2009, p129)

Introduction

In this chapter, we will explore what creative writing is, as well as some of the opportunities for creative writing that can arise in the primary classroom. Given the breadth of this topic, within this chapter alone, there is not the scope to address all of the ideas related to creative writing. Therefore, this chapter will focus upon visual texts and multisensory approaches, including visualisation, music and drawing as part of creative writing. We will look at writing composition as being central to creative writing, as well as how meaningful contexts, clear purpose and audience awareness are key to engaging children in the process of creative writing. By considering writing as an art, this chapter demonstrates what the writing process has in common with teaching approaches and contexts that are more typically associated with the arts.

What is creative writing?

When we consider what creative writing is, it is useful to begin by thinking about what creative writing is *not*. In some primary schools, the teaching of writing tends towards outdated approaches that give precedence to transcriptional elements through exercises based on grammar, punctuation, spelling and handwriting – these being a focus of tests such as the SATs. While transcription is an important part of the writing process, prioritising this at the expense of writing opportunities that are truly meaningful and motivating leads to children missing out on opportunities for creative expression. Moreover, teaching transcriptional skills purely as a set of worksheet-based exercises isolates transcription from relevant contexts for writing, and is not likely to engage learners. This is not creative writing.

Often the writing process itself is seen to be removed from approaches more commonly associated with the arts. A typical example is the role that drawing can have alongside writing. In one school that I visited, teachers give children permission to draw a picture only if they have finished their writing on time. Drawing is seen as an unnecessary extra task or a treat to be enjoyed by those children who are 'good' – or fast – at writing. This undermines the value of drawing both in the planning process for writing and as a part of the finished composition itself. It places pressure upon children who feel anxious and less confident with writing, and can cause them to feel inadequate and deprived if they miss out on opportunities to draw.

If we can instead see writing as an art, we will have more occasions to engage children in creative writing. Such an approach requires teachers to take risks and likewise encourage children to do so (Craft, 2000). Bob Jeffrey and Anna Craft (2004) suggest that creative pedagogies arise from making connections between teaching creatively and creative learning. Therefore, if through our teaching we approach writing as an art, this can inspire creative opportunities for writing, which in turn can spur children's own creativity. Further to this, in reflecting on his personal experiences of writing as an art, renowned author Michael Rosen (2019) identifies the importance of allowing children the space to daydream, as well as discovering and exploring the world around them as being central to creativity.

Meaningful contexts for writing are a significant part of children's engagement in creative writing. Instead of asking children to write just because it is part of the national curriculum, we need to present them with meaningful contexts, purposes and audiences for writing, placing composition at the forefront. An emphasis on composition does not neglect transcription; in fact, a compositional focus can enhance and contextualise transcription. For instance, writing should not merely imply that children must use functions such as fronted adverbials, but rather should encourage children to understand *why* to use fronted adverbials – and their effect upon the reader. Grammar and vocabulary choices in creative writing need to be contextual, and children can be shown how a seemingly simple word can have a significant effect on the reader if used in the right way. One such example occurs in Ruth Brown's picture book *A Dark, Dark Tale* (Brown, 1981), which uses repetition throughout to build suspense right up to the big reveal: an illustration of a startled mouse trying its best to evade the cat, who we as readers have followed through each dark, dark setting. The opportunities for creative writing explored in this chapter demonstrate meaningful contexts that give children a genuine purpose for writing and enable them to develop audience awareness, thereby aiming to inspire them as writers.

REFLECTION

Make a list of all the types of writing that you do. This can include writing that is paper-based or which uses technology.

What are your positive memories of writing? What are your purposes for writing, and why are these important? Who are the audiences for your writing, and how does this influence what and how you write? Do you have any negative feelings associated with writing?

This reflection might have invoked some negative memories of writing from when you were a child. You might have feelings of apprehension or even anxiety when faced with a blank page and asked to write. How can you ensure that the children you are teaching do not experience the same negative feelings? How might you encourage children to see the place and value of writing in their daily lives?

Visual texts and children's creative writing

Similarity and symbiosis between art and writing can be seen in visual texts, including picture books, comics and illustrated novels. The potential of visual texts to spark the reader's thoughts and imagination is identified by illustrator Chris Riddell in his lecture *The Age of the Beautiful Book*, (http://www.pearcelecture.com/the-lectures/2017-chris-riddell/) in which he describes books as 'covetable, collectable objects that furnish the room and the mind' (Riddell, 2017). As such, opportunities for children to read and engage imaginatively with a range of visual texts provide an important foundation for their own creative writing. Children's predisposition to play with visual texts that they encounter is evident in their compositions, and particularly the ways in which – when given the freedom to do so – they willingly combine text and image. Examples of this creative capacity as displayed by children are highlighted in research by Eve Bearne and Helen Wolstencroft (2007) and Teresa Cremin (2015). Children's natural enthusiasm for image/text combinations is something that teachers can draw upon in the classroom.

THEORY FOCUS: POWER OF PICTURES

The Power of Pictures project devised by the Centre for Literacy in Primary Education (CLPE) began in 2013 as a short course for teachers run by the CLPE's learning programme leader Charlotte Hacking and author Ed Vere. One aim of the course is to generate working partnerships between picture book authors and schools. This project is significant in its recognition of writing as an art and the interconnectedness between illustration and the written word. The project findings, cited below, are central to teachers' understanding of the potential of picture books in the classroom and the role of arts-based approaches in children's creative writing:

- Picture books are an important genre of children's literature and support the development of sophisticated reading skills.
- Children need time, space and planned opportunities to develop their ideas for truly creative and independent writing.
- When children are given opportunities to draw as part of the writing process, this helps them to formulate, develop and extend ideas for writing, making their independent, self-initiated writing richer.

(Johns-Shepherd, 2019, p3)

The Power of Pictures project (https://clpe.org.uk/powerofpictures) builds on what we know about the significance of picture books as a reading experience by demonstrating how picture books can provide an *art experience* for children. Time should be given for children to look closely at illustrations, since images that are expressive or detailed can provide creative contexts for children's own writing. An example of how picture books can be explored in this way is provided in the case study below.

CASE STUDY: *CASTLES* BY COLIN THOMPSON

This literacy lesson took place with a class of 9- and 10-year-olds. To begin with, I informed the children that we would be going on an imaginary journey to a castle; and to prepare for our visit, I wanted them to share what they already knew about castles. Had they visited one in real life, seen them on television or in books, or read stories about them? Beginning from the children's experience gave them immediate ownership over the context. I scribed a list of words that they associated with the physical features of castles, such as 'moat', 'tower', 'drawbridge' and 'turret',

(Continued)

(Continued)

and asked prompt questions, including: Who might live or work there? What stories do you know that are set in a castle? What characters and creatures are found there? Next, I introduced the castle that we would visit in our imaginations by showing an illustration of 'The Music Castle' from Colin Thompson's (2006) picture book *Castles* (**www.colinthompson.com/graphics/desktops/vvlmusic.jpg**) while playing a piece of music representing the sound of an orchestra tuning up (**www.youtube.com/watch?v=pRaLp8TAALs**). Once the children had studied this image for a few moments, I invited them to imagine jumping into the picture - that they were no longer in their classroom, but had been transported into this unusual setting, and could physically walk around to explore the castle. This combination of picture, music, movement and imagination enabled the children to engage in an immersive, multisensory experience of this fictional context. As they moved around the imaginary space, I encouraged them to think about what they could see, hear and feel (to the touch). They became increasingly animated as they enacted their experience of exploring this imagined environment.

Following this, the children used the illustration to suggest musical terminology, such as 'melody', 'harmony', 'lullaby' and 'resonate', and the names of musical instruments. I then explained that having visited this castle, we now needed to describe it for someone who has never been there, especially since it is so unusual. Working in pairs, I asked the children to write some ideas for what they had seen on their visit to 'The Music Castle' on sticky notes, drawing from the vocabulary charts that we had made to devise descriptive phrases. They then used sticky notes of different colours to write about what they could hear, thinking not only about the instruments, but also the characters that populate this castle and the sounds they themselves would make as they explore this environment. To support the children's development of ideas based on what they could feel, I prompted them to think about texture (e.g. smooth, jagged, bumpy, delicate, thin), temperature (e.g. warm, cool, cold), shape (e.g. curved, round) and material (e.g. wooden, brass, metal), modelling phrases such as 'smooth black clarinet with cold metal keys' and 'piano keys press down beneath my feet as I leap between each note'. I asked the children to omit the words 'I can see/hear/feel' so that each phrase began in a more creative and engaging way. This enabled the children to edit their writing from initial responses such as 'I can feel heat coming from a tuba dragon breathing fire', to more concise, poetic phrases such as 'heat from a fire-breathing tuba dragon'.

Next, I took a selection of suggested effective and interesting phrases from the children, scribing these on the board. I invited a child to read this piece of collaborative writing aloud and asked the class if they wanted to make any edits. I then revealed to the class that together, we had created a poem. My decision to structure the lesson in this way, rather than by saying from the start that we would write a poem, placed the focus upon the children's multisensory experience of this creative writing context.

Below is the poem written by the children:

'Tune Towers' by Elm Class, 2019

On the piano, little creatures singing operatically

An orchestra of many instruments playing a sweet melody of joy

Smooth brass texture of the golden trumpet

Over-sized clarinets for towers

Little creatures singing a lullaby to each other

Drum's vibrations rumbling through the ground

A dungeon at the bottom of the ancient, crackly double bass

High-pitched electric-guitar melodies

Curved shiny surface of a trombone playing harmonies

REFLECTION

Think of a picture book that you could use with children to adapt the approaches taken to *Castles*. Wordless picture books or illustrations - with little to no text - often work well as the context for this multisensory approach.

Personal story: drawing cats to write newspaper articles

I was observing a BA ITE student teacher on her very first teaching placement, working with a class of Year 4 children. The children had been reading the novel *Varjak Paw* by S.F. Said (2003), an adventure story about a cat on a quest to learn the 'Ancient Ways of Jalal', a combination of mindfulness and karate, so that he can save his family from a terrible fate. In the lesson, the student teacher told the children that they would plan a newspaper article and asked them to recap the features of report writing. Following the lesson, the student teacher noted how the children were already confident in their knowledge of report writing, having looked at this in detail the day before, and that the lesson seemed to lack momentum and purpose. We spoke about the need to provide the children with an exciting and meaningful context for writing so that they did not feel they were being asked to write just for the sake of it.

We concluded that in the next lesson, the student teacher would begin by telling the children – with some sense of urgency – that Varjak Paw has made the important decision to leave behind the safety of his home and venture into the world beyond for the benefit of his family. The children would need to document this significant event in the form of newspaper articles, giving them a clear purpose for writing. By coincidence, the class teacher had been off sick, and was therefore the perfect audience for the children's newspaper articles since she could read these on her return to find out what events she had missed.

The opening of the student teacher's lesson the following day had a marked impact upon the children's motivation and the content of their writing. In other words, their composition improved because from the outset they had a clear purpose and sense of audience for their writing. But another reason that the children's ideas for writing developed so well was because they had the opportunity to draw pictures on their newspaper template *before* they started writing. Drawing enabled the children to identify key plot points that they could write about in their newspaper article, supporting their ideas in relation to content and structure. For example, one child had drawn Varjak Paw's narrow escape as he crossed a road full of traffic, as well as the cat's first meeting with his friend Cludge the dog. The drawings made by the child became the foundation and reference point for the content of their writing, freeing them up for creative composition.

It is worth highlighting that *Varjak Paw* is an illustrated novel, with drawings by Dave McKean. Throughout the book, page layout has been given careful consideration through the combination of printed words and drawn images. For example, at a dramatic moment in which Varjak is almost hit by a car, the written text is pushed out of the way by the illustration; and when Varjak is transported to Mesopotamia, the illustrations appear as a faded backdrop to the printed text to evoke what is a dreamlike sequence. In this way, illustrated novels can provide an effective model for children when considering how images and text can be used together in creative ways to convey a story, much like in a newspaper.

REFLECTION

Think of an exciting event in a children's novel - possibly an event from an illustrated novel - that could be presented as a newspaper article. Thinking about purpose and audience, what would you say to the children to make them feel genuinely motivated to write about this event? Invite them to draw one or two key scenes as part of their newspaper article and ask them to talk about these with a partner *before* they start writing.

Through these reflections, you should now be more aware of ensuring that children write with a clear sense of audience and purpose in mind. The above example, as well as your own ideas, will hopefully have highlighted to you the value of children's novels as meaningful contexts and springboards for writing. Children's drawing alongside the written word provides them with important opportunities to discuss and communicate their ideas visually. In the next section, illustrator, author and comic artist Dan White explains how this concept applies in practice in relation to children reading and writing comic books.

Interview with Dan White, creator of *Cindy and Biscuit*

Comics can provide an exciting stimulus for children's own drawing and writing. In this interview, Dan White, creator of the comic book series *Cindy and Biscuit*, shares his creative approach to making comics. Dan's reflections show how the creative processes of the writer and artist are parallel and interwoven.

Q: *Where do your ideas for* Cindy and Biscuit *come from?*

A: It started life as a one-panel comic I drew called 'Cindy and Biscuit Save the World Again', showing a young girl holding a baseball bat, with her dog, and behind them the ruins of a Martian fleet that's tried to invade Earth. I liked the idea that a tiny girl and her dog would be capable of fending off an entire armada! At the time, my niece was about 4 years old, and I was struck by how fearsome and forthright little girls can be. I was keen to have a girl as the hero because I feel that there should be more representation of strong girl characters in comics.

Q: *Creative writing involves taking risks with characters and storylines. What risks do you take when you're writing comics?*

A: I'm a fan of monster movies and sci-fi, so I like to include little nods to horror. I think being scared can be exhilarating when you're young – it's a thrilling, raw experience, so I wanted to include that in *Cindy and Biscuit*. I don't want it to always be cuddly or comforting. I want to push the limits of being scary because I think kids like that. And even if you're scared in the moment, on reflection it's often had a positive, formative impact on you. That's how I felt about some of the monster movies I watched growing up.

Q: *What makes comics an interesting format for creative writing?*

A: Comics are really interesting because the words and images are completely symbiotic. When you create a comics page, you're aiming for something complete: the panels, the gaps between them, page layout, placement of words. It's all part of the same experience. Thinking about the reader, they're not just looking at words and pictures separately; often it's all happening *at the same time*. This means I can play around with the page, lead the eye in different ways and combine visual features creatively. I can tell the story in all sorts of ways: through actual words, images to convey words, images to convey images, juxtapositions, speech bubbles, thought bubbles, typography, directionality, time jumps, speed lines. All of this is the language of comics. I think comics are their own art form, which allows a lot of freedom in how you tell a story.

Q: *What is your creative process for writing comics?*

A: Often I'll have an idea that triggers the story, like a childhood memory, a riff on a monster story, or a narrative perspective such as Biscuit's viewpoint. I generally have an ending in mind, but sometimes the ending finds itself. I do recommend knowing how your story will end, though! If you know where you'll start and finish, you can have fun on the way – otherwise, you'll get lost! With shorter comics, I draw basic stick figure storyboards (thumbnails) to work out how the story will flow. Then I add some dialogue or key words to go with the panels, before developing the comic itself. For longer comics, I'll plot the events, the main beats, in words. Then I'll rough out the pages to see how the story will fit in the layout I've chosen, and where to condense or elaborate the narrative.

Q: What advice would you give to children creating their own comics?

A: Start simple. Think of a basic story or idea and try telling it in just one or two pages. Once you have the idea, you can work out *how* to tell the story through comics.

Page layout: Think about what a whole comics page will look like, not just one panel. That's what makes comics exciting – you're looking at the whole page at the same time.

Character: Decide on a main character you'd like to draw. It doesn't have to be complicated; it can be a stick person, a ball with eyes, your favourite TV character. Get used to drawing them a few times so you get to know them. You'll start to think about that character, and you'll see those characters come to life a bit. When characters come to life, stories begin to tell themselves.

In the next part of the interview, Dan explains how he uses a range of comic techniques in two of his one-page stories.

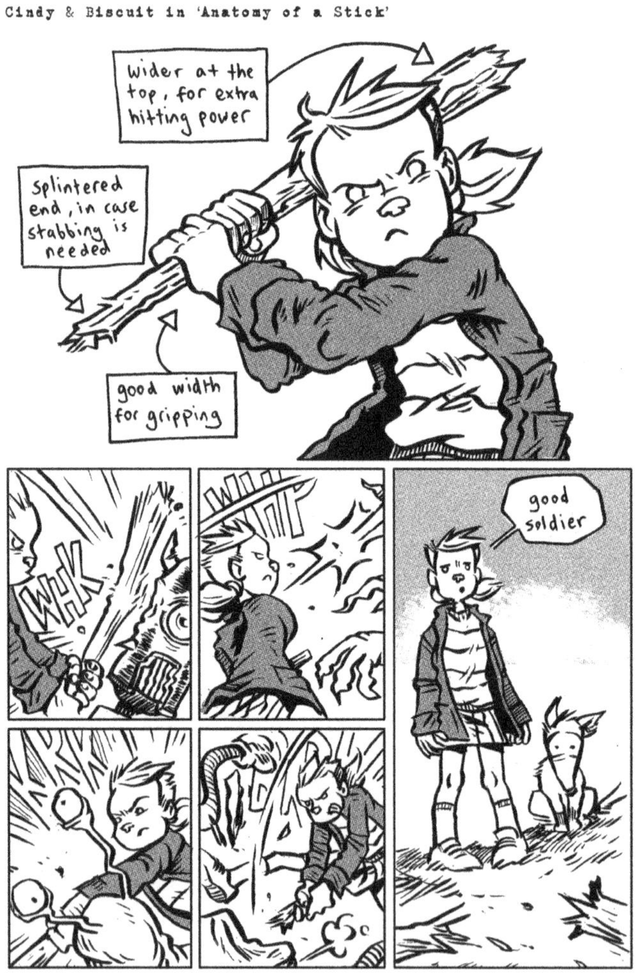

Anatomy of a Stick

Cindy routinely takes on monsters, aliens and ghosts, all with a stick. It's a point of humour that she always rushes into the fray, stick in hand. That's her only plan, and her innate foolhardy bravery is a big part of her appeal. In DC and Marvel comics, you'll see a cross section of a superhero's secret base or their car. I thought it would be funny to apply that here, but with a stick; so the first part is a splash panel with a narrative voice like an instruction manual, pointing out the different parts of the stick and why it's an effective weapon for battling monsters. I've deliberately used negative space to present this striking image of Cindy in action. She's not even in a panel here, she's outside of the comic in a way, which reflects her force of character and physical power. Then we have a sequence of action shots with Cindy bashing in monsters, robots and aliens. Having had a static moment at the top of the page, a pause with arrows and explanations, the story becomes kinetic with sound effects – the impact is an exciting moment of action. There's a change of tempo in the final panel, with Cindy and Biscuit looking at the stick, now broken in half, and she's saying, 'Good soldier', like it's a fallen hero. It shows how Cindy feels about these sticks – she's connected to them; and when a good stick is used up to battle monsters, she's paying it some respect. It's a humorous juxtaposition of this little girl within a war film parody, as a soldier looking at a fallen comrade. As an end piece, it's both funny and poignant.

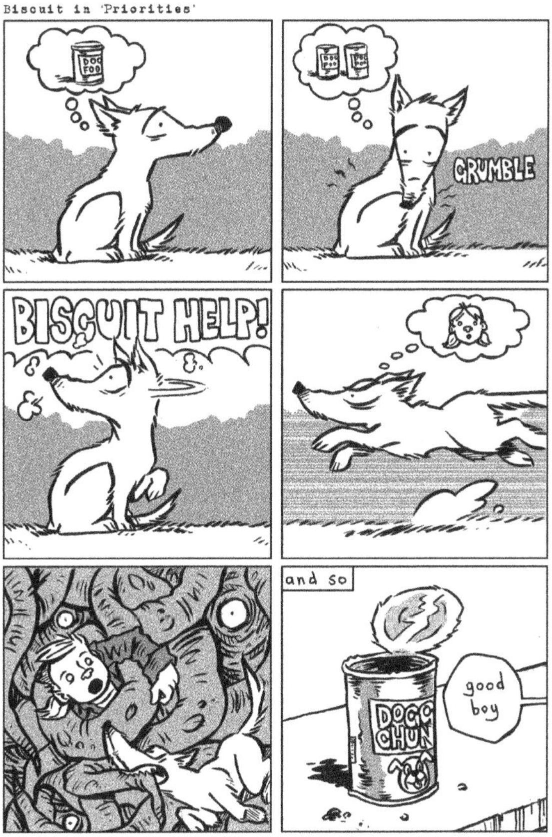

Priorities

This comic uses a classic six-panel grid composition, starting with a full character mid shot of Biscuit thinking about food. Biscuit is non-verbal and doesn't ever talk; so instead of using words, I've drawn tins of food within the thought bubbles – that's one way of telling the story. To indicate his growing hunger, there's a rumbling tummy sound effect with two tins of dog food. Changes within the first three panels are reasonably incremental, giving the effect that time is passing slowly. But from off-panel, you hear, 'Biscuit, help!' and he leaps into action with speed lines and a thought bubble to show he's thinking about Cindy. The fifth panel cuts to a completely different location and moment, with Cindy wrestling a tentacled monster and Biscuit helping her out. It's a silent panel, but silence is juxtaposed within a snapshot of heightened action. It's just one moment in this presumably long fight they have with this beast. The final panel jumps again to a different location and uses another storytelling device unique to comics: the text box in the final panel, 'and so ...' The text box changes the tone of the comic by introducing a narrator to conclude the story. The implication is that they've won the day because you have an empty can of dog food and the punchline, an off-panel voice saying, 'Good boy.' The assumption is that Cindy has now fed Biscuit – he's got his reward. The reason it's called *Priorities* is because Biscuit's preoccupation with food quickly changes when Cindy is in danger. In the end, Biscuit gets the food he wanted in the first place, so it's a tidy conclusion.

REFLECTION

Reread Dan's comics and the interview, then make notes in response to the following questions:

- Why might reading comics appeal to children?
- What can comics teach children about page layout, narrative structure, sequencing events, choosing vocabulary, expressive dialogue, and the role of drawing in telling stories?
- What steps would you need to model in a lesson where children create their own one-page comic story?

These reflections will encourage you to consider your own experience of comics. You may be used to reading in this mode, or perhaps it is new to you, in which case there are many wonderful comics for you to discover. You might think about the challenges and rewards of reading comics. Drawing is a popular approach to making comics, and collage is another effective arts medium for storytelling. Have a look at these collage comics by Philippa Rice: **http://mycardboardlife.com/archive**

Creative writing in the early years foundation stage

For children in the early years, multisensory arts-based approaches are part of their daily experiences at school through free-flow settings and child-led learning. Indeed, 'Children in the early years make no distinction between drawing, painting, modelling or writing as means of recording and exploring their experiences' (Cremin, 2015, p68). As such, children need to be offered creative and playful opportunities to engage in mark-making and motor skill development using a variety of materials, including coloured chunky chalks, Play-Doh, paints and brushes. Drawing is something that most children are able to do before they can form the letters of the alphabet required for conventional writing. Through drawing, very young children begin to understand that the marks they make on the page have meaning and are a powerful way for them to record and communicate their experiences and ideas about the world. Given this, it is equally important that these young children are presented with meaningful contexts and a sense of audience and purpose for their writing. Children's literature is a core resource in the early years, providing a springboard for creative writing alongside arts-based responses. For example, the *Helping Hands* series by Jess Stockholm includes titles such as *Moving Day*, *Party* and *Shopping*, which invite children to build their vocabulary and make early attempts at writing through creating drawings and lists related to each context (Stockholm, 2011c, 2011d, 2011e). Similarly, books in Stockholm's *First Time* series, such as *Doctor*, *Hospital* and *Vet*, can be shared with children alongside role-play areas set up to represent each of these real-life scenarios (Stockholm, 2011a, 2011b, 2011f). By immersing children in these reality contexts through a combination of children's literature and role play, opportunities for creative writing will emerge.

Story boxes are another way to provide engaging contexts for collaborative storytelling by children (Bromley, 1999a, 1999b). Beginning life as discarded shoeboxes, these can be painted, designed and filled with small-world characters that represent the real world (e.g. a fruit and veg stall, outer space), an imaginary scene (e.g. a pirate's cove, a wizard's castle) or a work of fiction. The story box then becomes the basis for dictated stories, a particularly important pedagogical approach that supports creative writing in the early years. During a dictated story, the teacher listens to and encourages children to verbalise their ideas based on a given scenario. The teacher scribes the children's ideas for them, so the children are free to compose creatively and are not held back by the additional physical efforts of transcription. From an arts-based perspective, children can be involved in making story boxes, which could be swapped between classes for others to explore. Hearing their stories read back to them is exciting for young writers, and can in turn motivate them to take steps towards physically writing – or transcribing – their ideas for themselves, leading to transcriptional development.

REFLECTION

Based on the above section, make a list of resources, teaching approaches and learning opportunities that can be applied within the early years. How can multisensory arts-based approaches in the early years be used with and/or adapted for children further up the school?

When you are in school, you may notice that role-play areas and opportunities for child-led enactments are scarcely found in Key Stage 2 classrooms. Give some thought as to why this is and think about how you could provide role-play opportunities in classrooms further up the school, as well as how these might lead to creative writing. Similarly, consider how dictated stories – another approach most often associated with the early years – can be beneficial to older children's creative writing development.

REFLECTION

What does creative writing have in common with teaching approaches and contexts more commonly associated with the arts? How can primary teachers use visual texts and multisensory approaches to provide children with opportunities for creative writing? Having read this chapter, return to the introductory quote by Ursula K. Le Guin and think about how her thoughts on reading and 'the art of words' apply to teachers in supporting children to develop creatively as writers.

DEEP DIVE

Intent

How are you planning for creative writing in your school/class?

Implementation

How are you facilitating teachers/your own practice to incorporate creative writing?

Impact

What is the projected impact? What are you expecting to see as a result of the changes that you have implemented?

CHAPTER SUMMARY

This chapter has invited you to see writing as an art by making links between visual texts, arts-based approaches and creative writing opportunities in the primary classroom. We have considered how teachers can use visual texts and multisensory approaches to give children agency as writers, as well as providing children with opportunities to develop creatively as writers.

Further reading

Arizpe, E. and Styles, M. (2016) *Children Reading Picturebooks: Interpreting Visual Texts*, 2nd edition. London: Routledge.

Cremin, T., Reedy, D., Bearne, E. and Dombey, H. (2015) *Teaching English Creatively*, 2nd edition. London: Routledge.

Ogier, S. and Ghosh, K. (2017) Exploring student teachers' capacity for creativity through the interdisciplinary use of comics in the primary classroom. *Journal of Graphic Novels and Comics*, 9(4): 293–309.

White, D. (2014) *Cindy and Biscuit*. London: Milk the Cat Comics.

13

CLASSROOM DRAMA: LEARNING THROUGH AS-IF BEHAVIOUR

ALASTAIR DANIEL

KEYWORDS: AS-IF BEHAVIOUR; DRAMA; EMBODIMENT; MEANING-MAKING; PROCESS; ROLE PLAY

CHAPTER OBJECTIVES

This chapter will help you to:

- understand the connection between drama and play through 'as-if' behaviour;
- explore how drama (as crafted play) can foster a creative learning community;
- recognise potential for experiential and embodied learning through drama;
- recognise how drama can be applied across subject areas and learning domains.

LINKS TO THE TEACHERS' STANDARDS

This chapter maps to the following Teachers' Standards:

TS1 Set high expectations which inspire, motivate and challenge pupils

TS3 Demonstrate good subject and curriculum knowledge

TS4 Plan and teach well structured lessons

See the Appendix for links to the ITT Core Content Framework.

> *Drama engages 'students not as disembodied thinking machines but as emotional and bodily creatures, capable of imagining as well as reasoning'.*
>
> (DeCoursey, 2019, p3)

Introduction

In this chapter, we shall explore how drama can be considered *crafted play* that is put to pedagogic use. Through examples from my own practice, I shall illustrate how drama enables children to explore possibilities and shape meaning in a range of contexts, and we shall examine the place of drama (and role play) in the early years foundation stage (EYFS) and the national curriculum. As part of this discussion, we shall consider the tensions – and find some common ground – between approaches that focus on drama as performance (related to communication skills) and drama as a process (through which ideas are explored). As Grainger (2003) states:

> *Drama ... represents an opportunity to construct powerful and imaginary worlds together, and enables speculation, modification and transformation of our understandings through examining different people's perspectives, alternative possibilities and the consequences of our actions.*
>
> (p45)

Defining drama and finding its roots in play

Many years ago, I was teaching a literacy lesson to a mixed year group when Luke, a Year 1 child who had been working in the art room with the teaching assistant, entered my classroom with an empty cornflakes packet tied to his back. He ran through the class and out of the opposite door, shouting, 'I'm a Ghostbuster! I'm a Ghostbuster!' Although this playful moment (which lasted only a few seconds) may seem trivial, it has proved to be a critical event in shaping my thinking about the relationship between drama and play in the classroom, a relationship which Edmiston (2007) makes explicit in his suggestion that 'Drama is the use of pretend play for curricular ends' (p338). Although Luke's behaviour was not, in any obvious way, directed towards 'curricular ends', his pretend play provides a useful starting point from which to discuss the nature of drama, and how – in DeCoursey's words – it recognises learners as 'emotional and bodily creatures, capable of imagining as well as reasoning' (DeCoursey, 2019, p3).

The most significant aspect of Luke's role-playing was his behaviour as if he was a Ghostbuster, and it is the 'as-if-ness' of pretend play that is at the very heart of drama and which separates it from other activities. Educational drama depends, as does pretend play, on being able to negotiate between imagined worlds and the real world. Throughout his playful as-if behaviour, Luke maintained awareness of both being himself in the real world (he tells us who he is) and playing the role of a Ghostbuster (he acts as if he is the character). This process of negotiation in drama allows the real world of the classroom to be overlaid with an imagined world so that a chair can become a throne, the classroom a ship's deck, and an empty cornflakes packet a 'proton pack', which is, of course, the equipment used by characters in the film *Ghostbusters* (1984).

THEORY FOCUS: THE AMBIGUITY OF PLAY

We can explore this connection between play and drama in more detail by relating Luke's as-if behaviour to the characteristics of play identified by Brian Sutton-Smith in his influential text *The Ambiguity of Play*. These are quirkiness, redundancy and flexibility (Sutton-Smith, 1997, p229).

- *Quirkiness*: Apart from treating a cardboard box as a 'proton pack', the quirkiness of Luke's play is revealed in his identification (as a 7-year-old) with an adult defeater of the supernatural. This quirkiness of play is directly transferred to drama as the classroom becomes a castle, a forest or any other setting - a story space that children populate with characters through their as-if behaviours.

As children get older and become more self-conscious, however, awareness of the quirky nature of as-if behaviour can become a barrier to effective drama. It is important, therefore, for the teacher to create a supportive classroom environment in which children feel safe enough to play and explore the possibilities of being in-role.

- *Redundancy*: For Sutton-Smith, redundancy is evident when a child discards or adapts elements of their play to make it more satisfying. Luke, for example, was unlikely to repeat exactly the same pattern of behaviour the next time he played Ghostbusters, but rather base his play on those elements that worked for him, either discarding or adapting those that did not give satisfaction. The ephemeral nature of drama means that we can adapt activities by repeating, pausing and rerunning sections, discarding those elements which are redundant. However, while elements of a drama may be identified as being redundant, the process by which these elements are chosen, as well as how the drama is then adapted, needs to be valued through reflection and dialogue.
- *Flexibility*: In drama, flexibility of thought is needed on multiple levels. Most importantly, as-if behaviour requires the child to think and respond to an imagined situation from someone else's point of view, or as themselves in an unfamiliar context. This flexibility towards role, then, requires the application of - and leads to the development of - empathy (Holland, 2009).

Flexibility is also needed when integrating physical space and symbolic items into the drama. Prior to his as-if behaviour, Luke had to adapt his imagined world to the materials that were available in the art room, choosing carefully those which could best represent the 'proton pack' in his play. Once the choices had been made and the equipment assembled, Luke had to demonstrate further flexibility, treating the assemblage of cardboard and string as a symbol for the 'proton pack' and then as a means of him taking on the role of a Ghostbuster.

Remembering the pedagogic purposes to which play is directed in drama, flexibility is also evident in the way that curriculum content is incorporated (Duffy, 2014). For example, in order to create a coherent drama about smugglers, children need to know something about the history of smuggling. Opportunities for relevant knowledge to be included in the drama, then, need to feature both in prior planning and in the drama as it is structured from moment to moment.

Finally, in drama, children need to be sufficiently flexible to react to circumstances as they arise, responding to the initial stimulus, the space in which the drama occurs, and - most significantly - the dramatic play of other people and the unfolding of events.

Having discussed the close relationship between play and drama, we will go on to consider the artistic nature of dramatic play following the reflection below.

REFLECTION

What do you understand by the phrases 'talking as if ...' and 'behaving as if ...'?

When you listen to children talking, to each other or to adults, are you aware of how they shift roles as they talk? Sometimes you can hear children imitating another person, whether a character in a favourite TV programme or a real person in their lives. This as-if behaviour is most obvious when young children are role-playing or manipulating small-world figures (or puppets), but it is also integrated into the everyday conversations of children and adults alike.

Drama and art: crafting play

Defining drama education within 'the arts' can seem quite a challenge. By adding the word 'crafted' to Edmiston's (2007) definition of drama, so that it becomes 'crafted pretend play for curricular ends', we can put choice and innovation at the centre of dramatic activity. By recognising the importance of crafting play in drama, its artistic nature is revealed, and we can establish a clear alignment with both Boyd's (2009) definition of art as 'cognitive play with pattern' (p15) and Craft's (2002) recognition of choice as a core element of creativity (p44).

The extent to which classroom drama activities are crafted varies. In his Ghostbuster imaginative play, for example, we can see how Luke made choices not only in constructing the 'proton pack', but also in the spontaneous acting out of the character to match his perceptions of the role of a Ghostbuster. Although this role was being crafted in the moment, we can see how Luke will have rejected some options (redundancy) and adapted his behaviour (flexibility) in response to the context – not least the layout of my classroom. At the other end of the spectrum, a school play goes through a rehearsal process in which choices are explored and elements are discarded and adapted to create the maximum impact for an audience. This, then, is how (in Boyd's terms), we 'play with pattern' in drama, making choices that create 'powerful and imaginary worlds' (Grainger, 2003, p45) which are coherent for both the participants and the audience (if the drama leads to a performance). This naturally leads us to consider how focusing on the process of drama shapes very different learning outcomes than a focus on drama as a product (performance).

The debate over whether we should focus on process or product was at the heart of conflicting visions of drama education when I started my teaching career in the early 1990s. Fortunately, these arguments are now more nuanced, with a broad recognition that drama activities contain aspects of both process and product. This means that decisions on how to frame drama, as well as whether we should emphasise process or product, are determined by the learning we intend to come out of planned activities.

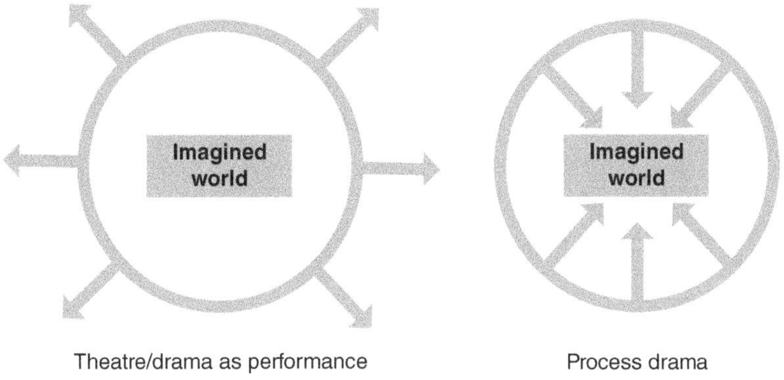

Figure 13.1 Drama worlds

When drama leads to an end product, children direct their as-if behaviours out from the imagined world and towards an audience (see Figure 13.1), as in theatre, and such a performance-based approach is a common feature of curriculum-focused drama (in addition to the school play). In activities where children create and present pieces of drama to each other, such as an episode from a children's book, the teaching points and criteria for assessment might concentrate on aspects of the performance (e.g. voice, language, gesture, use of space). However, we also need to consider what other learning could take place, as well as whether the outcome should be focused and assessed on performance skills alone.

Grainger (2003) suggests that drama 'enables speculation, modification and transformation of our understandings' (p45), and this focus on learning is at the core of drama education. While it is sometimes appropriate to concentrate on modifying or transforming children's understanding of their own performance skills (see the second case study below), learning will usually be more centred on what the performance reveals about the subject of the drama, whether that is a text, image or theme, and this focus should be reflected in the initial stimulus and the organisation of the task, as well as feedback on the task. This is not to say that performance skills are unimportant. It is through children's authentic engagement as 'emotional and bodily creatures' (DeCoursey, 2019, p3) that new meanings are made for them as performers and for their audience, and this bodily nature is reflected in their movement, posture, voice and breath as they perform. Whatever the learning intention of the performance, however, it is vital for the teacher to make space for reflection by both performers (on the crafting process by which choices were made) and audience (on the final product), and it is through such dialogic reflection that questions can be prompted, minds changed and understanding developed.

While performance-focused drama is turned outwards, representing the imagined world to an audience, process drama is turned inwards and remains within the imagined world itself (see Figure 13.1). Process drama, then, is focused on the actual experience of as-if behaviour during the activity, and without reference to theatrical merit. Rather than being confined to rehearsals, as in performance-oriented drama, flexibility is demanded of the children throughout process drama activities. Such flexibility towards role, action, space and objects is essential as the drama is enacted in the moment – as when Luke, while in-role as a Ghostbuster, was able to navigate the obstacles of my classroom by incorporating them into his imaginary play. This in-the-moment crafting is also evident in the way that children make choices between a range of possible as-if behaviours (redundancy). However, these principles of flexibility and redundancy also come into play as dramatic activities are repeated and adapted in order to explore ideas fully.

The need for reflection is as important in process drama as performance-oriented drama. During a process drama activity, each child is focused on responding within the imagined world. By encouraging children to reflect, we offer them an opportunity to review events within the drama with a fresh eye. This changes the in-role responses of children and helps them to understand the drama in a deeper way.

Drama in and across the curriculum

With the publication of the national curriculum in 2013, drama was reduced to a single paragraph within English. However, it is possible to take advantage of such minimal guidance. Although according to the national curriculum it is mandatory for children to experience drama, the lack of detail in the guidance opens a space for teachers to apply drama pedagogy wherever they see it as appropriate to children's learning. In addition, it is important to stress that the as-if behaviour of drama can be applied across the curriculum, just as any other aspect of literacy. Drama provides a valuable pedagogic tool in any subject-specific learning that would benefit from the embodied exploration of alternative perspectives, unfamiliar places or other times.

In the EYFS, the term 'role play' is used rather than 'drama', and this features in the areas of communication and language as well as expressive arts and design (this is the case for both the 2019 document and the proposed reforms of 2020). We have already discussed the relationship between drama education and imaginative play. The centrality of play within early years practice means that as-if behaviours are a natural part of children's being and learning. However, this does not mean that activities which exploit the learning potential of as-if behaviour should not be planned, including the set-up of role-play areas. One of the most significant drama-based approaches currently used in the early years is the 'helicopter technique', based on the work of early years teacher and researcher Vivian Gussin Paley (see **https://helicopterstories.co.uk**), in which children act out the stories that they have created alongside the teacher (see also Lee, 2015).

Learning and drama

While drama may be engaging and fun for some – though not all – children, teachers need to connect its use explicitly to children's learning. There is evidence that the strategic use of classroom drama can have a positive impact on children's writing (Cremin et al., 2006; Dobson and Stephenson, 2019), narrative understanding (Mages, 2006), vocabulary development (Cremin et al., 2013), mathematics (Erdo⊠an and Baran, 2009; Fleming, et al., 2004) and science (Branscombe, 2019), as well as contributing to an anti-bullying culture (O'Toole and Burton, 2005).

The common thread in these findings is the benefit of the experiential nature of drama pedagogy. In drama, rather than children being treated as 'disembodied thinking machines' (DeCoursey, 2019, p3), the whole child is engaged in the learning process – cognitively, emotionally, physically and socially. Such an immersive form of learning allows connections to be made in response to a range of curriculum-related stimuli, or 'pre-texts' (O'Neill, 1995), in ways that are not accessible in other learning approaches. The holistic engagement encouraged in drama may also explain its motivational force. This enables many children to commit themselves wholeheartedly to the activities; and through techniques such as Dorothy Heathcote's Mantle of the Expert (Taylor, 2016), children can create coherent worlds in which they have agency to experiment, discover things for themselves and make choices – choices that can have an immediate effect in the imagined world.

There are numerous drama strategies that can be employed in the classroom, including:

- still image/tableau/freeze-frame (all three terms are used);
- visualisation;
- role play;
- teacher in-role;
- thought-tracking;
- hot-seating;
- Mantle of the Expert (Taylor, 2016);
- story drama, such as teacher-directed story-making (Daniel, 2012) or 'story whoosh' (Winston and Tandy, 2012);
- the 'helicopter technique' (see Lee, 2015);
- mime, in which the performer uses their physicality to create a world, rather than relying on props or sets – and which does not need to be silent;
- roll on the wall;
- conscience alley.

Guidance for each of these strategies can be found in drama books (such as those listed in the further reading section at the end of this chapter) or online; but in the two case studies below, I am going to explore how I have used the first four (still image, visualisation, role play and teacher-in-role) in my own teaching.

CASE STUDY: KEY STAGE 1 – UNDERSTANDING SETTING

The pretext for this drama lesson was the oral storytelling of a tale, set in Baghdad, from *The Arabian Nights* (Haddawy, 1995). Following the storytelling, we talked about Baghdad and what we would have seen in the city 700 years ago if we were able to visit it. This preparatory section of the teaching sequence provided both context and content that the children could blend with their own imagined worlds (Duffy, 2014).

(Continued)

(Continued)

The opening drama activity was a visualisation in which children were led to create mental images of a magic carpet ride. Lying on the hall floor, the children closed their eyes; I told them that they were lying on a carpet and described a magic carpet ride. I described how the children's carpets rose from the floor and flew out of the school windows, over land and sea, and through time to the Baghdad of 700 years ago. To ensure the immediacy of the narration, I used the present tense and the 'you' form of address throughout the visualisation (e.g. 'You can feel the warm wind on your face').

When the children 'arrived' in Baghdad, I took them on a walking tour of the city, going down streets and alleys, seeing buildings such as mosques and libraries, and pointing out gardens and people's homes - my descriptions developing the pretext for the drama. The children then explored in pairs, with one child acting as a guide for the other. When the drama had reached its natural end, when the children had exhausted ideas of where they could go and what they could see, we returned to the school on another (shorter) magic carpet ride. We then reflected on where we had been, what we had seen, and the things that surprised us.

My roles in this activity were to create an engaging visualisation of the magic carpet ride and a model of how to tour the city, as well as supporting the ongoing drama. The visualisation required a continuous narrative with sensory information that would stimulate the children's imaginations (which had implications for my own preparatory work). Once I had modelled touring the city, I shifted roles to be better placed to support the ongoing drama. Taking on the role of someone who was lost in the city meant that I handed expertise to the children. Encountering me in-role, the children could lead me to my destination(s), creating imaginary streets as they did so, and apologising as they took wrong turns. This use of teacher in-role enabled me to interact in particular with those children who were struggling to maintain the role play, without dominating them and their responses.

CASE STUDY: YEAR 5 – DEVELOPING UNDERSTANDING OF AND CONFIDENCE IN EXPRESSING SHAKESPEARE'S LANGUAGE

In this drama workshop (which was part of a two-week project on *Macbeth*), children worked in groups of between four and six. Prior to this, they had taken part in an interactive storytelling performance of the play and discussed the themes of the story.

Each group of children was given a card with a short extract of *Macbeth* in the original language, which they read out loud as a group rather than in individual parts. They were given the chance to discuss the meaning of unfamiliar words or ask for help, and then chose the most important word or phrase in the extract. From this, they created a still image to represent their chosen word or phrase.

The strategy of still image is very flexible and can be used to represent moments in a narrative, ideas, relationships, or even scientific processes (Branscombe, 2019). In this workshop, the still images had an abstract quality as the children were led to create three-dimensional shapes or sculptures that represented their word or phrase, rather than specific characters in a scene. The group with an extract from Lady Macbeth's 'Out damned spot' speech, for example, chose the word 'blood', and created a fluid tableau of spilling blood.

While holding their positions in their still images, the children then verbalised their word or phrase, paying attention to their expression, connecting body and voice. The final step, before showing their piece, was for each group to bring their still image to life for as long as it took to say their word or phrase. Once the children had crafted their movement pieces, they created a whole-class performance, journeying through the story of *Macbeth* through these moving sculptures.

The children assessed themselves on primarily performance-related elements, such as voice, expression, and physicality and movement; but through reflective dialogue, these were explicitly linked to the children's understanding and interpretation of the text.

DEEP DIVE

Intent

How are you using drama to allow children to imaginatively explore the curriculum?

Implementation

Map opportunities across the curriculum where behaving 'as if' would allow children to explore alternative perspectives on curriculum content.

Impact

Consider whether children are able to evaluate curriculum content through taking different points of view.

CHAPTER SUMMARY

This chapter has focused on the relationship between the essential 'as-if-ness' of dramatic play and educational drama. While the playful nature of drama demands planned opportunities for children to demonstrate flexibility in their responses, it also depends on them not fearing the quirkiness of behaving as if they are someone else, somewhere else or somewhen else. Finally, we have recognised that in Edmiston's (2007) terms, this 'use of pretend play for curricular ends' (p338) needs to be crafted, and that children need opportunities to shape and then reflect upon their drama by adapting and discarding redundant content to better reflect the intended learning.

Further reading

Baldwin, P. (2004) *With Drama in Mind.* London: Continuum.

Barrs, M., Barton, B. and Booth, D. (2012) *This Book Is Not About Drama ... It's About New Ways to Inspire Students.* Markham, ON: Pembroke.

Johnson, C. (2018) Dynamic talk: speaking, listening and learning through drama. In D. Jones and P. Hodson (eds), *Unlocking Speaking Listening*, 3rd edition. London: Routledge, pp47–57.

Lee, T. (2015) *Princesses, Dragons and Helicopter Stories: Storytelling and Story Acting in the Early Years.* London: Routledge.

APPENDIX: LINKS TO THE ITT CORE CONTENT FRAMEWORK

Chapter 1: What is learning in the arts?

TS1 Set high expectations which inspire, motivate and challenge pupils
Learn that ... 1. Teachers have the ability to affect and improve the wellbeing, motivation and behaviour of their pupils. 5. A culture of mutual trust and respect supports effective relationships.
Learn how to ... **Communicate a belief in the academic potential of all pupils [...]** **And - following expert input - by taking opportunities to practise, receive feedback and improve at:** • *Creating a positive environment where making mistakes and learning from them and the need for effort and perseverance are part of the daily routine.*
TS3 Demonstrate good subject and curriculum knowledge
Learn that ... 1. A school's curriculum enables it to set out its vision for the knowledge, skills and values that its pupils will learn, encompassing the national curriculum within a coherent wider vision for successful learning. 5. Explicitly teaching pupils the knowledge and skills they need to succeed within particular subject areas is beneficial.
Learn how to ... **Deliver a carefully sequenced and coherent curriculum [...]** **And - following expert input - by taking opportunities to practise, receive feedback and improve at:** • *Providing opportunity for all pupils to learn and master essential concepts, knowledge, skills and principles of the subject.* **Help pupils apply knowledge and skills to other contexts [...]** **And - following expert input - by taking opportunities to practise, receive feedback and improve at:** • *Ensuring pupils have relevant domain-specific knowledge, especially when being asked to think critically within a subject.*

(Continued)

(Continued)

TS5 Adapt teaching to respond to the strengths and needs of all pupils

Learn that ...
1. Pupils are likely to learn at different rates and to require different levels and types of support from teachers to succeed.
2. Seeking to understand pupils' differences, including their different levels of prior knowledge and potential barriers to learning, is an essential part of teaching.

Learn how to ...
Provide opportunity for all pupils to experience success, by:

- *Observing how expert colleagues adapt lessons, whilst maintaining high expectations for all, so that all pupils have the opportunity to meet expectations and deconstructing this approach.*

Meet individual needs without creating unnecessary workload [...]
And - following expert input - by taking opportunities to practise, receive feedback and improve at:

- *Making use of well-designed resources (e.g. textbooks).*
- *Planning to connect new content with pupils' existing knowledge or providing additional pre-teaching if pupils lack critical knowledge.*
- *Building in additional practice or removing unnecessary expositions.*
- *Reframing questions to provide greater scaffolding or greater stretch.*

Chapter 2: The arts and education for sustainable development

TS1 Set high expectations which inspire, motivate and challenge pupils

Learn that ...
1. Teachers have the ability to affect and improve the wellbeing, motivation and behaviour of their pupils.

Learn how to ...
Communicate a belief in the academic potential of all pupils [...]
And - following expert input - by taking opportunities to practise, receive feedback and improve at:

- *Using intentional and consistent language that promotes challenge and aspiration.*
- *Creating a positive environment where making mistakes and learning from them and the need for effort and perseverance are part of the daily routine.*

TS3 Demonstrate good subject and curriculum knowledge

Learn that ...
1. A school's curriculum enables it to set out its vision for the knowledge, skills and values that its pupils will learn, encompassing the national curriculum within a coherent wider vision for successful learning.

Learn how to ...
Deliver a carefully sequenced and coherent curriculum [...]
And - following expert input - by taking opportunities to practise, receive feedback and improve at:

- *Working with expert colleagues to accumulate and refine a collection of powerful analogies, illustrations, examples, explanations and demonstrations.*

Support pupils to build increasingly complex mental models, by:

- *Discussing and analysing with expert colleagues how to revisit the big ideas of the subject over time and teach key concepts through a range of examples.*

Chapter 3: An eye on the past: curious explorations into 'the other'

TS3 Demonstrate good subject and curriculum knowledge

Learn that ...
1. A school's curriculum enables it to set out its vision for the knowledge, skills and values that its pupils will learn, encompassing the national curriculum within a coherent wider vision for successful learning.

Learn how to ...
Deliver a carefully sequenced and coherent curriculum [...]
And - following expert input - by taking opportunities to practise, receive feedback and improve at:

- *Providing opportunity for all pupils to learn and master essential concepts, knowledge, skills and principles of the subject.*
- *Working with expert colleagues to accumulate and refine a collection of powerful analogies, illustrations, examples, explanations and demonstrations.*

Support pupils to build increasingly complex mental models, by:

- *Discussing and analysing with expert colleagues how to revisit the big ideas of the subject over time and teach key concepts through a range of examples.*

TS4 Plan and teach well structured lessons

Learn that ...
2. Effective teachers introduce new material in steps, explicitly linking new ideas to what has been previously studied and learned.
3. Modelling helps pupils understand new processes and ideas; good models make abstract ideas concrete and accessible.

Learn how to ...
Plan effective lessons [...]
And - following expert input - by taking opportunities to practise, receive feedback and improve at:

- *Using modelling, explanations and scaffolds, acknowledging that novices need more structure early in a domain.*
- *Enabling critical thinking and problem solving by first teaching the necessary foundational content knowledge.*

Make good use of expositions, by:

- *Discussing and analysing with expert colleagues how to use concrete representation of abstract ideas (e.g. making use of analogies, metaphors, examples and non-examples).*

TS6 make accurate and effective use of assessment

Learn that ...
1. Effective assessment is critical to teaching because it provides teachers with information about pupils' understanding and needs.

Learn how to ...
Avoid common assessment pitfalls, by:

- *Discussing and analysing with expert colleagues how to plan formative assessment tasks linked to lesson objectives and think ahead about what would indicate understanding (e.g. by using hinge questions to pinpoint knowledge gaps).*

Chapter 4: Art as a way of learning across the curriculum

TS1 Set high expectations which inspire, motivate and challenge pupils

Learn that ...
2. Teachers are key role models, who can influence the attitudes, values and behaviours of their pupils.
3. Teacher expectations can affect pupil outcomes; setting goals that challenge and stretch pupils is essential.

(Continued)

(Continued)

TS1 Set high expectations which inspire, motivate and challenge pupils

Learn how to ...
Communicate a belief in the academic potential of all pupils, by:

- *Receiving clear, consistent and effective mentoring and how to set tasks that stretch pupils, but which are achievable, within a challenging curriculum.*

And - following expert input - by taking opportunities to practise, receive feedback and improve at:

- *Creating a positive environment where making mistakes and learning from them and the need for effort and perseverance are part of the daily routine.*

TS4 Plan and teach well structured lessons

Learn that ...
3. Modelling helps pupils understand new processes and ideas; good models make abstract ideas concrete and accessible.

Learn how to ...
Plan effective lessons [...]
And - following expert input - by taking opportunities to practise, receive feedback and improve at:

- *Enabling critical thinking and problem solving by first teaching the necessary foundational content knowledge.*

Chapter 5: Storytelling: the social art of language

TS1 Set high expectations which inspire, motivate and challenge pupils

Learn that ...
1. Teachers have the ability to affect and improve the wellbeing, motivation and behaviour of their pupils.
5. A culture of mutual trust and respect supports effective relationships.

Learn how to ...
Communicate a belief in the academic potential of all pupils [...]
And - following expert input - by taking opportunities to practise, receive feedback and improve at:

- *Creating a positive environment where making mistakes and learning from them and the need for effort and perseverance are part of the daily routine.*

Demonstrate consistently high behavioural expectations, by:

- *Receiving clear, consistent and effective mentoring in how to create a culture of respect and trust in the classroom that supports all pupils to succeed (e.g. by modelling the types of courteous behaviour expected of pupils).*

TS3 Demonstrate good subject and curriculum knowledge

Learn that ...
1. A school's curriculum enables it to set out its vision for the knowledge, skills and values that its pupils will learn, encompassing the national curriculum within a coherent wider vision for successful learning.
10. Every teacher can improve pupils' literacy, including by explicitly teaching reading, writing and oral language skills specific to individual disciplines.

Learn how to ...
Develop pupils' literacy [...]
And - following expert input - by taking opportunities to practise, receive feedback and improve at:

- *Modelling and requiring high-quality oral language, recognising that spoken language underpins the development of reading and writing (e.g. requiring pupils to respond to questions in full sentences, making use of relevant technical vocabulary).*

TS4 Plan and teach well structured lessons

Learn that ...
6. Questioning is an essential tool for teachers; questions can be used for many purposes, including to check pupils' prior knowledge, assess understanding and break down problems.
7. High-quality classroom talk can support pupils to articulate key ideas, consolidate understanding and extend their vocabulary.

Learn how to ...
Plan effective lessons [...]
And - following expert input - by taking opportunities to practise, receive feedback and improve at:

- *Using modelling, explanations and scaffolds, acknowledging that novices need more structure early in a domain.*
- *Enabling critical thinking and problem solving by first teaching the necessary foundational content knowledge.*

Stimulate pupil thinking and check for understanding [...]
And - following expert input - by taking opportunities to practise, receive feedback and improve at:

- *Planning activities around what you want pupils to think hard about.*
- *Including a range of types of questions in class discussions to extend and challenge pupils (e.g. by modelling new vocabulary or asking pupils to justify answers).*

Chapter 6: Music everywhere and every day

TS1 Set high expectations which inspire, motivate and challenge pupils

Learn that ...
3. Teacher expectations can affect pupil outcomes; setting goals that challenge and stretch pupils is essential.
4. Setting clear expectations can help communicate shared values that improve classroom and school culture.

Learn how to ...
Communicate a belief in the academic potential of all pupils [...]
And - following expert input - by taking opportunities to practise, receive feedback and improve at:

- *Using intentional and consistent language that promotes challenge and aspiration.*
- *Creating a positive environment where making mistakes and learning from them and the need for effort and perseverance are part of the daily routine.*

Demonstrate consistently high behavioural expectations [...]
And - following expert input - by taking opportunities to practise, receive feedback and improve at:

- *Teaching and rigorously maintaining clear behavioural expectations (e.g. for contributions, volume level and concentration).*
- *Acknowledging and praising pupil effort and emphasising progress being made.*

TS2 Promote good progress and outcomes by pupils

Learn that ...
1. Learning involves a lasting change in pupils' capabilities or understanding.
2. Prior knowledge plays an important role in how pupils learn; committing some key facts to their long-term memory is likely to help pupils learn more complex ideas.
6. Where prior knowledge is weak, pupils are more likely to develop misconceptions, particularly if new ideas are introduced too quickly.
7. Regular purposeful practice of what has previously been taught can help consolidate material and help pupils remember what they have learned.

(Continued)

(Continued)

TS2 Promote good progress and outcomes by pupils

8. Requiring pupils to retrieve information from memory, and spacing practice so that pupils revisit ideas after a gap are also likely to strengthen recall.
9. Worked examples that take pupils through each step of a new process are also likely to support pupils to learn.

Learn how to ...
Avoid overloading working memory [...]
And - following expert input - by taking opportunities to practise, receive feedback and improve at:

- *Breaking complex material into smaller steps (e.g. using partially completed examples to focus pupils on the specific steps).*

Build on pupils' prior knowledge [...]
And - following expert input - by taking opportunities to practise, receive feedback and improve at:

- *Encouraging pupils to share emerging understanding and points of confusion so that misconceptions can be addressed.*

Increase likelihood of material being retained [...]
And - following expert input - by taking opportunities to practise, receive feedback and improve at:

- *Balancing exposition, repetition, practice and retrieval of critical knowledge and skills.*
- *Increasing challenge with practice and retrieval as knowledge becomes more secure (e.g. by removing scaffolding, lengthening spacing or introducing interacting elements).*

TS4 Plan and teach well structured lessons

Learn that ...
3. Modelling helps pupils understand new processes and ideas; good models make abstract ideas concrete and accessible.
4. Guides, scaffolds and worked examples can help pupils apply new ideas, but should be gradually removed as pupil expertise increases.
6. Questioning is an essential tool for teachers; questions can be used for many purposes, including to check pupils' prior knowledge, assess understanding and break down problems.

Learn how to ...
Plan effective lessons, by:

- *Observing how expert colleagues break tasks down into constituent components when first setting up independent practice (e.g. using tasks that scaffold pupils through meta-cognitive and procedural processes) and deconstructing this approach.*

And - following expert input - by taking opportunities to practise, receive feedback and improve at:

- *Using modelling, explanations and scaffolds, acknowledging that novices need more structure early in a domain.*
- *Enabling critical thinking and problem solving by first teaching the necessary foundational content knowledge.*
- *Removing scaffolding only when pupils are achieving a high degree of success in applying previously taught material.*
- *Providing sufficient opportunity for pupils to consolidate and practise applying new knowledge and skills.*

Chapter 7: Science and the arts - closer than you think

TS2 Promote good progress and outcomes by pupils

Learn that ...
1. Learning involves a lasting change in pupils' capabilities or understanding.
2. Prior knowledge plays an important role in how pupils learn; committing some key facts to their long-term memory is likely to help pupils learn more complex ideas.

TS2 Promote good progress and outcomes by pupils

Learn how to ...
Avoid overloading working memory, by:

- *Receiving clear, consistent and effective mentoring in how to take into account pupils' prior knowledge when planning how much new information to introduce.*

TS3 Demonstrate good subject and curriculum knowledge

Learn that ...
2. Secure subject knowledge helps teachers to motivate pupils and teach effectively.
3. Ensuring pupils master foundational concepts and knowledge before moving on is likely to build pupils' confidence and help them succeed.
4. Anticipating common misconceptions within particular subjects is also an important aspect of curricular knowledge; working closely with colleagues to develop an understanding of likely misconceptions is valuable.

Learn how to ...
Deliver a carefully sequenced and coherent curriculum, by:

- *Receiving clear, consistent and effective mentoring in how to identify essential concepts, knowledge, skills and principles of the subject.*
- *Observing how expert colleagues ensure pupils' thinking is focused on key ideas within the subject and deconstructing this approach.*
- *Discussing and analysing with expert colleagues the rationale for curriculum choices, the process for arriving at current curriculum choices and how the school's curriculum materials inform lesson preparation.*

TS4 Plan and teach well structured lessons

Learn that ...
1. Effective teaching can transform pupils' knowledge, capabilities and beliefs about learning.

Learn how to ...
Plan effective lessons, by:

- *Observing how expert colleagues break tasks down into constituent components when first setting up independent practice (e.g. using tasks that scaffold pupils through meta-cognitive and procedural processes) and deconstructing this approach.*

Chapter 8: Poetry – the art of expression

TS1 Set high expectations which inspire, motivate and challenge pupils

Learn that ...
3. Teacher expectations can affect pupil outcomes; setting goals that challenge and stretch pupils is essential.
6. High-quality teaching has a long-term positive effect on pupils' life chances, particularly for children from disadvantaged backgrounds.

Learn how to ...
Communicate a belief in the academic potential of all pupils, by:

- *Receiving clear, consistent and effective mentoring in how to set tasks that stretch pupils, but which are achievable, within a challenging curriculum.*

And – following expert input – by taking opportunities to practise, receive feedback and improve at:

- *Creating a positive environment where making mistakes and learning from them and the need for effort and perseverance are part of the daily routine.*

(Continued)

(Continued)

TS3 Demonstrate good subject and curriculum knowledge
Learn that ... 2. Secure subject knowledge helps teachers to motivate pupils and teach effectively. 5. Explicitly teaching pupils the knowledge and skills they need to succeed within particular subject areas is beneficial. 10. Every teacher can improve pupils' literacy, including by explicitly teaching reading, writing and oral language skills specific to individual disciplines.
Learn how to ... **Deliver a carefully sequenced and coherent curriculum, by:** • *Receiving clear, consistent and effective mentoring in how to promote reading for pleasure.* **Develop pupils' literacy, by:** • *Discussing and analysing with expert colleagues how to teach different forms of writing by modelling planning, drafting and editing.* **And - following expert input - by taking opportunities to practise, receive feedback and improve at:** • *Modelling and requiring high-quality oral language, recognising that spoken language underpins the development of reading and writing (e.g. requiring pupils to respond to questions in full sentences, making use of relevant technical vocabulary).*
TS4 Plan and teach well structured lessons
Learn that ... 3. Modelling helps pupils understand new processes and ideas; good models make abstract ideas concrete and accessible. 4. Guides, scaffolds and worked examples can help pupils apply new ideas, but should be gradually removed as pupil expertise increases. 7. High-quality classroom talk can support pupils to articulate key ideas, consolidate understanding and extend their vocabulary.
Learn how to ... **Plan effective lessons [...]** **And - following expert input - by taking opportunities to practise, receive feedback and improve at:** • *Using modelling, explanations and scaffolds, acknowledging that novices need more structure early in a domain.* • *Removing scaffolding only when pupils are achieving a high degree of success in applying previously taught material.* **Model effectively [...]** **And - following expert input - by taking opportunities to practise, receive feedback and improve at:** • *Narrating thought processes when modelling to make explicit how experts think (e.g. asking questions aloud that pupils should consider when working independently and drawing pupils' attention to links with prior knowledge).* **Stimulate pupil thinking and check for understanding [...]** **And - following expert input - by taking opportunities to practise, receive feedback and improve at:** • *Planning activities around what you want pupils to think hard about.*

Chapter 9: Digital media and primary computing

TS1 Set high expectations which inspire, motivate and challenge pupils
Learn that ... 3. Teacher expectations can affect pupil outcomes; setting goals that challenge and stretch pupils is essential. 6. High-quality teaching has a long-term positive effect on pupils' life chances, particularly for children from disadvantaged backgrounds.

TS1 Set high expectations which inspire, motivate and challenge pupils

Learn how to ...
Communicate a belief in the academic potential of all pupils, by:

- *Receiving clear, consistent and effective mentoring in how to set tasks that stretch pupils, but which are achievable, within a challenging curriculum.*

And - following expert input - by taking opportunities to practise, receive feedback and improve at:

- *Seeking opportunities to engage parents and carers in the education of their children (e.g. proactively highlighting successes) with support from expert colleagues to understand how this engagement changes depending on the age and development stage of the pupil.*

TS3 Demonstrate good subject and curriculum knowledge

Learn that ...
2. Secure subject knowledge helps teachers to motivate pupils and teach effectively.
3. Ensuring pupils master foundational concepts and knowledge before moving on is likely to build pupils' confidence and help them succeed.
4. Anticipating common misconceptions within particular subjects is also an important aspect of curricular knowledge; working closely with colleagues to develop an understanding of likely misconceptions is valuable.

Learn how to ...
Deliver a carefully sequenced and coherent curriculum, by:

- *Receiving clear, consistent and effective mentoring in how to identify essential concepts, knowledge, skills and principles of the subject.*
- *Observing how expert colleagues ensure pupils' thinking is focused on key ideas within the subject and deconstructing this approach.*
- *Discussing and analysing with expert colleagues the rationale for curriculum choices, the process for arriving at current curriculum choices and how the school's curriculum materials inform lesson preparation.*

TS4 Plan and teach well structured lessons

Learn that ...
1. Effective teaching can transform pupils' knowledge, capabilities and beliefs about learning.
6. Questioning is an essential tool for teachers; questions can be used for many purposes, including to check pupils' prior knowledge, assess understanding and break down problems.
7. High-quality classroom talk can support pupils to articulate key ideas, consolidate understanding and extend their vocabulary.

Learn how to ...
Plan effective lessons, by:

- *Observing how expert colleagues break tasks down into constituent components when first setting up independent practice (e.g. using tasks that scaffold pupils through meta-cognitive and procedural processes) and deconstructing this approach.*

And - following expert input - by taking opportunities to practise, receive feedback and improve at:

- *Using modelling, explanations and scaffolds, acknowledging that novices need more structure early in a domain.*
- *Enabling critical thinking and problem solving by first teaching the necessary foundational content knowledge.*

Stimulate pupil thinking and check for understanding [...]
And - following expert input - by taking opportunities to practise, receive feedback and improve at:

- *Planning activities around what you want pupils to think hard about.*
- *Including a range of types of questions in class discussions to extend and challenge pupils (e.g. by modelling new vocabulary or asking pupils to justify answers).*

Chapter 10: Dance: the art of movement

TS3 Demonstrate good subject and curriculum knowledge

Learn that ...
2. Secure subject knowledge helps teachers to motivate pupils and teach effectively.
3. Ensuring pupils master foundational concepts and knowledge before moving on is likely to build pupils' confidence and help them succeed.
4. Anticipating common misconceptions within particular subjects is also an important aspect of curricular knowledge; working closely with colleagues to develop an understanding of likely misconceptions is valuable.
5. Explicitly teaching pupils the knowledge and skills they need to succeed within particular subject areas is beneficial.

Learn how to:
Deliver a carefully sequenced and coherent curriculum, by:

- *Receiving clear, consistent and effective mentoring in how to identify essential concepts, knowledge, skills and principles of the subject.*

And - following expert input - by taking opportunities to practise, receive feedback and improve at:

- *Being aware of common misconceptions and discussing with expert colleagues how to help pupils master important concepts.*

Support pupils to build increasingly complex mental models [...]
And - following expert input - by taking opportunities to practise, receive feedback and improve at:

- *Drawing explicit links between new content and the core concepts and principles in the subject.*

Develop fluency [...]
And - following expert input - by taking opportunities to practise, receive feedback and improve at:

- *Providing tasks that support pupils to learn key ideas securely (e.g. quizzing pupils so they develop fluency with times tables).*

TS4 Plan and teach well structured lessons

Learn that ...
1. Effective teaching can transform pupils' knowledge, capabilities and beliefs about learning.
2. Effective teachers introduce new material in steps, explicitly linking new ideas to what has been previously studied and learned.
4. Guides, scaffolds and worked examples can help pupils apply new ideas, but should be gradually removed as pupil expertise increases.

Learn how to ...
Make good use of expositions [...]
And - following expert input - by taking opportunities to practise, receive feedback and improve at:

- *Starting expositions at the point of current pupil understanding.*
- *Combining a verbal explanation with a relevant graphical representation of the same concept or process, where appropriate.*

Stimulate pupil thinking and check for understanding [...]
And - following expert input - by taking opportunities to practise, receive feedback and improve at:

- *Planning activities around what you want pupils to think hard about.*

TS7 Manage behaviour effectively

Learn that ...
3. The ability to self-regulate one's emotions affects pupils' ability to learn, success in school and future lives.
4. Teachers can influence pupils' resilience and beliefs about their ability to succeed, by ensuring all pupils have the opportunity to experience meaningful success.
5. Building effective relationships is easier when pupils believe that their feelings will be considered and understood.
7. Pupils' investment in learning is also driven by their prior experiences and perceptions of success and failure.

Learn how to ...
Develop a positive, predictable and safe environment for pupils [...]
And - following expert input - by taking opportunities to practise, receive feedback and improve at:

- *Establishing a supportive and inclusive environment with a predictable system of reward and sanction in the classroom.*
- *Giving manageable, specific and sequential instructions.*
- *Checking pupils' understanding of instructions before a task begins.*
- *Using consistent language and non-verbal signals for common classroom directions.*

Chapter 11: The arts and mathematics

TS1 Set high expectations which inspire, motivate and challenge pupils

Learn that ...
1. Teachers have the ability to affect and improve the wellbeing, motivation and behaviour of their pupils.
5. A culture of mutual trust and respect supports effective relationships.
6. High-quality teaching has a long-term positive effect on pupils' life chances, particularly for children from disadvantaged backgrounds.

Learn how to ...
Communicate a belief in the academic potential of all pupils [...]
And - following expert input - by taking opportunities to practise, receive feedback and improve at:

- *Creating a positive environment where making mistakes and learning from them and the need for effort and perseverance are part of the daily routine.*
- *Seeking opportunities to engage parents and carers in the education of their children (e.g. proactively highlighting successes) with support from expert colleagues to understand how this engagement changes depending on the age and development stage of the pupil.*

TS3 Demonstrate good subject and curriculum knowledge

Learn that ...
1. A school's curriculum enables it to set out its vision for the knowledge, skills and values that its pupils will learn, encompassing the national curriculum within a coherent wider vision for successful learning.
5. Explicitly teaching pupils the knowledge and skills they need to succeed within particular subject areas is beneficial.

(Continued)

(Continued)

TS3 Demonstrate good subject and curriculum knowledge

Learn how to ...
Deliver a carefully sequenced and coherent curriculum [...]
And - following expert input - by taking opportunities to practise, receive feedback and improve at:

- *Providing opportunity for all pupils to learn and master essential concepts, knowledge, skills and principles of the subject.*

Help pupils apply knowledge and skills to other contexts [...]
And - following expert input - by taking opportunities to practise, receive feedback and improve at:

- *Ensuring pupils have relevant domain-specific knowledge, especially when being asked to think critically within a subject.*

TS4 Plan and teach well structured lessons

Learn that ...
1. Effective teaching can transform pupils' knowledge, capabilities and beliefs about learning.
2. Effective teachers introduce new material in steps, explicitly linking new ideas to what has been previously studied and learned.

Learn how to ...
Plan effective lessons, by:

- *Observing how expert colleagues break tasks down into constituent components when first setting up independent practice (e.g. using tasks that scaffold pupils through meta-cognitive and procedural processes) and deconstructing this approach.*

Model effectively, by:

- *Discussing and analysing with expert colleagues how to make the steps in a process memorable and ensuring pupils can recall them (e.g. naming them, developing mnemonics, or linking to memorable stories).*

Stimulate pupil thinking and check for understanding, by:

- *Discussing and analysing with expert colleagues how to consider the factors that will support effective collaborative or paired work (e.g. familiarity with routines, whether pupils have the necessary prior knowledge and how pupils are grouped).*
- *Receiving clear, consistent and effective mentoring in how to provide scaffolds for pupil talk to increase the focus and rigour of dialogue.*

Chapter 12: Writing as an art: engaging children in creative writing

TS1 Set high expectations which inspire, motivate and challenge pupils

Learn that ...
1. Teachers have the ability to affect and improve the wellbeing, motivation and behaviour of their pupils.
3. Teacher expectations can affect pupil outcomes; setting goals that challenge and stretch pupils is essential.

Learn how to ...
Communicate a belief in the academic potential of all pupils [...]
And - following expert input - by taking opportunities to practise, receive feedback and improve at:

- *Creating a positive environment where making mistakes and learning from them and the need for effort and perseverance are part of the daily routine.*

TS3 Demonstrate good subject and curriculum knowledge

Learn that ...
2. Secure subject knowledge helps teachers to motivate pupils and teach effectively.
10. Every teacher can improve pupils' literacy, including by explicitly teaching reading, writing and oral language skills specific to individual disciplines.

Learn how to ...
Deliver a carefully sequenced and coherent curriculum [...]
And - following expert input - by taking opportunities to practise, receive feedback and improve at:

- *Working with expert colleagues to accumulate and refine a collection of powerful analogies, illustrations, examples, explanations and demonstrations.*

Develop pupils' literacy [...]
And - following expert input - by taking opportunities to practise, receive feedback and improve at:

- *Modelling and requiring high-quality oral language, recognising that spoken language underpins the development of reading and writing (e.g. requiring pupils to respond to questions in full sentences, making use of relevant technical vocabulary).*

Chapter 13: Classroom drama: learning through as-if behaviour

TS1 Set high expectations which inspire, motivate and challenge pupils

Learn that ...
1. Teachers have the ability to affect and improve the wellbeing, motivation and behaviour of their pupils.
5. A culture of mutual trust and respect supports effective relationships.

Learn how to ...
Communicate a belief in the academic potential of all pupils [...]
And - following expert input - by taking opportunities to practise, receive feedback and improve at:

- *Creating a positive environment where making mistakes and learning from them and the need for effort and perseverance are part of the daily routine.*

Demonstrate consistently high behavioural expectations, by:

- *Receiving clear, consistent and effective mentoring in how to create a culture of respect and trust in the classroom that supports all pupils to succeed (e.g. by modelling the types of courteous behaviour expected of pupils).*

TS3 Demonstrate good subject and curriculum knowledge

Learn that ...
1. A school's curriculum enables it to set out its vision for the knowledge, skills and values that its pupils will learn, encompassing the national curriculum within a coherent wider vision for successful learning.
10. Every teacher can improve pupils' literacy, including by explicitly teaching reading, writing and oral language skills specific to individual disciplines.

Learn how to ...
Develop pupils' literacy [...]
And - following expert input - by taking opportunities to practise, receive feedback and improve at:

- *Modelling and requiring high-quality oral language, recognising that spoken language underpins the development of reading and writing (e.g. requiring pupils to respond to questions in full sentences, making use of relevant technical vocabulary).*

(Continued)

(Continued)

TS4 Plan and teach well structured lessons
Learn that ... 6. Questioning is an essential tool for teachers; questions can be used for many purposes, including to check pupils' prior knowledge, assess understanding and break down problems. 7. High-quality classroom talk can support pupils to articulate key ideas, consolidate understanding and extend their vocabulary.
Learn how to ... **Plan effective lessons [...]** **And - following expert input - by taking opportunities to practise, receive feedback and improve at:** • *Using modelling, explanations and scaffolds, acknowledging that novices need more structure early in a domain.* • *Enabling critical thinking and problem solving by first teaching the necessary foundational content knowledge.* **Stimulate pupil thinking and check for understanding [...]** **And - following expert input - by taking opportunities to practise, receive feedback and improve at:** • *Planning activities around what you want pupils to think hard about.* • *Including a range of types of questions in class discussions to extend and challenge pupils (e.g. by modelling new vocabulary or asking pupils to justify answers).*

Source: www.gov.uk/government/publications/initial-teacher-training-itt-core-content-framework

REFERENCES

Abrahams, I., Potterton, B., Fotou, N. and Constantinou, M. (2019) *Scientific literacy: who needs it in a 'black box' technological society?* In *New Perspectives in Science Education*, 21–22 March, Florence, Italy.

Agard, J. and Nichols, G. (2004) *From Mouth to Mouth: Oral Poems from Around the World*. London: Walker Books.

Alexander, R. (ed.) (2010) *Children, Their World and Education: Final Report and Recommendations of the Cambridge Primary Review*. London: Routledge.

Applebee, A.N. (1978) *The Child's Concept of Story: Ages Two to Seventeen*. Chicago, IL: University of Chicago Press.

Art in Action (2019) *5 Benefits of Arts Education for Child Development*. Available at: https://artinaction.org/5-benefits-of-arts-education-for-child-development/

Association of Teachers of Mathematics (ATM) (2020) *Cuisenaire Rods: Gattegno and Other Films*. Available at: www.atm.org.uk/Cuisenaire-Rods---Gattegno-and-other-films

Atkinson, D. (2010) Extended, embodied cognition and second language acquisition. *Applied Linguistics*, 31(5): 599–622.

Atwood, S. (2011) *Ruskin's Educational Ideals*. Aldershot: Ashgate.

Bachmeier, E.E. (2016) *Tessellations: An Artistic and Mathematical Look at the Work of Maurits Cornelis Escher*. Available at: https://scholarworks.uni.edu/cgi/viewcontent.cgi?article=1208&context=hpt

Barlow, A. and Whitehouse, S. (2019) *Mastering Primary Geography*. London: Bloomsbury.

Barnes, J. and Scoffham, S. (2017) The humanities in English primary schools: struggling to survive. *Education 3–13*, 45(3): 298–308.

Barrance, R. (2020) *The Right to Protest: A Children's Rights Perspective on the School Climate Strikes*. Available at: www.bera.ac.uk/blog/the-right-to-protest-a-childrens-rights-perspective-on-the-school-climate-strikes

Bates, V.C. (2019) Standing at the intersection of race and class in music education. *Action, Criticism, and Theory for Music Education*, 18(1): 117–60.

Bearne, E. and Wolstencroft, H. (2007) *Visual Approaches to Teaching Writing: Multimodal Literacy 5–11*. London: Paul Chapman Publishing.

Behrens, P. (2020) *The Best of Times, the Worst of Times: Futures from the Frontiers of Climate Science*. London: Indigo Press.

Benton, M. (1978) Poetry for children: a neglected art. *Children's Literature in Education*, 9(3): 111–26.

Bonnett, A. (2008) *What Is Geography?* London: SAGE.

Bonwell, C.C. and Eison, J.A. (1991) *Active Learning: Creating Excitement in the Classroom*. Washington, DC: Jossey-Bass.

Bourdieu, P. (1973) *Cultural Reproduction and Social Reproduction*. London: Tavistock.

Boyd, B. (2009) *On the Origin of Stories: Evolution, Cognition and Fiction*. Cambridge, MA: Belknap Press.

Bradley, L. and Bryant, P.E. (1983) Categorizing sounds and learning to read: a causal connection. *Nature*, 301: 419–21.

Branscombe, M.V. (2019) *Teaching Through Embodied Learning*. London: Routledge.

British Science Association (BSA) (2019) *Science and the Arts Section*. Available at: www.britishscienceassociation.org/science-and-the-arts-section

Bromley, H. (1999a) Having a go with the box (1). *Primary English Magazine*. Available at: https://ukla.org/wp-content/uploads/Having_a_go_with_the_box_1_Helen_Bromley.pdf

Bromley, H. (1999b) Having a go with the box (3). *Primary English Magazine*. Available at: https://ukla.org/wp-content/uploads/Having_a_go_with_the_box_3_Helen_Bromley.pdf

Brown, R. (1981) *A Dark, Dark Tale*. London: Andersen Press.

Brownlee, L., Hardy-Dawson, S. and Stevens, R. (2018) *Apes to Zebras: An A–Z of Shape Poems*. London: Bloomsbury.

Bruner, J.S. (1966) *Toward a Theory of Instruction*. Cambridge, MA: Harvard University Press.

Bruner, J.S. (2004) Life as narrative. *Social Research: An International Quarterly*, 71(3): 691–710.

Bull, A. (2019) *Class, Control, and Classical Music*. Oxford: Oxford University Press.

Butterworth, L. (2020) *Spin, Weave, Stitch*. Available at: www.artandeducation.co.uk/values-for-art-education

Buttriss, J. and Callander, A. (2008) *A–Z of Special Needs for Every Teacher*, 2nd edition. Kent: Optimus Education.

Carden, C. (ed.) (2019) *Primary Teaching: Learning and Teaching in Primary Schools Today*. London: SAGE/Learning Matters.

Chang, E., Lim, M. and Kim, M. (2012) Three approaches to teaching art methods courses: child art, visual culture, and issues-based art education. *Art Education*, 65(3): 17–24.

Chappell, K. (2007) Creativity in primary level dance education: moving beyond assumption. *Research in Dance Education*, 8(1): 27–52.

Coelho, J. (2020) *Poems Aloud: An Anthology of Poems to Read Out Loud*. London: Wide-Eyed Editions.

Collins, A., Vanderheide, R. and McKenna, L. (2014) Hearing, listening, action: enhancing nursing practice through aural awareness education. *Contemporary Nurse*, 47(1–2): 108–18.

Cook, E.T. and Wedderburn, A. (eds) (1903–1912) *The Complete Works of John Ruskin: The Library Edition in 39 Volumes*. London: George Allen.

Cooper, B. (2018) *Primary Colours: The Decline of Arts Education in Primary Schools and How It Can Be Reversed*. London: Fabian Society.

Cooper, H. (1992) *The Teaching of History*. London: David Fulton.

Cooper, H. (2018) *History 5–11*. London: Routledge.

Cooper, H., Asquith, S. and Rowley, C. (eds) (2006) *Geography 3–11*. London: Routledge.

Copus, J. (2015) *The Hog, the Shrew and the Hullabaloo*. London: Faber & Faber.

Corbett, P. (2018). *Jumpstart! Poetry: Games and Activities for Ages 7–12*. London: Routledge.

Corbett, P. and Strong, J. (2020) *Talk for Writing Across the Curriculum*, 2nd edition. London: Open University Press.

Craft, A. (2000) *Creativity Across the Primary Curriculum: Framing and Developing Practice*. London: Routledge.

Craft, A. (2002) *Creativity and Early Years Education: A Lifewide Foundation*. London: Continuum.

Cremin, T. (2015) Creatively engaging writers in the early primary years. In T. Cremin, D. Reedy, E. Bearne and H. Dombey (eds), *Teaching English Creatively*, 2nd edition. London: Routledge, pp67–83.

Cremin, T., Goouch, K., Blackmore, L., Goff, E. and Macdonald, R. (2006) Connecting drama and writing: seizing the moment to write. *Research in Drama Education*, 11(3): 273–91.

Cremin, T., Swann, J., Flewitt, R., Faulkner, D. and Kucirkova, N. (2013) *Evaluation Report of MakeBelieve Arts Helicopter Technique of Storytelling and Storyacting*. Available at: www.makebelievearts.co.uk/Helicopter

Csikszentmihalyi, M. (1990) The domain of creativity. In R.S. Albert and M.A. Runco (eds), *Theories of Creativity*. London: SAGE, pp190–212.

Cultural Learning Alliance (CLA) (2019) *The Arts for Every Child*. Available at: https://culturallearningalliance.org.uk/wp-content/uploads/2019/10/Arts-for-every-child-CLA-Social-justice-briefing.pdf

Daniel, A. (2012) *Storytelling Across the Primary Curriculum*. London: Routledge.

Daubney, A. (2017) *Teaching Primary Music*. London: SAGE.

Daubney, A., Spruce, G. and Annetts, D. (2019) *Music Education: State of the Nation*. Available at: www.ism.org/images/images/State-of-the-Nation-Music-Education-WEB.pdf

Davies, N. (2013) *The Promise*. London: Walker Books.

Dawood, Z. (2020) Inheritance and new ways of learning. In N. Gill (ed.), *SLAM! You're Gonna Wanna Hear This*. London: Macmillan Children's Books, p4.

Dawson, I. (2004) Time for chronology? Ideas for developing chronological understanding. *Teaching History*, 117: 14–24.

de Botton, A. (2002) *The Art of Travel*. London: Penguin.

Decolonizing the Music Room (n.d.) *Black Lives Matter Statement*. Available at: https://decolonizingthemusicroom.com

DeCoursey, M. (2019) *Embodied Aesthetics in Drama Education: Theatre Literature and Philosophy*. London: Bloomsbury.

Department for Culture, Media and Sport (DCMS) and National Dance Teachers Association (NDTA) (2005) *Dance Links: A Guide to Delivering High Quality Dance for Children and Young People*. London: DCMS/NDTA.

Department for Education (DfE) (2013a) *Music Programmes of Study: Key Stages 1 and 2*. Available at: https://assets.publishing.service.gov.uk/government/uploads/system/uploads/attachment_data/file/239037/PRIMARY_national_curriculum_-_Music.pdf

Department for Education (DfE) (2013b) *The National Curriculum in England: Key Stages 1 and 2 Framework Document*. Available at: www.gov.uk/government/uploads/system/uploads/attachment_data/file/425601/PRIMARY_national_curriculum.pdf

Department for Education (DfE) (2014a) *Early Years Foundation Stage Statutory Framework (EYFS)*. Available at: https://assets.publishing.service.gov.uk/government/uploads/system/uploads/attachment_data/file/596629/EYFS_STATUTORY_FRAMEWORK_2017.pdf

Department for Education (DfE) (2014b) *National Curriculum in England: English Programmes of Study*. Available at: www.gov.uk/government/publications/national-curriculum-in-england-english-programmes-of-study/national-curriculum-in-england-english-programmes-of-study#contents

Department for Education (DfE) (2017) *Statutory Framework for the Early Years Foundation Stage*. London: Department for Education.

Department for Education (DfE) (2019a) *An Unequal Playing Field: Extra-Curricular Activities, Soft Skills and Social Mobility*. Available at: www.gov.uk/government/publications/extra-curricular-activities-soft-skills-and-social-mobility

Department for Education (DfE) (2020a) *Early Years Foundation Assessment and Reporting Arrangements 2021*. Available at: https://assets.publishing.service.gov.uk/government/uploads/system/uploads/attachment_data/file/940833/2021_EYFS_ARA_V1.0.pdf

Department for Education (DfE) (2020b) *Statutory Framework for the Early Years Foundation Stage – EYFS Reforms Early Adopter Version*. London: Department for Education.

Department for Education and Employment (DfEE) and Qualifications and Curriculum Authority (QCA) (1999) *The National Curriculum Handbook for Primary Teachers in England*. London: DfEE/QCA.

Dixon, L. and Hayes, A. (2014) *Bringing History Alive Through Local People and Places*. London: Routledge.

Dobson, T. and Stephenson, L.S. (2019) 'I think it fits in': using process drama to promote agentic writing with primary school children. *Literacy*, 53(2): 69–76.

Doherty, J. and Brennan, P. (2014) *Physical Education 5–11: A Guide for Teachers*. London: Routledge.

Donaldson, J. and Monks, L. (2005) *Sharing a Shell*. London: Macmillan Children's Books.

Doull, K., Russell, C. and Hales, A. (2019) *Mastering Primary History*. London: Bloomsbury.

Downing, D., Johnson, F. and Kaur, S. (2003) *Saving a Place for the Arts? A Survey of the Arts in Primary Schools in England*. Slough: NFER.

Duffy, P.B. (2014) The blended space between third and first person learning: drama, cognition and transfer. *Research in Drama Education*, 19(1): 89–97.

Dutton, D. (2010) *The Art Instinct: Beauty, Pleasure, and Human Evolution*. Oxford: Oxford University Press.

Dymoke, S., Barrs, M., Lambirth., A. and Wilson, A. (2015) *Making Poetry Happen: Transforming the Poetry Classroom*. London: Bloomsbury.

Dzvimbo, M.A., Monga, M. and Mashiza, T.M. (2017) Perpetual 'outcasts': the impact of climate change on rural children in Zimbabwe. *Journal of Public Administration and Development Alternatives*, 2(2): 60–9.

Early Education (2012) *Development Matters in the Early Years Foundation Stage (EYFS)*. Available at: https://foundationyears.org.uk/files/2012/03/Development-Matters-FINAL-PRINT-AMENDED.pdf

Eaude, T. (2017) Humanities in the primary school: philosophical considerations. *Education 3–13*, 45(3): 343–53.

Eckhoff, A. and Urbach, J. (2008) Understanding imaginative thinking during childhood: sociocultural conceptions of creativity and imaginative thought. *Early Childhood Education Journal*, 36(2): 179–85.

Edmiston, B. (2007) Mission to Mars: using drama to make a more inclusive classroom for literacy learning. *Language Arts*, 84(4): 337–46.

Edwards, D. (ed.) (2006) *A Choice of Poets*. Cheltenham: Thomas Nelson & Sons.

Eisner, E.W. (1972) *Educating Artistic Vision*. New York: Macmillan.

Eisner, E.W. (2002) *The Arts and the Creation of Mind*. New Haven, CT: Yale University Press.

Elliott, D.J., Silverman, M. and McPherson, G.E. (2019) Philosophical and qualitative perspectives on assessment in music education. In D.J. Elliott, M. Silverman and G.E. McPherson (eds), *The Oxford Handbook of Philosophical and Qualitative Assessment in Music Education*. Oxford: Oxford University Press, pp1–26.

Encyclopædia Britannica (n.d.) *The Arts*. Available at: www.britannica.com/topic/the-arts

Engel, S. (1995) *The Stories Children Tell: Making Sense of the Narratives of Childhood*. New York: W.H. Freeman & Co.

Engel, S. (2011) Children's need to know: curiosity in schools. *Harvard Educational Review*, 81(4): 625–45.

English, F.W. and Bolton, C.L. (2016) *Bourdieu for Educators: Policy and Practice*. London: SAGE.

Erdo⊠an, S. and Baran, G. (2009) A study on the effect of mathematics teaching provided through drama on the mathematics ability of six-year-old children. *Eurasia Journal of Mathematics, Science and Technology Education*, 5(1): 79–85.

Eva-Wood, A.L. (2008) Does feeling come first? How poetry can help readers broaden their understanding of metacognition. *Journal of Adolescent & Adult Literacy*, 51(7): 564–76.

Fisher, R. (1998) *Teaching Thinking: Philosophical Enquiry in the Classroom*. London: Cassell.

Fleming, M., Merrell, C. and Tymms, P. (2004) The impact of drama on pupils' language, mathematics, and attitude in two primary schools. *Research in Drama Education*, 9(2): 177–97.

Folkestad, G. (2006) Formal and informal learning situations or practices vs formal and informal ways of learning. *British Journal of Music Education*, 23(2): 135–45.

Gamble, N. (2019) *Exploring Children's Literature: Reading for Knowledge, Understanding and Pleasure*, 4th edition. London: SAGE.

Gayford, M. (2016) *A Bigger Message: Conversations with David Hockney*, revised edition. London: Thames & Hudson.

Gentle, K. (1986) *Children and Art Teaching*. Kent: Croom Helm.

Georgakopoulou, A. (2015) Small stories research: methods – analysis – outreach. In A. De Fina and A. Georgakopoulou (eds), *The Handbook of Narrative Analysis*. Oxford: Wiley-Blackwell, pp255–71.

Ghazi, T. (1999) *Footprints in the Forest: A Chembakelli Story*. London: ActionAid.

Ghostbusters (1984) Directed by Ivan Reitman. Los Angeles, CA: Columbia-Delphi Productions.

Gibbons, A. (2011) *The Piano*. Available at: www.youtube.com/watch?v=0uHCMt3wm04

Gill, N. (ed.) (2020a) *SLAM! You're Gonna Wanna Hear This*. London: Macmillan Children's Books.

Gill, N. (2020b) *'The Language of Fire, Fury and Freedom': Nikita Gill on the Power of Performance Poetry and Her Vital New Anthology SLAM!* Available at: www.panmacmillan.com/blogs/books-for-children/nikita-gill-slam-poetry-performance-poetry

Glover, J. (2000) *Children Composing, 4–14*. London: Routledge.

Godec, S., King, H. and Archer, L. (2017) *The Science Capital Teaching Approach: Engaging Students with Science, Promoting Social Justice*. London: UCL.

Goldin, G.A. (2002) Representation in mathematical learning and problem solving. In L.D. English and E.A. Warren (eds), *Handbook of International Research in Mathematics Education*. Mahwah, NJ: Erlbaum, pp197–218.

Goodhart, D. (2020) *Head, Hand and Heart: The Struggle for Dignity and Status in the 21st Century*. London: Allen Lane.

Goodwin, P. (ed.) (2011) *The Literate Classroom*, 3rd edition. London: Routledge.

Gove, M. (2009) *Speech to the Royal Society for the Arts*. Available at: www.thersa.org/_data/assets/pdf_file/0009/213021/Gove-speech-to-RSA.pdf

Graham, G., Holt/Hale, S.A. and Parker, M. (2020) *Children Moving: A Reflective Approach to Teaching Physical Education*, 10th edition. New York: McGraw Hill.

Grainger, T. (2003) Creative teachers and the language arts: possibilities and potential. *Education 3–13*, 31(1): 43–7.

Gregory, P., March, C. and Tutchell, S. (2020) *Mastering Primary Art and Design*. London: Bloomsbury.

Gussin Paley, V. (1990) *The Boy Who Would Be a Helicopter: The Uses of Storytelling in the Classroom*. Cambridge, MA: Harvard University Press.

Gyford, P. (2009a) *John Evelyn's Fire of London*. Available at: www.pepysdiary.com/indepth/2009/09/02/evelyns-fire/

Gyford, P. (2009b) *Diary Entries from September 1666*. Available at: www.pepysdiary.com/diary/1666/09/

Hackathorn, J., Solomon, E.D., Blankmeyer, K.L., Tennial, R.E. and Garczynski, A.M. (2011) Learning by doing: an empirical study of active teaching techniques. *Journal of Effective Teaching*, 11(2): 40–54.

Haddawy, H. (1995) *The Arabian Nights II: Sindbad and Other Popular Stories*. New York: W.W. Norton & Co.

Hallam, S. (2010) The power of music: its impact on the intellectual, social and personal development of children and young people. *International Journal of Music Education*, 28(3): 269–89.

Halliday, J. (2017) How to improve the school results: not extra maths but music, loads of it. *The Guardian*. Available at: www.theguardian.com/education/2017/oct/03/school-results-music-bradford

Halsey-Dutton, B. (2016) Concepts of creative risk-taking: issues-based instructional strategies for pre-service educators. *Art Education*, 69(1): 38–44.

Hamilton, A., Jin, Y. and Krieg, S. (2019) Early childhood arts curriculum: a cross-cultural study. *Journal of Curriculum Studies*, 51(5): 698–714.

Harel, I.E. and Papert, S.E. (1991) *Constructionism*. Norwood, NJ: Ablex Publishing.

Harnett, P. (2000) History in the primary school: re-shaping our pasts – the influence of primary school teachers' knowledge and understanding of history on curriculum planning and implementation. *History Education Research Journal*, 1(1): 7–9.

Haven, K. (2007) *Story Proof: The Science Behind the Startling Power of Story*. Westport, CT: Libraries Unlimited.

Hayes, D. (2010) The seductive charms of a cross-curricular approach. *Education 3–13*, 38(4): 381–7.

Hess, J. (2014) Radical musicking: towards a pedagogy of social change. *Music Education Research*, 16(3): 1–22.

Hetland, L., Winner, E., Veenema, S. and Sheridan, K.M. (2007) *Studio Thinking: The Real Benefits of Visual Arts Education*. New York: Teachers College Press.

Hicks, D. (2012) *Sustainable Schools, Sustainable Futures: A Resource for Teachers*. Available at: http://assets.wwf.org.uk/downloads/sf_full_version.pdf?_ga=2.235689858.2017660587.1561474117-1636918014.1561474117

Holder, N. (2020) *If I Were a Racist …* Available at: www.nateholdermusic.com/post/if-i-were-a-racist

Holland, C. (2009) Reading and acting in the world: conversations about empathy. *RiSE: The Journal of Applied Theatre and Performance*, 14(4): 529–44.

Holland, C. (2021) *Chris Holland the Storyteller*. Available at: www.wholeland.org.uk/storyteller/

Intergovernmental Panel on Cimate Change (IPCC) (2014) *AR5 Synthesis Report: Climate Change 2014*. Available at: www.ipcc.ch/report/ar5/syr/

Jeffrey, B. and Craft, A. (2004) Teaching creatively and teaching for creativity: distinctions and relationships. *Educational Studies*, 30(1): 77–87.

Jickling, R. and Sterling, S. (2017) Post-sustainability and environmental education: framing issues. In R. Jickling and S. Sterling (eds), *Post-Sustainability and Environmental Education: Remaking Education for the Future*. London: Palgrave Macmillan, pp1–11.

Johns-Shepherd, L. (2019) *The Power of Pictures: Summary of Findings from the Research on the CLPE Power of Pictures Project 2013–19*. London: CLPE.

Jordanova, L. (2006) *History in Practice*. London: Hodder Arnold.

Jorgensen, E.R. (2015) Intersecting social justices and music education. In C. Benedict, P. Schmidt, G. Spruce and P. Woodford (eds), *The Oxford Handbook of Social Justice in Music Education*. Oxford: Oxford University Press, pp7–28.

Jové, G. and Farerro, M. (2018) Rethinking education through contemporary art. *International Journal of Art and Design Education*, 37(2): 333–44.

Katz, J.T. and Khoshbin, S. (2014) Can visual arts training improve physician performance? *Transactions of the American Clinical and Climatological Association*, 125: 331–42.

Kawamura, Y. (2015) *Meine schönsten Bilder-Märchen*. Hamburg: Ellermann.

Kelly, A. (2009) Sounds geographical. *Primary Geography*, 68: 35–6.

Kelly-McHale, J. (2018) Equity in music education: exclusionary practices in music education. *Music Educators Journal*, 104(3): 60–2.

Kent, G. and MacIntosh, M. (2005) Art and geography: children's own places. *Primary Geography*, 56: 26–7.

Kidd, D. (2020) *A Curriculum of Hope: As Rich in Humanity as in Knowledge*. Carmarthen: Independent Thinking Press.

Kim, K.H. (2011) The creativity crisis: the decrease in creative thinking scores on the Torrance Tests of Creative Thinking. *Creativity Research Journal*, 23(4): 285–95.

King's College London (2019) *Science Capital: An Introduction*. Available at: www.sciencecentres.org.uk/resources/science-capital/science-capital-introduction/

Koehler, M.J. and Mishra, P. (2009) What is technological pedagogical content knowledge? *Contemporary Issues in Technology and Teacher Education*, 9(1): 60–70.

Kosmas, P. (2018) Implementing embodied learning in the classroom: effects on children's memory and language skills. *Educational Media International*, 56(1): 59–74.

Kress, G. (1997) *Before Writing: Rethinking the Paths to Literacy*. London: Routledge.

Laban, R. (1948) *Modern Educational Dance*. London: Macdonald & Evans.

Labov, W. (2013) *The Language of Life and Death: The Transformation of Experience in Oral Narrative*. Cambridge: Cambridge University Press.

Lavin, J. (ed.) (2008) *Creative Approaches to Physical Education: Helping Children Achieve Their True Potential*. London: Routledge.

Le Guin, U.K. (2009) A message about messages. In *Cheek by Jowl: Talks and Essays on How and Why Fantasy Matters*. Seattle, WA: Aqueduct Press, pp125–30.

Lee, J., Hicks, D., Henriksen, D., Mishra, P., Cain, W., Fahnoe, C., et al. (2015) Historical soundscapes for creative synthesis. *TechTrends*, 59(5): 4–8.

Lee, T. (2015) *Princesses, Dragons and Helicopter Stories: Storytelling and Story Acting in the Early Years*. London: Routledge.

Lewis, G. (2015) *Gorilla Dawn*. Oxford: Oxford University Press.

Lewis, G. (2017) *Sky Dancer*. Oxford: Oxford University Press.

Li, D. (2018) Using issues-based art education to facilitate middle school students' learning in racial issues. *International Journal of Education & the Arts*, 19(12): 1–12.

Lindström, L. (2012) Aesthetic learning about, in, with and through the arts: a curriculum study. *International Journal of Art and Design Education*, 31(2): 166–79.

Little, S. (2020) Why multilingual pupils need to encounter books in their language in formal education contexts: stories from a multilingual library. *English 4–11*, 69: 10–13.

Lockwood, M. (2008) *Promoting Reading for Pleasure in the Primary Classroom*. London: SAGE.

Lockwood, M. (2011) *Bringing Poetry Alive: A Guide to Classroom Practice*. London: SAGE.

Lykesas, G., Tsapakidou, A. and Tsopmanaki, E. (2014) Creative dance as a means of growth and development of fundamental motor skills for children in first grades of primary schools in Greece. *Asian Journal of Humanities and Social Studies*, 2(1): 211–18.

Mages, W.K. (2006) Drama and imagination: a cognitive theory of drama's effect on narrative comprehension and narrative production. *Research in Drama Education*, 11(3): 329–40.

Malaguzzi, L. (1994) *Your Image of the Child: Where Teaching Begins*. Available at: https://reggioalliance.org/downloads/malaguzzi:ccie:1994.pdf

Maloney, J.H., Peppler, K., Kafai, Y., Resnick, M. and Rusk, N. (2008) Programming by choice: urban youth learning programming with scratch. *Proceedings of the 39th SIGCSE Technical Symposium on Computer Science Education*, 11–16 March, pp367–71.

Mann, E.L. (2016) Creativity: the essence of mathematics. *Journal for the Education of the Gifted*, 30(2): 236–60.

Mannis, C.D. (2002) *One Leaf Rides the Wind: Counting in a Japanese Garden*. New York: Viking Press.

Marshall, J. (2010) Five ways to integrate: using strategies from contemporary art. *Art Education*, 63(3): 13–19.

Matthews, A. and Ross, T. (2010) *Shakespeare Stories*. London: Hachette Children's Group.

McDougle, L. (2020) *Songs with a Questionable Past*. Available at: https://docs.google.com/document/u/0/d/1q1jVGqOgKxfiUZ8N3oz0warXefGIJill2Xha-3X5nUY/mobilebasic?fbclid=IwAR2W-s3A_AvkAF_PNkLeY6U_a7pJB5ta9cYaRNV3LwHPF_QQ7fPvaCGSFEk#bookmark=id.tt77aa19uddc

McPherson, G.E. and Welch, G.F. (eds) (2018) *Music Learning and Teaching in Infancy, Childhood, and Adolescence: An Oxford Handbook of Music Education, Volume* 2. Oxford: Oxford University Press.

Moll, L.C., Soto-Santiago, S. and Schwartz, L. (2013) Funds of knowledge in changing communities. In K. Hall, T. Cremin, B. Comber and L.C. Moll (eds), *International Handbook of Research on Children's Literacy, Learning and Culture*. London: Wiley-Blackwell, pp172–83.

Montague-Smith, A., Cotton, T., Hansen, A. and Price, A.J. (2018) *Mathematics in Early Years Education*, 4th edition. London: Routledge.

Music Mark (n.d.) Ofsted *Music Deep Dive Resources and Information*. Available at: www.musicmark.org.uk/resources/ofsted-music-deep-dive-resources-and-information/

National Society for Education in Art and Design (NSEAD) (2019) *The NSEAD's Manifesto for Real Change, for Our Subject*. Available at: www.nsead.org/news/news/a-manifesto-for-real-change-for-our-subject/

O'Neill, C. (1995) *Drama Worlds: A Framework for Process Drama*. Portsmouth, NH: Heinemann.

O'Toole, J. and Burton, B. (2005) Acting against conflict and bullying: the Brisbane DRACON project 1996–2004 – emergent findings and outcomes. *Research in Drama Education*, 10(3): 269–83.

Ochs, E. and Capps, L. (2001) *Living Narrative: Creating Lives in Everyday Storytelling*. Cambridge, MA: Harvard University Press.

Ofcom (2020) *Children and Parents: Media Use and Attitudes Report 2019*. Available at: www.ofcom.org.uk/research-and-data/media-literacy-research/childrens/children-and-parents-media-use-and-attitudes-report-2019

Ofsted (2011a) *History for All: History in English Schools 2007–2011*. Available at: www.gov.uk/government/publications/history-for-all-strengthes-and-weaknesses-of-school-history-teaching

Ofsted (2011b) *Learning to Make a World of Difference 2007–2011*. Available at: www.gov.uk/government/publications/geography-learning-to-make-a-world-of-difference

Ofsted (2012) *Music in Schools: Wider Still, and Wider*. Available at: https://assets.publishing.service.gov.uk/government/uploads/system/uploads/attachment_data/file/413347/Music_in_schools_wider_still__and_wider.pdf

Ofsted (2019a) *Inspecting the Curriculum: Revising Inspection Methodology to Support the Education Inspection Framework*. Available at: https://assets.publishing.service.gov.uk/government/uploads/system/uploads/attachment_data/file/814685/Inspecting_the_curriculum.pdf

Ofsted (2019b) *Intention and Substance: Further Findings on Primary School Science from Phase 3 of Ofsted's Curriculum Research*. Available at: https://assets.publishing.service.gov.uk/government/uploads/system/uploads/attachment_data/file/777992/Intention_and_substance_findings_paper_on_primary_school_science_110219.pdf

Ofsted (2019c) *The Education Inspection Framework*. Available at: https://assets.publishing.service.gov.uk/government/uploads/system/uploads/attachment_data/file/801429/Education_inspection_framework.pdf

Ogier, S. (ed.) (2019) *A Broad and Balanced Curriculum in Primary Schools: Educating the Whole Child*. London: SAGE/Learning Matters.

Ojala, M. (2018) Eco-anxiety. *RSA Journal*, 164(4 (5576): 10–15.

Ormerod, J. (2005) *Doing the Animal Bop*. Oxford: Oxford University Press.

Owens, P. (2018) A chameleon subject with a rigorous heart. *Primary Geography*, 97: 30–2.

Pacheco, H.S. (2006) Conventions of typography related to traditional poetry. In *WonderGround Proceedings Book of the International Conference of Design Research Society*, 1–4 November.

Paine, L. (2014) *Complete Guide to Primary Dance*. Leeds: Human Kinetics/NDTA.

Papert, S.A. (1980) *Mindstorms: Children, Computers, and Powerful Ideas*. New York: Basic Books.

Percival, J. (2020) *Understanding and Teaching Primary History*. London: SAGE.

Peterson, C. and Seligman, M.E.P. (2004) *Character Strengths and Virtues: A Handbook and Classification*. Oxford: Oxford University Press.

Piaget, J. (1930) *The Child's Conception of Physical Causality*. New Brunswick, NJ: Transaction Publishers.

Pickard, A. and Maude, P. (2014) *Teaching Physical Education Creatively*. London: Routledge.

Quigley, A. and Stringer, E. (2018) *Making Sense of Metacognition*. Available at: https://impact.chartered.college/article/quigley-stringer-making-sense-metacognition/

Riddell, C. (2017) *The Age of the Beautiful Book*. Available at: www.pearcelecture.com/the-lectures/2017-chris-riddell/

Robinson, K., Minkin, L., Bolton, E., French, D., Fryer, L., Greenfield, S. and Green, L. (1999) *All Our Futures: Creativity, Culture and Education*. Available at: http://sirkenrobinson.com/pdf/allourfutures.pdf

Robinson, K. (2009) *The Element: How Finding Your Passion Changes Everything*. London: Penguin.

Root-Bernstein, R. (2008) Arts foster scientific success: avocations of Notel, National Academy, Royal Society and Signma Xi members. *Journal of Psychology of Science and Technology*, 1(2): 51–63.

Rosen, M. (2011) *Create a Poetry-Friendly Classroom*. Available at: www.booktrust.org.uk/what-we-do/childrens-laureate/former-laureates/michael-rosen/poetry-friendly-classroom

Rosen, M. (2014) How we teach the arts is as important as the fact we're doing it. *The Guardian*. Available at: www.theguardian.com/teacher-network/zurich-school-competition/teach-arts-michael-rosen-education-worthwhile-students

Rosen, M. (2015) *A Great Big Cuddle*. London: Walker Books.

Rosen, M. (2019) Writing as an art form: an author's perspective. In S. Ogier (ed.), *A Broad and Balanced Curriculum in Primary Schools: Educating the Whole Child*. London: SAGE/Learning Matters, pp133–45.

Rosen, M. and Oxenbury, H. (illustrator) (1989) *We're Going on a Bear Hunt*. London: Walker.

Royal Geographical Society (RGS) (2020) *Map Skills*. Available at: www.rgs.org/schools/teaching-resources/map-skills/

Royal Society (2012) *Shut Down or Restart? The Way Forward for Computing in UK Schools*. Available at: https://royalsociety.org/topics-policy/projects/computing-in-schools/report/

Said, S.F. (2003) *Varjak Paw*. London: David Fickling Books.

Sanderson, A. (1995) *Banana Splits: Ways into Part-Singing*. London: A&C Black.

Sanson, A.V. and Burke, S.E. (2020) Climate change and children: an issue of intergenerational justice. In N. Balvin and D.J. Christie (eds), *Children and Peace: From Research to Action*. Cambridge: Springer, pp343–62.

Scottish Executive (2007) *Building the Curriculum 2: Active Learning in the Early Years*. Available at: www.education.gov.scot/Documents/btc2.pdf

Shneiderman, B. (2019) *Leonardo Joined Art with Engineering*. Available at: https://theconversation.com/leonardo-joined-art-with-engineering-113967

Sissay, L. (2008) *Listener*. London: Canongate Books.

Smith, D.L. (2011) Material culture and issues-based art education. *International Journal of Arts Education*, 9(2): 92–100.

Smith-Autard, J.M. (2002) *The Art of Dance in Education*. London: A&C Black.

Solt, M.E. (1968) *Concrete Poetry: A World View*. Bloomington, IN: Indiana University Press.

Spielman, A. (2017) *HMCI's Commentary: Recent Primary and Secondary Curriculum Research*. Available at: www.gov.uk/government/speeches/hmcis-commentary-october-2017

Steen, L.A. (1988) The science of patterns. *Science*, 240(4852), 611–16.

Stockholm, J. (2011a) *Doctor*. Swindon: Child's Play.

Stockholm, J. (2011b) *Hospital*. Swindon: Child's Play.

Stockholm, J. (2011c) *Moving Day*. Swindon: Child's Play.

Stockholm, J. (2011d) *Party*. Swindon: Child's Play.

Stockholm, J. (2011e) *Shopping*. Swindon: Child's Play.

Stockholm, J. (2011f) *Vet*. Swindon: Child's Play.

Style, E. (1988) *Curriculum as Window and Mirror*. Available at: https://nationalseedproject.org/Key-SEED-Texts/curriculum-as-window-and-mirror

Sullivan, G. (2001) Artistic thinking as transcognitive practice: a reconciliation of the process–product dichotomy. *Visual Arts Research*, 27(1): 2–12.

Sutton-Smith, B. (1981) *The Folkstories of Children*. Philadelphia, PA: University of Pennsylvania Press.

Sutton-Smith, B. (1997) *The Ambiguity of Play*. Cambridge, MA: Harvard University Press.

Taguma, M., Litjens, I. and Makowiecki, K. (2013) *Quality Matters in Early Childhood Education and Care*. Available at: www.oecd.org/education/school/SWEDEN%20policy%20profile%20-%20published%2005-02-2013.pdf

Taylor, T. (2016) *Mantle of the Expert: A Transformative Approach to Education*. Norwich: Singular Publishing.

Teach Primary (2011) *Pie Corbett's Animal Poems*. Available at: www.teachprimary.com/learning_resources/view/pie-corbetts-animal-poems

The Guardian (2009) *Dr Vandana Shiva at the Copenhagen Climate Summit*. Available at: www.youtube.com/watch?v=6XduZe7gSuw&feature=emb_title

Thompson, C. (2006) *Castles*. London: Random House Children's Books.

Thurman, L. and Welch, G.F. (eds) (2000) *Bodymind and Voice: Foundations of Voice Education*, 2nd edition. London: VoiceCare Network, National Center for Voice and Speech.

Tilkin, G. and Paulus, M. (2012) *Telling Tales: Stories for Learning in European Schools*. Available at: https://issuu.com/aldenbieseneu/docs/manual-tales-eng_final

Turner, J., Keogh, B., Naylor, S. and Lawrence, L. (2011) *It's Not Fair – or Is It?* Stafford: Millgate House.

Turner-Bisset, R. (2005) *Creative Teaching: History in the Primary School*. London: David Fulton.

Tutchell, S. (2014) *Young Children as Artists: Art and Design in the Early Years and Key Stage 1*. London: Routledge.

UNESCO (2014) *Good Practice Stories on Education for Sustainable Development in India*. Available at: https://in.one.un.org/wp-content/uploads/2016/10/232544e.pdf

UNESCO (2019) *What Is Education for Sustainable Development?* Available at: https://en.unesco.org/themes/education-sustainable-development/what-is-esd

UNICEF (1990) *The United Nations Convention on the Rights of the Child*. Available at: www.unicef.org.uk/wp-content/uploads/2010/05/UNCRC_united_nations_convention_on_the_rights_of_the_child.pdf

United Nations (UN) (2015a) *The Paris Agreement*. Available at: https://unfccc.int/process-and-meetings/the-paris-agreement/the-paris-agreement

United Nations (UN) (2015b) *Sustainable Development Goals*. Available at: https://sdgs.un.org/goals

Vandevelde, S., Van Keer, H., Schellings, G. and Van Hout-Wolters, B. (2015) Using think-aloud protocol analysis to gain in-depth insights into upper primary school children's self-regulated learning. *Learning and Individual Differences*, 43: 11–30.

Voices Foundation (2020) *Our Commitment to Anti-Racist Practice, Diversity and Inclusivity*. Available at: www.voices.org.uk/vf-blog-commitment-to-anti-racist-practice-diversity-and-inclusivity

Vygotsky, L.S. (2004) Imagination and creativity in childhood. *Journal of Russian and East European Psychology*, 42(1): 7–97.

Watts, R. (2005) Attitudes to making art in the primary school. *International Journal of Art and Design Education*, 24(3): 243–53.

Watts, R. (2018) A place for beauty in art education. *International Journal of Art and Design Education*, 37(1): 149–62.

Winston, J. and Tandy, M. (2009) *Beginning Drama 4–11*. London: Routledge.

Winston, J. and Tandy, M. (2012) *Beginning Shakespeare 4–11*. London: Routledge.

Woodford, P.G. (2005) *Democracy and Music Education*. Bloomington, IN: Indiana University Press.

Wyse, D., Jones, R., Bradford, H. and Wolpert, M.A. (2018) *Teaching English, Language and Literacy*, 4th edition. London: Routledge.

Zipes, J. (1995) *Creative Storytelling: Building Community, Changing Lives*. London: Routledge.

INDEX